HAINT PUNCH

HAINT PUNCH

Richard Murff

Burnaby Books

For Maggie and Littlebit

Haint (n.) Southern colloq.: A ghost or spirit. A creature unholy.

For the mob is eternally virtuous, and the only thing necessary to get it to favor some new and super-oppressive law is to convince it that that law will be distasteful to the minority that it envies and hates.

--H.L. Mencken

ONE:
#DAMNDEKE

In the bowels of the Capitol Building's parking garage Burt Carlson, congressman from the great state of Nebraska, sent out a single aide to check conditions. The young man returned with the all clear and the congressman strode out of the open elevator with his aide following at a respectable three steps. This was about the time all 5' 3" of the insufferably cute reporter came around a concrete pillar and sidled up to the aide. "Hi, Tim."

"Oh hi, Lucy!" he said, delighted until the horns of the current dilemma became clear. "Ahh hell!"

Carlson looked back from a determined gait to see Lucy trotting to keep up. "Dammit Tim, you're supposed to keep these vultures away from me! You're fired!"

"Congressman!" she stuck out a hand, "Lucy Burton from the *Daily Brute*. Do you - "

"Jesus! You're tiny!" Carlson looked back but kept walking.

"It's the low end of average, Congressman!"

"For a smurf!"

"Do you have any response to Ms. Higgins's accusations of sexual harassment and possible cruelty to animals?"

"Unfounded, untrue. Ms. Higgins is just a star-struck intern. I've been dealing with this since I played basketball at –"

"Any comment on the elk penis she claims you sent to her apartment?"

The congressman stopped and looked at Tim. "Why the hell is *she* still here?"

"Couldn't say."

"Why not?"

"You fired me, sir," Said Tim, "I'm no longer executing your commands."

"Then why are *you* still here?"

"Well, sir, since I won't be working tonight, I was gonna see if Lucy here would like to grab a drink after the interview."

"Why Tim, I'd love to –"

"Quiet, you! Tim, this isn't an interview. You're re-hired. I believe in second chances. Now get rid of her!"

"Congressman!" Lucy barked, "You can't go sneaking in and out of work forever. The longer you hide from this, the worse it's gonna get. Just give me a statement, your side of the story... something to give the mob something to discuss before they crucify you."

"Yeah, sure, play the media game by your rules. Apologies and ratings eh? What if I don't give you anything? It'll all blow over and you know it."

"I'm almost positive the elk penis will not go un-noted."

"Just you watch."

"Sir, it was tied with a bow."

Carlson stopped and faced Lucy head on. "You want a statement? Here it is and you listen good: I don't need tricks like that...I get my fair share!" The former point guard for the University of Nebraska straightened his tie, threw his shoulders back and called for Tim, who was five feet away cradling his face in his hands.

"Burt mah boy!" came a voice from behind Lucy that caught Carlson cold. The senior senator from the great state of Mississippi, Aubrey Laudermilk, was a thickset man: Let's just call him fat, with a mane of silver white hair. His suit was made of great rumbled bolts of blue and white seersucker. He had jowls like a hound dog and an accent that caused the northern and western segments of the Republic to wonder if he kept marbles in said jowls for any good reason. Many years ago, one senator from Idaho found himself co-sponsoring a bill with Laudermilk and actually watched hours of old Foghorn Leghorn cartoons in a semi-successful attempt to better understand the man. With him was Mississippi's junior senator, the tidy and slightly shell-shocked David Davison. "Burt, what have you gotten yo'self into?" Laudermilk laughed, "Lawd, Davison here just lost his primary 'cause he couldn't keep it in his pants. Granted, your pants might'un been a bit cramped with all that elk penus."

"Senator Laudermilk," Carlson said, nodding to Lucy, "the press."

"Burt, if she's trackin' you down in parking garages, she already knows something." Then to Lucy, "Ms. Burton is it? Of the *Brute*? I'm Aubrey Laudermilk of Mississippi."

Sweet Jesus! Lucy thought, is there actually a twinkle, and honest to God, physical twinkle in his eye? "Charmed, Senator." Charmed? Where the hell did that come from?

"Burt, you need to take yaw medicine. Or you'll be sent back to the private sector like Davison here. I promise you the workday duddn't end at 2:30 in the real world."

The color went out of Davidson's face. "Private sector! I thought you were working on an appointment."

"Settle down Davison. We'll get you sumthun' nice. Like American Samoa or Ambassador to Paraguay."

"Paraguay? I can't talk the wife into moving to Paraguay! She had an awful experience in Mexico once."

"Paraguay iddn't Mexico, you half-wit."

"To Sandra, everything south of Houston is Mexico." Davison said sadly.

"Well you shoulda thought about that before you took up with that casino lobbyist. Lawd." Laudermilk turned to Tim, who'd recovered enough to be merely rubbing his eye sockets, "Tim is it? Listen, I don't care what Burt's got scheduled for 7:30 in the a.m., but clear it. He's gonna grant 20 minutes to Ms. Burton of the *Brute*. Got it?"

"Oh, I don't know Aubrey," Carlson said. "The Chief doesn't want us granting interviews right now."

"'The Chief?' Damn Carlson, He ain't runnin' daddy's real estate business for cryin' out loud! He's the President - Gawd help us!"

"Okay, the President – "

"And the President ain't your boss, Carlson!" Laudermilk put a thick finger in the congressman's face. "The people of Nebraska are. And I work for the State of Mississippi like Davison did before he humped himself out of a job... and possibly a marriage."

"Oh God..." Davison groaned.

"Now... I don't know what you two poonhounds got planned for tonight, but can it. Davison, you go home to your wife and you might what to stop by the jewelry store on the way out. Burt, you aren't goin' public. Come to my house, we'll feed you and figure out what you're gonna tell Ms. Burton here in the morning." Laudermilk shook his heavy jowls. "Jay-sus. Elk Penus. What happened to just tellin' a gal she got pretty eyes and lettin' her talk? You know they like to talk? Why you gotta go straight for the underpants? Have some style, boy! Good thing yo' daddy and I go back a way…"

"Seven thirty? The Congressman's office?" Lucy confirmed.

"That's what the man says." Said Tim and trotted off to catch up with the shamed congressman and the lame-duck senator wandering off with Laudermilk like a pair of second-string athletes caught out by the coach after curfew.

WENDY X HAD driven to Bardstown, Kentucky that morning and located the hotel fairly quickly, but he was gone. From there she drove out of town to the Rock Ridge Bourbon distillery. The surrounding countryside was green and rolling and exactly how she'd expected it to look. She hated it. It was a hot day, the late August sun beat down on the black metal rickhouses where the distillers laid up their whiskey for years in order to mellow. The countryside actually smelled faintly of bourbon. Smelled, Wendy thought, like frat boys trying to get laid.

She was a small, mousy creature in her late twenties wearing skinny jeans and an artist's smock. Despite the heat, a black beret was bulled down over curly fawn hair. Parking her Prius in front of the company store, she went inside and pretended to shop. Her massive purse – sustainably sourced and hand-crafted in Ecuador according to the Mother Goddess store in Knoxville, Tennessee – attracted the attention of the lone security guard who didn't know anything about a Mother Goddess but thought it looked like the sort of thing a shoplifter might carry. He sulked around, watching the enormous bag closely. Finally, Wendy had enough. She spun around and she planted her feet wide apart. "What do you want?" she barked. "Why are you following me?"

"Can I help you find something?" the guard sputtered.

"No! Back off. You're victimizing my personal space! This is an assault!"

"Okay." He didn't really back off. It was a very large purse.

She wandered over some other rustic, wooden shelves and picked out a bottle of bourbon to look normal. Then she drifted around the flasks, glassware and tee shirts. Behind the sales counter, Wendy spied a chipper gal, probably an undergraduate who was entirely too put together to be intelligent. "You might be able to help me." Wendy asked almost sweetly, "I'm not really here to shop. Where is the business office?"

"Well, this is the visitor's center. It's important to us that our customers to know how Rock Ridge is made. This really isn't a business office."

Wendy could see the rental car out in the lot. She knew *he* was on the property. "So, there are no offices on-site?"

"Well, the owner keeps an office here for interviews and events." She absently pointed down the hallway. "If you take the distillery tour, you get to see it. Mr. Calhoun is here a fair amount, he likes to meet our customers. In fact, I think he's here today."

"Is he free?"

"Well, I'm not his secretary, so I can't tell you what his calendar looks like. But... if you take the distillery tour, you can see the office. It's forming up over there in about ten minutes. Last tour of the day."

Wendy drifted away from the racks of branded pullovers and coasters. There was an enclave with two restrooms, and down a short hallway the door was mostly open to an office that was just too awful: A wood paneled man-cave with overstuffed leather chairs. Two men were laughing and sipping dark bourbon from tiny glasses. The older one was in his sixties and wore a golf shirt with a Rock Ridge Bourbon logo and the other, in his mid-thirties, in one of those blue and white seersucker sport coats one-percenters still insist on wearing in the South; the whole thing looked like a monumental erection to the patriarchy. She crossed over to the men's room and was pushing the door open when the guard called out. "Ma'am... excuse me. That's the men's room. I mean, wait... you're dressed like a lady... I think."

The two stared at each other for a long moment while Wendy tried to figure out what to do about the troglodyte. Flummoxed for an escape, she ducked into the ladies' room just as she heard the two men emerge laughing from the Mr. Calhoun's office. At the sink, she took a couple of deep breaths and looked at her purse. She'd done this before, this was just a hiccup. Now that that hillbilly guard had his eye on her, she was going to have to play it cool. C'mon, think! She took off the damp beret and splashed cold water on her face. It really was too hot for the hat but it looked *so* revolutionary, very Che. Very X. Eventually, she emerged from the restroom with her breathing under control. The guard was still lingering.

"Ma'am, that tour is about to start." He said with a friendly smile. Oaf.

Wendy joined the group and tried to ignore the gaggle of misogynistic college students ahead of her. The tour group was led into a high-tech room with the stills before shuffling out into the heat toward an enormous black warehouse – the tour guide called it a rickhouse – that looked like it could have been a hundred years old. Inside the cramped wooden confines, the air was musty and yeasty. Wooden barrels of whiskey sat on tightly fitted racks up to the low ceiling and above them, they were told, were six more floors of the same. "In the heat of the summer," the tour guide was saying, "the bourbon expands into the charred wood of the barrel. In the cold of the winter in contracts drawing back out. And we regularly roll the barrels. That movement is what turns what is essentially moonshine into the bourbon we all love so much, mellows it out and gives it that marvelous color."

"Makes me want to fire up a stogie." Said one of the college boys.

"Oh, don't do that," said the tour guide, you'd blow the place sky high."

In the tight confines of the rickhouse, Wendy's her panic returned as the college boys gasped and groaned like they were in heaven. She gripped the purse close to her body and, at the same time, wanted it to be as far away from it as possible. She began to lag behind the group in the soft darkness. While the perky tour guide talked about heat transference and charring white oak barrels, Wendy's rooted around in her purse and retrieved a heavy package wrapped in brown paper. Carefully, she stuck it behind one of the barrels before catching up with the group, but kept her eye suspiciously on a tall guy who seemed to be micro-aggressively unaware of her existence.

THE OFFICES OF the *Daily Brute* were mostly dark after hours, but dotted with the odd light still burning across the cube farm. At the far end of the long, cramped room Editor-in-Chief Anna Degrasse sat in an office that ate up all the window space in the narrow building overlooking a narrow D.C. street. Through its glass walls, Degrasse watched over her hipster bastion of mewing new media sorts, looking about as adult and out of place as possible in black slacks and white silk blouse. The transparency of the glass wall, she said, illustrated her "open door" policy with her employees. Although she never fully explained why its glass door was nearly always shut.

At the far end at the long room, Deke Kipling dropped his battered leather Ghurka bag and briefcase on a pristine desk and retrieved a bottle of bourbon. He headed toward Degrasse in her glass box and forced a smile, rapping on the door before going in. "Greetings from Kentucky." He said, waving the bottle.

"Well, what have you got?" Degrasse asked.

"Charming as always. The QED is that basically Kentucky is making so much bourbon that it comes dangerously close to running out of water every summer." Deke poured out a couple of tumblers.

"Okay, environmental disaster, I like it." Degrasse pressed the intercom on her phone, "Francis, will you check on which liquor companies advertise with us?"

"Mom!" came the distressed voice on the other end of the line. "I told you it's Frank now!"

"Your name is whatever I say it is!" She turned back to Deke. "It is so hard to find good help these days. Where was I?"

"You were going to put me on staff."

"I'm almost certain that wasn't it."

"Look, Ms. Degrasse, I'm sick of freelancing and you're sick of this conversation. Why don't you take me on as a staff writer? I'll open up the *Daily Brute's* New Orleans desk."

"Deke, you aren't a team player and you know it. When was the last time you promoted one of your stories over the social media? I mean, I can barely get the rest of the staff off to actually write anything they didn't pull of the Internet. Of course, it's shit, but it gets clicks!"

Deke laughed, "I'm not sure that social media is where I need to be right now."

"Well damn Deke – where should you be?"

He squished into his chair, "Is hashtag: *damndeke* still a thing?"

"Yes! You really are clueless, aren't you?"

"Ms. Degrasse, my phone crashes twice a day."

"Did someone hack it?"

"Lord if I know. At any rate, I need a new one so I'm a little behind on making myself obvious at 280 characters a pop. Besides, have you ever been a man online? All the bigoteers take you for a rapist or at least criminally creepy."

"That's ridiculous, women are constantly harassed on social media."

"So why is anyone one on it?"

"God only knows but they are. Why, my son Francis is a regular social media guru."

"I said a man."

"Oh, quit whining." Degrasse said with a lingering sip of her drink, "*Vodka, Bears and Furry Hats* spent eight weeks on the bestseller list. Granted not very high on the list, but *I* paid for your plane ticket. And by the way, Mr. Kipling dear, those ridiculous books you write wouldn't sell have as much if I hadn't made you fashionable."

"You're paying me in exposure, how modern. Look, someone actually has to write these books. After expenses, I'm basically working for the *Brute* for free."

"Where have you been, Deke? Nobody gets *paid* anymore… welcome to the new economy. That's why we're pushing the social media… It's all about the platform! Awareness! Go start a funding campaign to cover your expenses. Hashtag: *damndeke* is lighting it up!"

"I'm not sure I want to beat that drum too loudly."

"Deke, you are a very nearly award-winning writer, you might come out ahead with a fundraiser.

"You want me to raise money so that I can write a story for the *Daily Brute*?"

"You'll never know unless you're out there being a twit. Or a twat. Is that what they call the online social justice set on that hellscape?" She looked at Deke hard, "Oh, what am I asking you for? Francis knows all about that foolishness."

Deke grabbed the bourbon. "Here, lemme top you up, Ms. Degrasse. Courtesy of Rock Ridge. How long can sobriety stay fashionable?"

"I don't like your tone, young man." She contemplated the bourbon. "Now quit fussing. I'm thinking of replacing all of you with AIDCB."

"Beg pardon?"

"AIDCB – Artificial Intelligence Driven Click Bait - AIDCB"

"It certainly sounds more efficient than what I do."

"Oh, it is. We're going to brand our AI program 'FRANCYS.'"

"After your son?"

"No, we're spelling it with a Y." One of Degrasse's rare girlish smiles rent her face. "He *hates* it."

Beyond the glass wall, Lucy Burton came into the newsroom and stopped to look at the bags resting on her desk like a pair of rotting whale carcasses on an otherwise neatly ordered beach. She looked up and saw Deke beyond the glass wall and headed across the cube farm. Sticking her head in, she said, "Hey, Deke. Your bags are on my desk."

"I have too. I don't have one, you see. I'm freelance."

"That sounds like a damn Deke problem, not a Lucy problem."

"Don't you start. Can I buy you a drink?" Deke poured out another glass.

"Thanks. Wow, that's good." Lucy looked at Degrasse, "Have you told damn Deke about the lawyers?"

"Lawyers? Is it bad?"

"Deke, are lawyers ever good?" Degrasse asked, "Professor Blanche Barker – you may remember that you profiled her in that little article of yours…"

"You know you published the story, right?"

"…has decided to sue the *Daily Brute*." She sighed, "I think it's because you won't join in on some ridiculous online slapfight – which would be click-bait gold, Francis tells me!"

"Can you actually sue someone for that?" asked Deke. He was curious.

"Well…no…." said Degrasse. "But she *can* sue for libel for alleging that she or her organization has any ties to a domestic terrorist organization … what was it? The OLA … What does that even stand for?"

"Ovarian Liberation Army." Deke explained.

Lucy laughed, "Do the white nationalists know this? Aren't they still trying to dox you too?"

"Well, Dr. Barker suing *me*." Degrasse looked at Lucy. "Seriously Lucy, what do the feminists have against me? I'm a feminist icon!"

"Icon?" asked Lucy.

"I mean, I can see why these women hate Deke – he wrote the article and gave it that silly title. Just look at him in his wadded seersucker, flying around like some half-in-the-bag country squire who can't keep help, or afford dry cleaners."

"Ma'am, I'm right here." Deke scratched his head, "I don't have anything against feminists. And yes, Ballyhoo, or whatever the white rights crew is calling themselves this week, are still trolling me for the 'We're No Wankers' piece. I'd have thought you'd be happy the traffic."

"Listen up, my aggressively moderate friend, it's Blanche Barker who is suing us this week." She quaffed the last of her bourbon and waved the glass at Deke who gave her another slug. "I guess that's my problem. When you get back to New Orleans, write me a draft for Kentucky. And weren't you kicking something around about some illegal casinos down there? Why is that interesting? I thought Louisiana had legalized gaming?"

"They do. So something other than cards must be going on. My guess is whores and drugs. I've also heard that you can buy a voodoo hex on a horserace.

"Cocaine, hookers and voodoo? Ok, I'll bite." She smiled fleetingly. "Oh, and one more thing, I got your email and we are not running Kentucky under the title 'Flogging the Bung.'"

Lucy stifled a laugh.

"It's an industry term, I swear."

"Be that as it may…"

"Look, I'll write Kentucky, but after that I'm driving up to Clarksdale for a dove shoot."

"I'm not paying you to go hunting."

"You aren't paying me at all! I need a break and I haven't missed a Labor Day shoot since I was twelve. I'll call you about the ghost casinos when I get back to New Orleans."

"Fine. We wouldn't want to wreck your boyhood memories. Go fry up some catfish and buy some ribbon for Ellie May Clampett. Meanwhile, I'll put someone else on the story."

"No, you won't. I'm your only guy in New Orleans and you're too cheap to fly anyone down there." Before Degrasse could hurl her cocktail glass at Deke's head, he said, "Hey Lucy – you ought to come with me. Can you shoot? Press isn't officially allowed, but Senator Laudermilk will be there – the last one he missed was for Vietnam. It's gotten to be quite a political to-do down in the Delta. All the politicos and kingmakers in Mississippi will be there, for what that's worth. I'll bet that Betty Sue Wallace is trying to get an invite as we speak."

Before Lucy – eyes now very wide – could answer, Degrasse put her drink down with a rap. "Deke, dear, you've been hunting with Senator Aubrey Laudermilk – the 'Old Bear' of the Senate – every year since you were twelve and never thought to mention it?"

"What can I say? I'm freelance."

"Being an idiot has nothing to do with your W-9." She waved at Lucy grandly, "Didn't you think that our newbie political correspondent might need to know this?"

"Our?"

"I'm not that new…" Lucy grumbled.

"Deke," Degrasse continued, "did you just forget that Laudermilk is a senator?"

"It's easier to do than you might think. Listen Lucy, I'll call Ferg and tell him I've got an 'and guest.'"

"Who?"

Degrasse thundered, "Deke! As of now I'm putting you on the Mississippi senate race!"

"No!" Lucy and Deke screamed in unison.

Degrasse's eyes gleamed, smiling brighter than she'd ever smiled at Francis. "You know there is a rumor that Laudermilk is planning a run for the White House."

Lucy calmly topped off Degrasse's highball, "Ms. Degrasse, I've been following Betty Sue Wallace for months now. I picked up the trial of that deranged, wannabe Southern Belle before anyone thought she could knock Davison out in the primary. It hasn't been easy, either. Do you have any idea how hard it is to come up with good copy from a woman who thinks that all political issues can be reduced to a metaphor about Gamaw's deviled eggs?"

"Nonsense." Degrasse said, swirling the tiny bit of ice in her glass. "You two will be equal partners. Right Deke?"

"It's all equal until someone has to clean the birds."
Deke sighed. "Look, Ma'am, this is Lucy's story. I'm
gonna take it easy, bag my limit and drink some of that
wicked whiskey barrel punch Mr. O'Conner makes. I'm
off the clock."

Lucy relaxed. "So you'll be drunk most of the time?
Really? Deke? You promise?"

"...and well armed."

"My, that sounds perfectly reasonable." Said Lucy.
"Just remember to point the gun upward."

"Kiss the sky with brass!" Deke stood and quaffed
the rest of his bourbon. "Alright boss-lady, give me a few
days on Kentucky." He and Lucy walked back to her
cube where she wordlessly pointed out the offending
baggage. "So, listen." Deke said, ignoring the finger.
"I've got an early flight tomorrow."

"I've got an early interview with Congressman
Carlton. It's part of my job. You know, one of those
things you don't have."

"Right. Please don't make me get into hotels and
taxis. I'll get into a fight with Degrasse over expenses and
we both know that I'll lose. The woman is terrifying. Can
I sleep on your couch? Or bathtub? Or the perfumed
embrace of your bosom? C'mon, I'll make you dinner."

Lucy gathered her purse and pointed to the exit.
"The couch is good. And I've eaten your cooking, so
what you'll do is make reservations...AT A PLACE
THAT TAKES RESERVATIONS."

"Fair point."

They got outside and Lucy turned to Deke. "Where
are we eating? Nothing in a basket. And I want cloth
napkins, understand Mr. Hashtag Damn Deke?"

"Don't forget oppressed white men hate me too."

"Always making friends, aren't ya?"

"Yeah, they love me to death. I'm getting it in stereo these days." Deke looked into the window of Milo's Greek Cuisine, "You want to eat here?"

Lucy kept walking, "Do you not know what a reservation is?"

"Well, let's get a cab then. You work in a shit neighborhood."

"That's most of D.C."

He hailed a cab and slid in behind Lucy. As they drove away, small groups of young men began to come out of the shadows and filter into the alley Deke and Lucy just passed.

"Seriously Deke," Lucy said, "be careful with those ghost casinos. That sounds like the mafia."

"I just got back from Syria... Don't worry about me I'll wear my Kevlar turtleneck."

"I'm serious."

Deke turned and took Lucy by the shoulders, "Tomorrow I fly into the belly of the beast."

"You mean home?"

"Well, yes. Eventually, though, my luck will run out." Deke looked theatrically into the night.

Lucy failed to keep a smile at bay. "Now that was a good line!"

"Thank you."

Lucy settled into the seat. "You think you're pretty clever, don't you? You just fly into town after a month – having infuriated every women's group in the country and drinking whiskey with the fellas - and you just assumed I'd be free? Is that it?"

"Hoped is a better word."

"I'll have you know that I was invited out for cocktails tonight."

"I don't doubt it. You're a catch Lucy Burton of the *Brute* ...and yet here you are..."

"Here I am."

"So what happened to your gentleman caller?"

"Date got cancelled. I was whacked with an elk penis."

"I'm listening."

"Well, not *literally*."

"Lucy, how do you *figuratively* get whacked with an elk penis?"

"What time is that flight, Buddy?"

TWO:
BOYS BEHAVING BADLY

Into the alley beside Milo's Greek Cuisine they came in groups of two and three until about fifteen were gathered around the forcefully vaping figure of Theodore T. Landry. The gang stood silent in matching dark army fatigue pants and bright, wild aloha shirts.

"Who is Ballyhoo?" a tall skinny man named Danny Spewe asked Teddy.

"Hold on, Spewe! We gotta wait for Trevor." Said another boy.

"Put that damn vaporizer away, Teddy!" Said someone else.

"Shut up!" said Spewe, "We gotta wait for Trevor."

"For how long?"

"As long as it takes!" he snarled and smoothed his shiny, almost shellacked hair.

A door in the back of the alley opened and out came the unremarkable figure of Trevor pulling off his baby blue and white Milo's golf shirt and wrestling himself into a pink and yellow aloha shirt with toucans on it. "Sergeant at Arms present!" Trevor said in a voice far deeper than natural.

Teddy crammed the vaporizer into the pocket of his khakis and sucked in his stomach. He knew what was coming because the secret initiation into Ballyhoo was something of an internet sensation.

"Who is Ballyhoo?" Spewe asked, smoothing his hair again.

"BALLYHOO!" came the response in unison.

"Do you know who we are, Mr. Landry?" Spewe continued, "Despite what the mainstream media says, we are not white supremacist. We are not a hate group. We exist solely to be a voice for the voiceless American of European Descent – and to preserve that noble but beleaguered culture. And the first step in that struggle is to stand up for yourself. And as white men we need to stand up for our women. And to do that we need to be hard for the coming bugaloo!"

"BALLYHOO! BUGALOO" the twenty-something's howled.

"And Ballyhoo needs focus. That's why we don't masturbate excessively, to stay hard."

As he was taking this new approach to life in, Teddy failed to notice the rest of boys willfully avoiding eye-contact with each other.

Spewe looked around, "That way we stay hard!" Teddy thought the phrasing of the speech needed a little work.

"Ballyhoo!" they shouted unenthusiastically at their feet.

"We are a fraternity of peace, of brotherhood." Spewe continued, "We will fight to preserve the Euro-centric culture – of the Germans and the Celts, of kin and hearth – that we hold dear. The mainstream media will tell you this is bad, but it is *pure*. And that terrifies them. They don't understand because purification is hard. You need to wash away the soft, liberal dogma that would replace us with Jews and Blacks. Wash away the thought that masculinity is toxic. We seek only justice – and you must be clean to enter this League of Justice." At this Spewe went silent for a long time. "To purify yourself, Theodore T. Landry, you must endure the Ballyhoo fistbath."

"FISTBATH" The boys shouted.

"And you must keep your head about you as well. So, you will be required to recite the members of the Justice League as the fistbath showers you with blows. Are you ready?"

Before Teddy could answer, the gang screamed "FISTBATH!" in unison and closed in. Someone punched him in the stomach. Another gouged his love handles with a thumb. All around him the blows came and Trevor called, "Can you keep your head?" and slapped him in the crotch.

"Superman!" Teddy said as another gut punch landed. It really was hard to remember the names of the Super Friends in the thrall of a fistbath. "Robin! Batman!" another whack. "...uhh."

"There is no Uggh in the Justice League!" Whack.

"Robin." Thwack.

"You said that!" Yoink.

"Aquaman!" Inappropriate squeeze.

"More!" Someone got Teddy in the jacobs again – which he was expressly told wouldn't happen.

"Wonder Woman!" he called.

"That's right" someone said, "Ballyhoo boys *luuuuve* the pussy!"

"Agghhh…"

"More names!" screeched Spewe.

"Solomon Grundy!" Ooff!

"Hey!" Trevor shouted, "Solomon Grundy was the Legion of Doom!"

"Dumbass."

"Toyman!"

"Wrong again" said Trevor and went in for another groin punch.

"Wait," someone said, "there was a hero named Toyman."

"Naw, he was a villain."

"Yeah I know. But he was also a tween superhero."

With his hands cupping his crotch, Teddy looked up, "Yeah, I meant that one!"

Danny Spewe was a long, thin creature without much muscle to speak of. "But Toyman wasn't a Super Friend!" he screamed as the palm attached to that long arm arched around. What a good slap from Danny Spewe lacked in power, it more than made up for in inertia.

AN HOUR LATER Teddy Landry, newest member in full of Ballyhoo, sat aggressively vaping in the offices of brash political news start-up SLAMNEWS! Before crashing into the media scene, the office had simply been known as Teddy's apartment and as far as the landlady knew, it still was. A long, seductive cloud of vapor came from his nostrils and mouth and drifted up before him. It made him feel like modern day Sherlock Holmes with the nicotine soothing his nerves so he could focus his mind fully on the task at hand. Secretly, he even thought that it made him look like the famous hero, as opposed to just looking like someone sucking on a large plastic spark plug. The translucent casing was the same alarming orange color that matched the SLAMNEWS! logo. With no advertisers, staff or any revenue to speak of, many in the "establishment" press called it a blog – but Teddy had vision. He'd tapped into a rich vein of anger in the American psyche, and his brand of no holds barred journalism was getting noticed. He could also see that he was hungry and just where was his calzone?

He pulled the second cushion off the vintage corduroy SLAMNEWS! love seat and ran his hand through its crevasses. Along with some lint, Paleolithic gum, and a button, he mined a handful of change dating back to the Employable Era. He put this with the rest of the change and few dollars on the coffee table. He counted the money again and shuffled over to the jar near the bed with a strip of duct tape bearing the message *do not touch!* He touched and opened and pulled out two more dollars. He was sorting the meager stash out into well-organized piles when the knocking came.

"Tut's Pizza!"

Teddy opened the door to see a young man standing with a sack. "Two for one calzone and bread sticks, right? That'll be $17.75." Teddy began to count out the money. "Hey," the delivery guy said, "you're that SLAMNEWS! guy!"

"You don't have to shout it." Teddy said.

"Wow, you did a number on that senator from Mississippi – Davison... cost him the primary. Where'd you get that video?" asked the guy. Teddy shot a stream of vapor into the young man's face as he counted out his change. "What is that scent? Periwinkle?"

"Don't worry about it. It's a custom mix." Teddy said.

"That's adorable. Listen I'm a big fan of SLAMNEWS!" he shouted it again. "My boss says you're a real twat...so does my mom actually."

"Is your mom a longshoreman with a mouth like that?"

"Teaches third grade. Ah, don't worry about it Teddy –"

"Theodore–"

"I think you're an entertaining twat, Teddy. Those hashtag slap fights you get into are hilarious."

Teddy snatched the warm, greasy bags away. "They aren't supposed to be funny. What the crap do you know? You're a pizza delivery guy."

"And you're a blogger."

"Are you expecting a tip?"

"Not since you started paying me in nickels and seat cushion hair."

Teddy slammed the door. He was starting to have doubts about the all caps logo on the website. People were always yelling it at him – that wiseacre pizza boy had almost parted his hair. One calzone went in the fridge, along with half the second one, and each of the two breadsticks assigned to a portion. One thing about his poverty was that he was starting to lose some the baby fat he thought had always prevented people from taking him seriously as an investigative journalist. He ate the allotted portion of dinner and scrolled through the feed on his phone to find a *Daily Brute* breaking story about the congresswoman from the great state of Oregon. Apparently, the narcolepsy from which the congresswoman claimed to suffer to explain her habit of falling asleep during votes was really just garden-variety alcoholism. "Perfect example of the mainstream media attacking the GOP!" Teddy muttered to himself before realizing that the congresswoman in question was a Democrat. "Damn, those Godless heathens are what's wrong with this country." He muttered with approval. "Who wrote this?"

He looked at the byline picture of the Lucy Burton, which made her look more adorable than specifically hard-hitting. He tried to suck in his stomach, but it was still sore from the fistbath.

Then the phone lit up with the area code he'd been waiting for. It was not, however, the voice he'd been expecting.

"Oh… hey *Mr.* Wallace. What's up?"

"Listen Teddy, or Theodore, or whatever you're calling yourself this week, you really ought to learn not to sound so disappointed when you hear it's not my wife on the line."

"Well, I called Betty Sue…ehem…Mrs. Wallace."

"And I'm returning it, dab-burn it! As you can well imagine, Theodore, the candidate has been very busy since winning the primary. But I did want to touch base with you…"

"I've left six messages for your wife! If it weren't for me…"

"Of course, your positive coverage of Betty Sue's anti-establishment message has been wonderful. We *are* grateful. Which is why I'm calling… to thank you."

"To thank me? If you want to thank me you can grant me an exclusive interview. I need this SLAMNEWS! needs to stay ahead of the news cycle to attract capital."

"Ah yes. The go fund me page, yes, I saw that." he said. "So SLAMNEWS! isn't generating the traffic it did a month ago with that video of Davison? Where'd you get that dash-burn thing anyway?"

Teddy appreciated his not yelling the name, but Casper Wallace said it in the same sedative monotone in which he always spoke, a soft voice that seemed to be hiding something. He also had the feeling that this was not the time to admit a weakness. "I have my sources. And SLAMNEWS! is doing great!" He brushed his hand through his flaming red hair. "I just want to stay on top of things. You know, keep the coverage momentum moving."

"Well, it would help us if you shifted your momentum from brow beating the party elite in the election. The Chief says he doesn't like it." Casper said deliberately. "The incumbent is out – we've made our point. Davison is heading home, change is heading to Washington. We're running against Leo Kabler – a democrat – now, not the GOP."

"I know that! Everyone knows that! I'm already digging around but you've got to have something on Leo,

Mr. Wallace, a lead or something. He's a congressman from the gulf coast. You own, what, 150 gas stations or truck stops across the Southeast. You must have something I can use! Isn't your entire state just one big gossipy quilting bee?"

"Look, you son of a buck," said Casper, "I'm a businessman, not a political operative. I appreciate that you don't have the backing of a large, or reputable, news organization, so I'm making a small donation to your site. Anonymously, of course. I can talk to Betty Sue about an interview, but nothing exclusive, we need the national press."

"Hey, SLAMNEWS! *is* the national press, it has a global reach."

"So does my niece's Christian fashion blog. I meant mainstream press."

"Ahh, the fake news... look, give me something on Kabler! Just a rumor I can investigate!"

"Lemme make some calls and see if we can't come up with something. Now look, Betty Sue and I are going to try to be in Clarksdale this weekend for Labor Day dove shoot —"

"Ho ho! Betty Sue Wallace, anti-establishment maverick has gone status quo already!"

"This is Mississippi politics, Teddy. I don't expect to hear any more of your bull ca-ca about it. Of course, I can call the *Daily Brute* for an interview. Didn't you work for them once upon a time?"

Yes, yes he had. He'd resigned on a matter of principle, yet a nasty rumor persisted — no doubt spread by that dominatrix Degrasse — that he'd been sacked on a matter of ethics. Or more to the point, falsifying a quote. "No, no. I understand," said Teddy, "dance with the Devil for the greater good."

"I don't even like to joke about the Devil. Too hot for my God-fearin' blood. I'll make the donation tonight."

CASPER WALLACE hung up the phone. He could hear his wife on the hotel balcony overlooking the French Quarter, wo-hooing to the crowd below. Casper had retreated back into the suite hoping not to disturb the party on the balcony and, apparently, he hadn't. He was happy for his wife's primary victory. He was. For his own lot he was decidedly less optimistic. The O'Conners were very establishment people and Betty Sue was making a national name for herself being an angry rash their kind couldn't quite reach.

None of this was new. Once the children were out of diapers and in school, Betty Sue — now standing like a curvy, pilates obsessed Brunhilde over Chartres Street — had used the considerable force of her personality to shape a pleasantly innocuous Methodist church into her personal organ of social dominance in Jackson, Mississippi. Casper secretly suspected that the Women's Guild had placed the idea of national politics in her ear to get their church back.

Although the campaign manager/good Christian in him wanted to suggest she put the bright red hurricanes down and come inside, the downtrodden husband in him was glad she was getting drunk with the other wives and leaving him alone. He wasn't even on vacation. Bayoil Energy may have wanted its loyal vendors to get drunk on their ticket once a year, but Casper hadn't built his empire up from his dad's nine Digger Gas Stations by getting blind drunk in front of business associates. He was really hoping that he could convey the same sense of focus to his wife on her primary victory lap.

"Caspah, Shug?" he heard her coo from the balcony. His blood, warmed by only the occasional beer over the weekend ran cold. "Who were you talkin' to?"

"Teddy Landry."

"What are you messin' with him for? He's small fry."

"If it weren't for that video he pushed, you might not have won. The kid might prove useful yet. Let's keep him on the line."

She came in to the suite, hips swaying, a gentle bounce in her soft bosom, her hair – like a child's art project of yellow cotton candy and Aqua Net – remained immovable. "But Shug, I *did* win the election. *We* won it. Now, we need to get some real allies on the national level. We can do without Teddy and his desperate little frat boys. Have you gotten me, us, that invitation to that O'Conner Hunt? Can't do politics in Mississippi without it."

"I'm working on it, dear."

"We've come too far to lose to some jew from Biloxi."

"Betty Sue, now what did I tell you about saying things like that?"

"Sorry Shug. But this is a safe place, right?"

He glanced at the balcony full of drunk women. "I don't see how it is."

It didn't matter. She was right on top of Casper now, so she only had to whisper it. Casper hated when she got close enough to whisper. Well, he loved it… and she knew it… which is why he hated it. Her breath came low. "Surely a man like you, who moves as much fuel as you can call one of these Bayoil execs and wrangle us an invite… surely *you* can. Why, on that very balcony is Peggy Kipling – she said her husband is from Clarksdale. Surely they know *someone*." Casper swallowed hard. "Come on out to the balcony, that's where the party is."

"I don't think that I need to stand up right now."

He was staring down her cleavage as her lips, inches from his ear, whispered. "I'll bet you don't. You make some calls and I'll see what we can do about *that* later." She cupped his crotch.

"Okay." He said meekly. Betty Sue straightened up and put her hands on her hips. She picked up the phone and cooed into the receiver. "Aren't you a dear, honey? You already know what room it is. I need another round of hurricanes…" She turned to count the three women still on the balcony "…make it four. Pronto. We'd hate to dry out up here." She put her finger in the cradle and handed the phone to Casper. "Your turn to make some magic, Shug."

For the moment, Casper found the magic very diverting. Then his eyes fell to the muted television set on CNN: It was showing live aerial coverage of a massive fire. What looked like two enormous warehouses were entirely engulfed in flames as fire crews uselessly sprayed the blaze with water. Across the bottom of the screen rolled: Bourbon Warehouse Explodes. Rock Ridge Distillery. Bardstown, KY….

Once the magic had gone away enough to stand up, Casper went downstairs to the bar to find Peggy Kipling's husband and buy him a drink.

Downstairs in the bar, Ashley Kipling was having his temples massaged by the big Cajun boom known as Ronald Basco's drunk voice. "… Aint that right, Ash?"

Ashley was almost certain that it was not, in fact, right. "Look, sir, this is a Bayoil vendor event, you're the CEO of Bayoil, you can't just leave."

Basco looked at his watch, "Hell, I've got all these sum' bitches so drunk they don't know if they pitchin' or catchin'. Dey don't know if I'm here or gone. It's been a long weekend and you know I gotta fly to D.C. to snow that Congressman Kabler. I just wanna go find a quiet card game to relax, okay?"

"Okay. But you know there are *legal* casinos in New Orleans…"Ashley had been known as 'White Bread' in his college fraternity.

"Not like this one they ain't, a real gentleman's game" said Basco in a conspiratorial whisper that dropped even lower. "…And I hear that they got a voodoo queen, she'll put a hex on a racer horse for ya, before you go to the bookies."

"A hex, like a curse? Ashly said, "That doesn't sound legal."

"Ash, you're the lawyer, I'll let you make it legal."

"Will you quit saying that?!"

Basco slapped him on the shoulder, "Look, my car is here."

"Mr. Basco, we're being sued by the last driver for termination without cause."

"I fired her 'cause' I'm the boss." And he was off.

Ashely swiveled back to the bar to find himself face to face with Casper Wallace. "Hey, Casper, you seem relatively sober. What the hell did Betty Sue do with my wife?"

ON ESPLANADE STREET, running along the edge of the French Quarter, stood a well-preserved house with its shades drawn against the night. Louis Guillory was standing in the rear of its front hall, flanked by two dimly lit parlors on either side. Both were crowded with green baize tables and a roulette wheels serving a few dozen gamblers. Three heavily made up girls who looked like strippers with the night off were running in and out of the kitchen with cocktails, swerving around a rock-hard man – tattoos peeking out of the collar of his black suit – sitting at a heavy oak table displaced by one of the roulette wheels.

Guillory was wearing an elegantly rumpled, flax colored linen suit without a tie and ignoring the flirty waitress when the front door opened and in walked Ronny Basco. "Mr. Basco!" he said coming across the room, "glad you came." He turned to the flirty waitress,

"Listen, could you see Pencil and get $2,500 in chips for Mr. Basco here?" Flirty looked nervously at the wolfish creature at the oak table. "Mr. Basco's credit is good. And see what he wants to drink."

"I tell ya darlin' I do like some bourbon." boomed Basco.

Guillory guided him into the parlor, "You seem like a poker man, am I right?"

"Yeah. I tried that baccarat once, just like in the Jimmy Bond movie. Sheeiitt! That was expensive lesson."

"Well, let's play to our strong points. Look, I've had a few calls with Congressman Kabler's people, after y'alls sit-down Wednesday morning –"

"Iddn't Kabler a rampant environmentalist?"

"Yes."

"Duddn't he hate me?"

"He's about to hate you a lot less. He needs support for his senate run."

"I guess you're a good guy to know, Guillory. It's a shame you can't work for dad. You do good work. Still, whuy is it so important I fly to D.C. and where a damn tux with those sum'bitches?"

Flirty showed up with a double bourbon with a single fist-sized cube of ice.

Taking Flirty gently by the arm Guillory said, "Listen, Mr. Basco is a friend of mine, you take care of him, understand?" Then back to Basco, "I think you're gonna get lucky tonight."

A few hours later, the crowd was thinning out in the parlors and Pencil was still sitting over the bank like a snarling wolf. His brother Claude sat with a cheek propped on the table like a softer, prissier version of Pencil in a pristine white linen suit, pale blue shirt and pastel tie perfectly knotted and matched to his pocket square.

Pencil pulled at the collar of his perfectly average white shirt. "I don't like it."

"Your suit?" asked Claude. "I don't like it either, but your collection of unwashed thrash metal tee-shirts won't do."

Pencil snorted and fingered the thick, smooth plastic of the chip. "These cost twice as much as the ones we use at the truck stop. And we're out in the open too. I'm telling you, Claude, we ought to get back to the simple life of craps games, and running girls and a little junk. Harmless. No one even knew we were there."

"Grand Terre is going to be different." Claude fussed with his pocket square, "Have I ever steered you wrong?"

"Alright, I'll admit that the off-shore gaming operation was a hell of an idea. But we was still *off shore*... nobody knew we was there 'cept the oil companies and no one was gonna fuss at them. But Jesus man, we're right on Esplanade Avenue! We're exposed!"

"Now keep your voice down. It's only through the weekend. We're also mobile." Claude stopped popped off the table. "Congressman Casey, I knew we couldn't keep you away. Where have you been all night? Look Pencil, the congressman drove in from Lake Charles." The congressman bought into the game and Pencil watched the chips go into one of the parlors.

"Exposed!" Claude laughed, "You're damn right we are! There are two congressmen – one from Mississippi – a state senator, three judges and at least one partner from half the law firms in New Orleans that matter in this room. We may be exposed, but we're also bullet proof. And thanks to these private games, so are the truck stops and the off-shore gaming ops."

"We payin' a lot for that protection." Huffed Pencil.

"You never were one to see the big picture. Congressmen are a bargain – small audience, cheap media buy in – but the incumbency rate is about 95%. Once you buy one you've got him for about 20 years. If it doesn't work out, you throw a casino lobbyist at him." Claude laughed, "I guess that Guillory is good for something."

"I don't like *him* either." Said Pencil.

"You don't like anyone who can read, Pencil. Besides we're getting a lot more than what that redneck Sheriff was getting us."

"*Redneck* Sheriff? You really think you've moved up in the world, doncha, Claudel?"

"It's Claude and I'd leave the thinking to me, Pencil. Now quit talking, you'll get coon-ass all over my new suit."

Guillory came out of the parlor and approached the brothers. "Claude, a word?" He moved past Pencil into a vast unused showroom of a kitchen, retrieved his phone and sent one of the tired waitresses out on another lap.

"Louis," said Claude, "I hope you didn't fuck this up. This is important."

"More important than the first three times you told me?" He pecked at the phone.

"Don't get smart. I didn't *have* to take you on."

"You did if you wanted to get out of truck stops."

Before Claude could answer he showed him the images now streaming across the screen of his phone. Both watched a happy, fairly drunk and slightly richer Ronny Basco in an interesting tangle in the master bedroom with Flirty the waitress. "Really," Claude said, "You are turning this honest game into something sordid."

"That's rich coming from a pimp."

"*I've* never done time." Said Claude. "And you can go back. I wouldn't worry about it though, Louis. You aristocrats and we crooks are a lot alike: Spoiled, self-absorbed, access to cash we didn't work for."

"Let's not jump the gun with blackmail. Basco likes to place a bet so he may just tie himself up tighter than we ever could. Well, I've seen enough. Looks like he's closing the deal."

Claude eyed him suspiciously. "You mean you aren't staying for the money shot? Be a dear and see where do they keep the popcorn around here? Will ya look at that, it looks like a fat blood sausage. Should he see a doctor?"

He slipped the phone into his jacket and stepped around the oak table where Pencil Dechamp still kept vigil and hopped up the stairs. Coming out of the bathroom, he was confronted by a young man and woman who looked eerily alike. "Look, Mr. Guillory, gambling was one thing," said the young man, "But we didn't say anything about a brothel!"

"Ahh, the Harwell twins. Young Benjamin, I like your entrepreneurial spirit. Mom and dad aren't using the house for a month so make it profitable. Five grand apiece while mom and dad are cruising the Mediterranean. Good thinking, but remember you took the money – so don't worry about what is going on in mom and dad's room. You might wash the sheets though."

"That's so gross." Said the young woman.

"The lovely Annaliese, is it? You're growing up to be a proper young lady. I can see that you're both upset. I just don't care. When they get back, I assume that you plan on telling mom and dad that you've rented their beautiful house – and it is a beautiful house – wasn't it featured in *Garden & Gun*? So you want to tell mom and dad that you've rented their house out to a pair of cajun mafia goons to run an illegal casino – but not a brothel – because Young Ben and Annaliese have standards. How close am I?"

"You can't do this!" spat Benjamin. He never saw Guillory's hand move, but suddenly his larynx was pressed in a tightening grip. He grasped at the arm but his strength was flowing out of him.

"It's already done, kid. You took the money so just enjoy the ride." He looked at Annaliese. "I reckon you're the practical one. Get some shopping in and don't worry about the rest of it. We'll have the cleaning service come by and get the place ship shape."

He let go of Benjamin, who slid to the floor sucking for air.

THREE:
A WELL-ARMED POLITICAL THREE-WAY

The taxi turned off Magazine Street, and Deke could see home. Or at least he could see his brother's home. Behind the beautifully restored house of Ashley and Peggy Kipling, stood the not remotely restored carriage house apartment of Deke Kipling. The main house looked exactly like the home of a successful corporate lawyer for an oil company in New Orleans should: It was tasteful, fashionable but not overly so, and utterly predictable. Deke suspected that one day, when the couple first realized they were flush with money, Peggy had seen the home of a successful corporate lawyer in an interior design magazine and said, "That's the one." And Ashley, knowing that his wife had an eye for this sort of thing, said, "Yes dear." Which is, in fact, only a slightly foreshortened version of how it actually happened.

It was a little before noon when Deke paid the cab fare on the street, walked up the drive past his brother's house with his bags and climbed the spiral staircase to the veranda on which sat some potted mint. Behind the shutters, Deke opened the narrow french doors into a long, narrow room fronted with tall windows. Inside there wasn't much of a kitchen which served as a bar, an ancient green leather sofa and a section of cypress log being used as a side table. Along the baseboards were a few pictures and some ducks he'd never gotten around to hanging. The only thing on the walls was a couple of eight-point antlers, an elk, and a rack with two double barrel shotguns: an ornate Holland & Holland Royal, and a very unremarkable side by side. There was some coffee in the avocado green fridge, but nothing solid he dared eat.

He went down to the big house where he spied his sister-in-law sitting forlornly at the kitchen table contemplating a large glass of sparkling water. "You don't look too hot." said Deke coming in the back door with a knock.

"Ohhh. Hi Deke. Glad to see you're still alive." Peggy didn't look up, she was still staring down the enormous insulated tumbler fizzing away in front of her.

"Are you?"

"Check back in an hour. Did you fly in from Kentucky?"

No, D.C. I left Kentucky yesterday afternoon. Why?"

"You were at the Rock Ridge distillery, right? Did Ash tell me that?"

"Yeah."

"Last night one of their warehouses blew up... the blaze managed to get the next one over. We tried to call you last night but couldn't get through."

"Lord... I was just there. Was anyone hurt?"

"Killed a security guard. We were worried about you, Deke."

"Thank you. I'm fine. My phone has been acting up for a few weeks. Do they know what caused the fire?"

Peggy continued to stare at the fizzing water and drank off a long pull. "Details fuzzy."

"In general, or in your head?"

She pointed to her skull.

"What did you get up to last night?"

"Vendor event. Dear Lord. The wife of that fella from Digger Truck Stops is a force of nature. And she's running for Senate. Ash said he'd get them an invite to the O'Conner shoot. Tell your mom and dad to keep their heads down."

"Aren't y'all coming?"

"Nooooo!" she laughed. Then winced. "Owwwah. I'd never make it back alive. Not with Betty Sue Wallace stalking the grounds. You and Ferg need to keep her clear of the haint punch. She's got a hollow leg."

"She can't be that bad. I thought she was a Bible-thumper."

"I didn't think they made evangelical sex-pots. They're ... terrifying."

"I have to make a phone call."

Deke scooted out the door and was already back up the spiral staircase when Peggy said to an empty kitchen, "Okay. Deke, we're glad you're back. Might be time to upgrade that phone of yours."

Upstairs, Deke realized he'd forgotten to commandeer a sandwich, which was a shame because in Peggy's weakened state he could have made off with the smoked salmon and she'd have never noticed. He dialed the phone and was greeted with a hale, "The Intrepid Deke Kipling! Good to hear from you! Am I gonna see you this weekend?"

"Absolutely! Listen, Ferg, I have a friend I'd like to bring with me, a gal named Lucy Burton."

"Ahh, Deke's in love again...skipping along God's daisy chain. Marriage is a lovely institution. I can very nearly stand it."

"Is Missy coming?"

"No sir. She's taking the kids to her parents. You know how she feels about Daddy. Frankly, I'm inclined to agree with her, but I've built up a tolerance. But you,

Deke Kipling, are you starting a little family of your own?"

"It's not like that. She's a friend from work."

"Oh God, you're dating a writer. Do y'all sit around and say clever things at each other?"

"I'm not dating anyone, you boob. She's a friend. She does work for the *Daily Brute* though."

"Gee Deke, I don't know. Daddy might get pissed."

"I thought about that, Ferg. Now hear me out. What are you doing these days?"

"Your poor Ferguson Beaumont O'Conner is yet again between jobs."

"That's what I thought."

"Why would you think that?"

"You've been between jobs ever since your dad sold the firm."

"I've had jobs since then."

"Yes. Several."

"As you say."

"Look, Ferg, I know that traditionally no press has been allowed, but let's think this through; you need a job, and if you can get these politicos some good national press, in a controlled environment – on their turf – well, you might be able to get on with one of them as a PR guy. And the money in Washington is obscene."

"I'm listening."

"So, I was thinking I'd invite Lucy – as a date so she'll slide under the whole no press radar. Now she's been following the Mississippi Senate race for *The Brute* – Laudermilk'll love her – she's from South Carolina... smart and beautiful." Ferg stayed quiet. "Look, if she causes some bad noise, just blame it on me."

"It's not a bad idea. The problem is that Daddy – and he'll never admit this – has been fidgety as hell since he sold O'Conner & Locke. Darla is about to string him up. Now I'm unemployable and he's bored. He's angling

with Laudermilk to get a White House appointment as
Secretary of Agriculture or some such nonsense. It's all
hush hush."

"Even better, Ferg!" Said Deke, "If Beau O'Conner
is Ag Secretary or at least works for the office, then you
can pretty much write your own ticket. Hook up with
one of those lobby groups and have a ball."

"What, exactly, to lobbyists do? It's not like I went to
law school."

"They get politicos drunk and laid and then ask for
favors. Sometimes write check with other people's
money."

"Wow. I've basically got a Ph. D in all of that."

"I know you do Ferg. That's why I brought it up."

"Sure, bring her along but let's not say anything
about it now. I'll beg forgiveness later. Missy will be so
pleased that I have prospects. She says your ole Ferg
lacks focus. Oh, that reminds me... your brother Ashley
talked to Daddy – the Wallaces *are* coming. This Lucy
Burton friend of yours is sitting on one big, well-armed
political three-way. That's a great story, my man."

"Hell yeah it is. And you're right there in the middle
... making things happen."

"Sure. Deke, there is one thing I don't get. Why
don't *you* write it?"

"I'm off the clock. This is Lucy's thing. I'm trying to
help her out."

"Alright Sir Galahad. I'll let Daddy know you've got
a date."

Deke hung up and began to scour the Internet for
any developments on the Rock Ridge fire. After about 20
minutes he called Degrasse, who answered laughing.
"Oh Deke, this is too funny. I'm looking at a – I think
Francis calls it a *meme* – it's a badly drawn cartoon of a
buffoon in seersucker sportcoat... just like you've got ...

giving himself oral. It's a hashtag: *damndeke*. I'll send you the link."

"Please don't."

"But it's hysterical!"

"Mrs. Degrasse! Focus! The Rock Ridge distillery just blew up last night. Probably arson, massive fire. I need to go back to Kentucky. This is big."

"Well, safe travels.... Maybe you'll get a book out of it." Since the publication of *Vodka, Bears and Furry Hats*, this had become Degrasse's standard way of refusing expenses. "Your *awareness* is through the roof."

Deke hung up and was looking at his phone in a pathetic funk when it lit up with a New York area code. He always answered New York.

"Deke," came the confident voice on the other end, "this is Kenneth Macastle, from *Front Street* magazine. Listen I'm here in New York and was hoping to catch you at home."

"Good timing. I'm in town. How are you?"

"Fine. Like I said, I'm in the city and wanted to buy you a drink."

"Great, would love to. What are you doing down south, if you don't mind my asking?"

"I'm eating Deke. Eating well. Normally I leave the food writers alone to do their thing, but when we're talking about NOLA... well... it's good to be editor-in-chief. I'm in town tonight and flying to D.C. in the morning to attend some God-awful boring fundraiser for an opera house... or underfunded children. It all runs together. Anyway, I'd like to take you out to dinner tonight. Listen, I loved your 'Hell's Belles' piece. I understand you've drawn some fire from women's groups for that one. Hashtag: *damndeke*. Clever."

"Yeah, that's what I hear."

"Not a big social media guy, eh?"

"There is only so many times a fella can hear detailed instructions on how to turn his testicles into ear rings."

"Well, hell hath no fury. But even bad trending is good trending, right? Listen, I wanted to talk to you about another story. How does the Antoine's sound? We'll call it seven? Good."

Deke was fumbling around trying not to sound too eager. "That...let's see...that ought to work."

IT HAD BEEN a beautiful morning in Virginia. The kind of beautiful morning that Dr. Blanche Barker usually loved. Today, however, she was praying to Goddess to bring an end to the week and a three-day weekend to break the news cycle. She looked out the window at the students moving about below. It was still hot in Virginia, but things would cool off. Surely they would. Blanche had ended the term last spring a heroine, thinking at the time that her Institute for Sexual Ownership and Parity would get the voice it needed to stand up against campus patriarchy and pan-gender abuse.

She plopped behind her desk, fuming. In front of her lay a copy of *Tabula* from last April. It's sensitive coverage of a campus rape had mobilized the students around the country to protest those spoiled, misogynist bastards in their fraternity mansions that looked, at least in Virginia, just a little too much like Ole Marster's big house. She should have known that the next writer to come to campus, the one in seersucker sport coat of all things, was one of *them*. In the first interview, in the ISOP office, he'd seemed alright, then she'd got wind from her assistant that he was also talking to the accused boys.

"First of all," she'd explained with painful clarity that even a man could understand, "the victim's memory wasn't sloppy, it was traumatized. Of course, it was. It was a traumatic event. So perhaps she got her names wrong. She was trying to live her life, not fill out a police report."

"What about the Evans boy?"

"Okay, yes. That little Evans kid *was* in Newport News for a family funeral the night of the attack. But someone was guilty – and Evans was certainly guilty of *something*."

"Of what, do you think?"

"Well, patriarchal micro-aggressions are very pervasive. Universal, really."

"So he's guilty, just not of the crime accused?"

"They are *all* guilty of something."

"Even the fella she made up?" he'd asked.

"She didn't make *him* up, she just changed the name."

"So, there *is* a real name. Just not one the university of Facebook can find. Do the police know this name? or is it just you?"

"Something *did* happen that night."

"I don't doubt it, Dr. Barker. Was it something like the jello shots and Adderall?" he'd had the gall to ask. "Because that would cause a draft horse to hallucinate."

That's when Blanche felt the ground began to shift beneath her feet. Then the reporter leaned forward and asked a question that had absolutely nothing to do with the matter at hand. "Tell me about the OLA."

She coughed. "The what?" She arranged the pencils on her desk.

"Ovarian Liberation Army: A radical underground feminist army running around blowing up the men's rooms in various symbols of male dominance around the country."

Blanche said nothing.

"You know, the toilet bombers."

"Yes, I guess I have *heard* of them," she said "and, quite frankly, I applaud their work. I believe that it is a legitimate form of protest against the oppressive patriarchy. No one's been hurt − and men never listen until they think their precious genitals are at stake."

Deke considered this. "Fair point."

"But Mr. Kipling, the sign on my door says Institute for Sexual Ownership and Parity − ISOP − not OLA."

The knock on the door brought Blanche back to that pretty August morning as her teaching assistant, Summer Greene came in. Blanche always held that the most beautiful woman was a strong, confident one who owned her sexuality. And she meant it. The problem with Summer was that she was beautiful in other − more obvious − ways. A former child actress, she had face like an angel, tall and slim. She had hips that fashion designers hate but drive men − *men* − wild. Blanche had warned her that rutting Neanderthals were not the group she wanted to drive wild. Summer didn't look angry enough, not with those big doe eyes. Still, as an undergraduate, she'd laid some creep flat with a roundhouse kick to the skull for swatting her bottom. It had been winter, she'd been wearing riding boots. He needed bridgework. You couldn't take that away from her.

"Well, Dr. Barker," Summer said, "I sent off the grant request to the Athena Foundation. Now that the elk penis thing has run its first lap, we're all set to launch another round on social media against Congressman Carlson."

"What's the new hashtag?"

"Well that was a tough one. I mean hashtag: *elkpenis* is great − and it's still getting a lot of traffic − but it's hardly universal. Then there is *nopenis*, which might alienate the straight and cis-gendered women. So, we settled on *notyourpenis.*

Blanche thought about it. "I like it. Succinct, focused, vaguely mocking. Run with it."

Summer took the phone from under the book she was holding sent a single word text. "And it's done. And, umm, there is something else. Have you been following that big fire at the whiskey distillery in Kentucky?"

"Why would I care if a bunch of half-drunk Southern boys lose a few million gallons of brown water?"

"Well, you might want to start following it. The daytime security guard told investigators that 'some gal'" air quotes "tried to go into the men's restroom before the explosion. This plays out in the security video – but it hasn't been released yet."

"And?" Blanche asked indignantly after clearing her throat. She straightened her coffee cup realigned a pencil.

"Well," Summer shuffled around, "the police aren't making comments, but the press has speculated that the woman was OLA."

"This is the Institute for Sexual Ownership and Parity, not the OLA. That's what I told that damn writer."

"I know. I was tipped off by the sign on the door. But Deke Kipling didn't seem to believe you and since that story came out, the media has pretty much pegged you as director of both the ISOP and the topside face of the underground OLA."

"Hard to stay underground with all these hashtags flying everywhere."

"Social Justice Warriors will be heard. So, will the Hell's Belles."

"I know what he titled that damn story! Quit reminding me! It's awful."

"I don't know about that, Dr. Barker. I like the name – the fury of hell meets the Southern belle. We *are* in Virginia."

"You're from California." spat Blanche

"Hate him if you want to, but that Kipling ass described you as the Boudicca of Hell's Belles. And you aren't even a redhead! Sounds like high praise to me."

"Deranged Boudicca." Blanche corrected, failing to see said bright side. She turned to the wide, flat computer monitor on her desk open to the *Daily Brute*. "How is a website somehow more substantial than this!" She said waving the well-thumbed copy of *Tabula*. "Last spring I was Dr. Blanche Barker, Professor of Women's Studies and Chairwoman of ISOP. Champion of Oppressed Women everywhere. Then that victimized sophomore gets a few facts wrong, a few names –"

Summer winced, "...and dates and places and a fictional social media creation..."

"Oh shut up! Now I'll forever be known for being tied to an underground group of toilet bombers." She slapped the magazine on her desk. "So, someone blew up a whiskey warehouse?"

"Dr. Barker, I don't *know* anything. I'm just telling you what is all over the Internet right now. If it was a bomb, and she was trying to blow the men's room, it looks like she's OLA. If that's the case, then those harmless acts of protest have now killed someone."

"It sounds to me like some woman was rightfully ignoring outdated sexual segregation laws and a couple of buildings that were, more or less, seven story Molotov cocktails caught fire. I'm not going to worry about a bunch of Internet chatter. We've got real work to do. Did you send me that penis twat? Twerk...whatever." Blanche cleared her throat and stared at the computer screen. "Do you know who the girl is?"

"No, the investigators aren't saying yet. We're working on it."

"That damn story. Now everyone thinks we're tied up in this. The grant money is going to steer clear until this blows over. I've got to drive to D.C. to kiss the ass of that sawed-off little runt Leo Kabler so he gets off the environment and back on women's issues in Mississippi like he was last spring. You know I hate to back a man if a woman is running for office, but that Betty Sue Wallace will set us back a hundred years. What makes a woman do that to her own tribe?"

"Who can say?" said Summer. "#damndeke is still making the rounds."

"Yeah... good work on that count. So, what have you got on that misogynistic ass?"

"Nothing really. He's written a couple of books that appear to be travelogues to really awful places. Sort of made his name with an account of his working at a KKK summer camp in Arkansas called 'The C Word'..."

"So, he's a white supremacist too?"

"No. The C word wasn't 'Clan.' He was pretty brutal on them. And there his book, *Vodka, Bears and Furry Hats* is about the annexation of Crimea." She waved a copy of the book. "There aren't any bears in it."

"My Goddess, did you *buy* that?"

"I had too. After the 'Hell's Belles' article came out, Cynthia's boyfriend Kurt checked Kipling's books out of the library and burned them as an anniversary gift."

"Who says there aren't any good men around anymore? You know that ass got a royalty on that book, Summer? Why don't you buy him a drink while you're at it? I told you to research him, not support his children."

"He doesn't have any children. He's a bachelor."

"Obviously. What self-assured woman would want to marry him?"

"You never can tell about these things… He's cute."

"Oh keep it in your pants." Blanche fumed. "So, what do we know?"

"He lives in New Orleans. You know we have an ISOP chapter at Tulane, we could bomb the men's room at the student union as a protest."

"ISOP doesn't bomb toilets." Blanche hissed.

Summer rolled her eyes. "I can see if anyone at the Tulane chapter has a OLA connection."

"Well, I don't want anything to do with *that.*"

It had taken Summer sometime after becoming Dr. Barker's teaching assistant to realize that "Well, I don't want anything to do with *that.*" Was code for: *Mission approved. Proceed.* At least that's what she thought it meant. In truth, Blanche had never spoken or written down said code, but only acted it out in a lively, if vague, game of charades in an apple orchard one crisp fall day. Once Blanche was fairly certain her acolyte had the gist of the cipher, she hissed dramatically, "But this is no game, Summer Greene, and we're going to win it." At the time, Summer thought it prudent to not point out that the remark made no sense at all.

AT 3:45, MARGO KIPLING knocked on her uncle's door and poked her head in. She was sixteen but there was no telling her that. Around her zoomed her 12-year-old twin brothers zoomed into the apartment. "Uncle Suitcase! You're alive!" They screamed. "We heard you blew up drinking whiskey." Said Peter.

"Which would be a shame." added Derrick, "After all the places you've been… to get blown up in Kentucky. Geez."

"Thank you for your concern boys. Margo, thanks for watching the plants, the money is on the fridge."

"It's not about money," she said swiping the bill from under the magnet on the door, "I just wanted to welcome my favorite uncle home. Now I can sleep easy." She left with Peter, but young Derrick lingered.

"Hey Uncle Deke, I'm your namesake…"

"You aren't named after me. You're named after Grandaddy."

"Hey, we're all Derrick's here. So why don't *I* get the paying job?"

"Because Margo does exactly what she's paid to do. When you did it I came home and all my mint was all shriveled."

Derrick grabbed some scissors and went out on the veranda, returning with some well-tended sprigs in hand. Then he proceeded to make, somewhat deliberately, a mint julep. "Try this."

"Wow. This is fantastic. Boy, do your parents know about this…um…skill?"

"No sir."

"Now, I'm not suggesting that you lie to your mom and dad, but you might want to keep this one under your hat."

Young Derrick then proceeded to make a precocious argument to be hired on as the house bartender before his uncle threw him out.

RONNY BASCO'S BODY was finding it difficult to sweat enough to clean out the system. Even his proven hangover regime of a vodka tonic, long steam bath and a cold shower at the club hadn't worked. By the time he'd made it back to the Bayoil offices, he was already fading fast. And had only been at his desk, vaguely staring out over downtown New Orleans, for about 20 minutes when the secretary pinging in to announce "Louis Guillory here to see you."

Basco didn't remember responding, but there the man was in his office. "You don't look like you've found your appetite, Mr. Basco."

"Ohh, it be young again." Basco said without last night's booming *bon homme*.

"I don't know, you had a pretty lucky night."

"Well I don't mind tellin' ya that I came out ahead." He rubbed his temples. "Where'd you say this place was? We're not headed out to the bayou are we?"

"No sir. Just over in the Quarter. Parking being what it is, we ought to walk."

"It's hot."

"Not sure you want to bring her here, though. She's not real corporate."

"No." Basco muttered, "you're right about that. We'll stop on the way and get a bit to eat."

Guillory laughed. Said bite was, in fact, the piece of pickled okra jammed into the bloody mary. Then the pair pushed further into the quarter to a door in a wall so nondescript as to be next to impossible to notice if you weren't actively looking for it. It led to an alley way that opened into a badly maintained courtyard and on the far in to its uneven bricks, a small ramshackle house.

Inside the room adhered to a school of design known *Badly Neglected Creole* filled with some mismatched chairs and plain wooden shelves filled with, as far a Basco could tell, random voodoo shit. In the only chair that looked even remotely comfortable, sat a middle aged African American woman in a kaftan with her hair swept up in a faded read cloth. Were Basco wired to think this way, he might wonder if the woman seemed just a little too much out of central casting for a voodoo queen. As it was, he simply saw exactly what he thought he ought to be seeing. Now she was saying something and he had no idea what.

"I'm sorry?"

"What horse." She said with a thick backcountry accent, "what race?"

"Are you Madame Lemuex?"

"*Oui*. What horse, what race?"

"Now how does this work?

"You tell me what horse, what race. You pay me and I give you *ouange*. You place bet. You win big."

"Does it work?"

"What have you heard?"

"Your voodoo works."

"And I heard Ronny Basco likes to win."

He winced as Madame Lemuex said his name. He sat for a while, sweating and glanced over at Louis, who signaled to the side of his suit jacket. Basco pulled out a thick envelope. "Lotta money in here." he said.

Lemuex smiled. "Lotta magic in here too."

"Magic." Basco repeated and they all sat staring at each other until he handed over the envelope. At this Lemuex said something and another, younger woman came in and took the money. "Now, we fix your race."

Basco winced as she said that too. He hadn't known exactly what to expect, and somewhere in his imagination saw something like what his evangelical mother had told him was very "Catholic." With Lemuex muttering some damn gibberish or another, she stuck an old, enormous tooth into a small cloth sachet of rice. She tossed it to him. "You keep that in your pocket when you make your bet. You keep it in your pocket for the race."

Lemuex fell silent again but didn't move from the chair. Guillory stood leaning against one of the shelves, hands in his pockets. The silence in the room stretched out uncomfortably for a man not given to introspection. Finally, when Basco could stand it no more he laughed. "Well, Madam Lemuex, if this works I'll be back for football season."

He'd meant it as a parting joke to crack the silence, but Lemuex said without breaking her iron gaze, "This is very hard. To do this isn't to spook one soul but many. This is dangerous. One spooked soul does what it does.

Many spooked souls become a mob. Mobs are hard to control, even for *Li Grande Zombie*." She let that sink in then shrugged here shoulders, "But it can be done."

Basco smiled at this, but the microphone, hidden amongst the jumble of the shelves didn't pick it up.

KENNETH MACASTLE looked and acted exactly like Deke thought the editor-in-chief of a slick, storied big city monthly ought to look and act. Everyone in New York thought he was a cartoon of himself: handsome, but not pretty, and erring on the side of spastic. "Deke! Good to meet you." He popped up from the table and pumped Deke's hand. "Hey, thanks for meeting me on such short notice. I've had this idea I wanted to run you while I was in town."

It had been years since Deke had been in the dark red 1840 room at Antione's with its old portraits and muted lights set to a gas-lamp luminescence. "I'm surprised you want to talk to me with the bigoteers in full cry."

"Who? Oh, the Social Justice Warriors? Oh, they'll calm down and move on to something else. What are you drinking? Again, great work on 'Hell's Belles.'" The print out of the story was on the table. "but I have to ask, how'd you know that the campus assault story was bullshit?"

"Well, I didn't. It just seemed a little too theatrical. The story said the accused never responded. Who wouldn't respond to an accusation like that? If they were guilty there would have been a 'She's got no proof.' If they were innocent it would have been a loud 'I don't know what you're talking about.' But no comment? Those kids didn't even know they were part of the story until it came out."

A short-potbellied waiter in a white shirt and black bowtie set down a sausage and cheese plate and a couple of sazeracs. "Well, great investigative work, Deke. I took the liberty of ordering, but perhaps you drink mint juleps down here."

"Not normally. My nephew makes a great one. He's twelve."

"Wow," that smile lingered. "you people really start young down here."

"We have too, shortened life expectancy."

"Huh…" Macastle tapped the print out. "I've got the story right here. Just reread it. Not quite a tear sheet, but it'll do these days. And right under a banner ad for a product called…Smut Butter…which appears to be some sort of personal lubricant." It was a mocking little chuckle.

"I try not to click through if possible. So what's your idea?"

Macastle pinched his brow and drummed his fingers on the table. "Well, I wouldn't call it undercover work. But I understand…" He took a drink. "Jesus, that's stiff. Listen I understand that you've got some contacts in Clarksdale, Mississippi."

"Yeah. I grew up there. Heading up this weekend. Why?"

"Ah yes. And what does your father do?"

"He's a farmer. Do you want a Southern dove shoot story…cocktail party with guns…? I didn't think *Front Street* went in for that outdoorsy stuff."

Any pensive hesitation Macastle showed was burned away with a shining look and a winning smile. "We don't really. This is more politics. Do you know a fella named Beau O'Conner?"

"Yeah, he's a family friend. His son and I grew up together. That's where I'm heading actually. The bad news is that the O'Conner shoot is press free."

"Great!" said Macastle and tipped his glass. "C'mon, drink up. *Front Street* is buying. What we'd like is a story about Mississippi politics, told from *that* hunt. I mean it's been a hellu'va year right? We've got some cartoonish real estate mogul as president who spends most of his term sandbagging his own party. Down in Mississippi, the Republican incumbent is knocked out in the primary over a sex tape with a casino lobbyist by a renegade hottie who is now running against a career congressman gunning for the Senate. It's been a long time since Mississippi had a Democratic senator. Look at Alabama, though. Hell, given whose winning elections these days, Betty Sue *could* win."

Deke laughed. "If she does she's only stopping in the Senate long enough to powder her nose before making a play for the White House."

"Right." Macastle said, slapping the table and taking a deep quaff. "That's the kind of humor you bring to your writing." It occurred to Deke that as the editor of a magazine that had only published one the 43 stories he'd pitched them in the last three years, and that was by accident, Macastle seemed to be a devoted fan of his work. "Behind it all is Senator Laudermilk, the Old Bear of the Senate – in a cloud of persistent rumors about a presidential run. It's a great story Deke, and I think that you're the one to tell it. Think about it: A lot of media will want to know how this is going to play out, but you will be *our man* on the inside."

"Mr. Macastle I'm honored, but there it is strictly no press allowed."

"You're already going...*Front Street*'s man on the inside."

Deke managed to get the glass to his lips before tittering "Oh my!" and polishing off his sazarac. "Well, I didn't mean to do that." *Jesus Deke, get a hold of yourself.*

"Two more!" Macastle signaled to the waiter and gave Deke a wink. "You're hesitating, what's the problem?"

"Oh, no problem. It's ahh...I have to live with these people, you know."

"I thought you lived here in New Orleans."

"Okay, I want to be invited back."

"Oh, certainly. I understand. Don't do anything you aren't comfortable with, Deke my man. I just thought it was a good fit. Well, whatever's right. We were thinking a few thousand words..."

"...a few thousand?"

"Oh yeah, I see a long lead here. Plus photos."

"Mine?"

"Of course. They have to be, we can't get anyone else into the hunt, can we?"

"It's a dove shoot, not a hunt."

"Right. You see, that's the kind of useless crap you know."

"Thanks. I do see your point."

The next round of drinks came and Macastle started talking about cheese – he was an ardent fan with hard won opinions on the subject. Then he signaled for the check. "Deke, it was nice to meet you even if the dove hunt – sorry shoot –story doesn't pan out."

"We'll, I've got some heaps of ideas. Like, for instance, I was at the Rock Ridge distillery before it blew up. They think it's a bomb, now there is a great story..."

"- A warehouse fire?"

"Illegal gambling."

"Gambling is legal in Louisiana." Macastle seemed genuinely baffled. "Hell, I thought that everything was legal down here."

"Well," said Deke, "I just started chasing the thread, Mr. Macastle, but I've heard rumors of some voodoo queen throwing hexes around. Smells like point shaving to me."

"- voodoo sports fixing?"

"Well, those are the rumors."

Macastle stared at Deke for a long time before that smile began to spread across his face again. "Great! Listen shoot the features editor a query on that. How's Anna Degrasse? I'll bet she's keeping you busy. You wouldn't have time for a series anyway."

"Series?"

"On the web at least until the election and then a revisit again in print with a post-mortem in the spring. And I can promise that it *will not* be brought to you by the good people at Smut Butter. But if you don't feel comfortable... I'll figure something else out."

The waiter came across the floor with the check. Macastle craned over to get his wallet. It wasn't that the drinks had muddled Deke's thoughts – his thoughts were anything but milky. He could see, very clearly, the broad sunlit uplands of journalism in an organization with enough advertisers too afford to put itself into print. Advertisers like Rolex or those designers who make really skinny suits. How in the hell was he going to explain Smut Butter to his mother? *That* was murky. Very clearly, Deke could see an organization that would, on occasion, employ fact-checkers and copy-editors and much less routinely run lists claiming to be feature stories. And not just any print rag either, this was *Front Street*: the prestige, the portfolio, and the damn covered expenses. They'd published Faulkner and Fitzgerald – *before* he sobered up.

As the pot-bellied, bow-tied man set the bill on the table Deke looked up and said, "We'll have another round."

The waiter shrugged his shoulder, picked up the bill and shuffled away. Macastle settled into his seat and flashed a charming smile. "So, Deke Kipling, how do *you* see the story working?

FOUR:
GUARDIANS OF AN UNGRATEFUL CITIZENRY

THE OLD BEAR sat in a booth in the back of an out of the way cinderblock monument to fried chicken called Mac's. Aubrey Laudermilk liked fried chicken. You needed lots of pepper in the flour and the fat had to be "hawter than hell." Which is the way that Mac's did it. Mrs. Laudermilk was under the impression that most days her husband ate a salad at the capital. And he did, just not as "most" as he let on. Occasionally some homesick politico from Alabama or Georgia would wander into the place after hearing the Old Bear's magnolia accent singing its praises through the halls of power. For the most part, though, Mac's was Laudermilk's home terrain away from the buzzing hive of D.C.

Across from him sat Burt Carlson, who was looking uncharacteristically hangdog. When he'd first come to the Hill after winning his late father's seat, Laudermilk had taken the freshman under his wing out of respect to his old hunting buddy. Young Carlson, however, had proven better on the campaign trail than behind the desk. He had needed a lot of advice. So, he'd grown used to the fried smell of the place that seemed to be a narcotic to the Old Bear. Two beers and a basket of fried pickles sat between them. "What am I going to do?" Carlson moaned. "What. Am. I. Gonna. Do?"

"Eat your pickles son. You need your veg. It's like salad." The Old Bear never *technically* lied to Mrs. Laudermilk.

"I talked to that reporter yesterday morning, the little one, just like you said – and she absolutely hammered me this morning in the *Daily Brute.*"

"She was always gonna hammer ya, Carlson! And if you didn't put some strong medicine on the wound, it was gonna fester and good."

"The Chief is gonna be pissed."

"Well… he can't vote for ya either way, he's from New York."

"The press is having a field day over the walking stick excuse." Carlson moaned. "Do they really make walking sticks out of elk penis?"

"Hell, I don't know. They make them out of bull penus. I've got a distant cousin whose got one. He swears it's traditional, got it for a wedding gift so…there you go. You'd be shocked what people will excuse if they think it's tradition."

"Traditional. Jesus Laudermilk! I'm a laughing stock. I look like a twit!"

"Better than looking like a sexual predator."

"Who'd vote for a twit?"

"For God's sake, Boy! You're a congressman! Evidently *at least* 51percent of the voting population has no problem putting a twit in office. Take your ego out of it. Folks are talkin' about penus walking sticks and other terrible ideas from the olden days. Ya ain't the center of the story anymore."

"I swear if I ever see that little gnome again."

"Ya ain't gonna do a damn thing. She was just doin' her job. Lawd only knows what you were thinking to get into this mess. That young lady covers the Hill, so you're gonna see her again. And you're gonna be nice. I don't know how you stay mad at a face like that anyhow."

"You aren't trying hard enough."

"Hah! Maybe I'm not."

"What's going to happen now?"

"It's gonna blow over or it's not. Hell, look on the bright side, I hear one of these white fella groups are holding a rally down in Biloxi: the Ballyhoo Bugaloo – or some damn thing – at the Jeff Davis Presidential Library so you'll be outta the news by the weekend."

"I better. Have you seen the social media campaign against me?"

"Da' whut?"

"Social media, Senator. You've got an aide who takes care of it."

"Really? I'm gonna hafta take your word on that."

"It's hashtag: *notyourpenis*. Top trending … thing… right now."

Laudermilk worked on what he'd just been told for a pickle and two swallows of beer. He sighed. "Son, I don't know what in the hell you just said. Whuts hashbrowns got to do with it?"

"No, hashtag. Number sign. Pound symbol. You know, social media!"

"The telephone internet?"

"Yeah! It's driving the news cycle! It's not like the old days. A quarter of a million people have shared blurred images of genitals and phallic shaped food with my name attached and the hashtag *notyourpenis* or hashtag *elkpenis*."

The Old Bear chewed another fried pickle and washed it down while trying to get his sage head around the terrifying world Carlson was describing. "Come again?"

"A meme. It's like a pop culture political cartoon… but different." Carlson pulled out his phone for a tutorial. It began with a photo of the majestic elk with a bow tie on its knob, and deteriorated from there.

After a labored and detailed explanation, Laudermilk finally put his hand up. "So lemme see if I got this... potential voters taking pictures of a cake or breakfast sausage... shaped like *your* boner... and sending it to each other... and that.... *that* ... is driving the news cycle of this great Republic. Is that what you're tellin' me?"

It had sounded a lot less ridiculous the way Carlson had explained it. "Yes, sir."

Laudermilk took another drink. "Well, mah boy, I don't care who you are. That's just funny."

"It's humiliating."

"Yeah...but funny."

"I'm ruined."

"How many of those little pictures are in your district?"

"How should I know? Senator Laudermilk, you've always been good to me, but you should probably distance yourself from me for a while."

"Why? No one is accusing me of shuffling big game peckers."

"Jesus. Liberal hack job media."

"Where in the hell do you even get an elk penus anyway? Did you bag a buck last season and tell the processor, 'keep the John Thomas got somethun' in mind for that bit.'"

In fact, that is exactly what had happened, but Carlson wasn't to admit it out loud. He mumbled in his beer. "Listen, in years past, there hasn't been any press at the O'Conner shoot, right?"

"Never has been before." Laudermilk said, contemplating a pickle.

"I tell ya, I can't go to this opera gala tonight. Just can't face the press."

"Probably best. As for me and Mrs. Laudermilk we're headed home this afternoon." Carlson didn't answer, just peeled his beer label. "Ahh, snap out of it. You made your bed...or unmade it, I reckon. Look on the bright side – you get to suffer in silence. Poor Davison iddn't suffering in silence. Or more to the point, Mrs. Davison iddn't."

The waitress brought two plates of hot fried chicken, slaw and beans. "Speaking of the trials of David Davison..." Carlson was eager to change the subject, "What's gonna happen to him? Think he can run as an independent?"

"Not a chance. He's not that interesting. Davison couldn't bag a girl on election night gone right and then that beauty started mooning around him like he's the most charming guy on the planet." Laudermilk sighed, "That girl was a honey pot."

"So who set him up?"

"Hard to say, mah guess is that your Chief is in the way back of it. Sum' bitch is sandbaggin' his own party." Laudermilk pointed a thick finger at Carlson. "And you're helpin' him."

"No... so... What are Betty Sue Wallace's chances?"

"Oh Lawd, she'll might win, but only one term, I hope. She's too erratic. At least Kabler is greedy enough to be controlled."

Carlson stopped, shocked. "Are you saying that because he's Jewish?"

"Kabler iddn't Jewish. His grandfather was German. That old bastard fought *for* the Krauts. They brought him over to that POW camp they had up in Memphis. I shit you not."

"Really, I could have sworn..."

"If you had a skeleton *like that* in your closet and someone mistook you for a nice Jewish fella, would *you* correct 'em? Damn Nazis are worse than an attic full of Confederates."

"How do you know this?"

"It's my job to know."

"And why in the hell was there a POW camp in Memphis?"

Laudermilk shrugged his shoulders. "Damned if I know, it was a little before my time."

"Laudermilk, you've really got your fingers in a lot of pies, don't you?" Carlson said. The Old Bear only shrugged again. "You know," he said quietly, hunched over his plate, "There is a rumor that you're looking into a presidential bid in the next general…"

Laudermilk stopped with the chicken thigh between his fingers. "Careful. Nothing smells like a rumor mill."

"Senator, whose side are you on?"

He smiled. "The winning side."

And up until that moment, Carlson had never known that chicken leg quarter was bite sized.

BETTY SUE WALLACE did not like to be kept waiting on an ordinary day, and these were not ordinary days. She was on the cusp of her legacy, everyone knew that. Even her friends at church seemed intent on regularly reminding her of the greatness to come. And yet, here she was, waiting with Casper's executive assistant for him to get off the phone.

The Digger Corporation's main offices in downtown Jackson, Mississippi were modern but modestly forgettable. Which had always irked Betty Sue as it forced her into a lot of humble bragging about how the company was a lot bigger that it looked. She was telling Casper's enraptured assistant that "the ship of state" metaphor was flawed, that America was like a Thanksgiving table, and the fundamentals of bring Americans together weren't much different from hosting an elaborate holiday supper.

Then that unremarkable door opened and Casper said, "Sorry about-"

"Don't you ever close that door on-"

"Dab burn it, Betty Sue! Will you get in here!" Casper retreated inside. "And close the door behind you." He plopped down behind his desk to see his wife standing by the open door. "Please."

She shut the door. "Well, it's a good thing that I'm the candidate, Mr. Grumpy."

"I won't argue that."

"Shug… is there a problem?" She pulled the chair close to the desk and leaned forward on her elbows.

"I don't know." Casper said quietly. "That political strategist, Guillory, where did you find him?"

"Well, he had bona fides, Casper. He worked for Congressman Thibodeaux campaign over in Baton Rouge."

"Well, that was easy, Old Burns was caught with a pair of Vietnamese lady-boys."

"Thibodeaux still won."

"Yeah, I suppose. Wait, isn't he under indictment for money laundering?"

"Well, Shug, that's hardly his campaign strategist's fault, is it?"

"No, I don't guess so." mumbled Casper.

"And he *is* the one who dug up that video on Davison."

"It's playing dirty, Betty Sue."

"It's playing to win."

Dab Burn, if her breasts didn't just get larger. Casper thought. "Yeah, I guess so. Listen I just called the guy and asked him if he could dig up any dirt on Leo Kabler like he did on Davison."

"What'd he say?"

"He said that Kabler isn't quite as stupid as Davison. He said that few are."

"So is he going to get us something or not?"

"He's working on it."

"It's not like it has to be true, Shug. And whatever it is, leak it so someone other than that boob Teddy Landry."

"Well, Honey. Teddy Landry doesn't fact-check."

Betty Sue stood and planted her hands on her hips. "Who does anymore?" She smiled down on her husband, "You think we can use the lady-boy story again?"

SOMETIMES, thought Teddy, even D.C. could glitter. He brushed his flame red hair back and strode up to the Will-Call booth. The fellow in the glass box office looked vaguely familiar. "Press Credentials for Theodore T. Landry, with Slam News." He'd quit saying it in all caps.

The fellow gave a very convincing glance at the credentials laid out before him. "I'm sorry, I haven't got any credentials for SLAMNEWS!" All caps.

"Say, do I know you?" said Teddy suspiciously. He tried to inject his eyes with a hard and worldly cruelty.

"Not very well. You stiffed me on a tip the other day when you paid for a couple of calzones with belly button lint."

"You're gonna hold my media credentials because I didn't over tip?!"

"Didn't *over* tip?"

"I'll call the management."

"I'm afraid you'll have to. They're the only ones that can help, Teddy Boy. I don't issue the credentials, I just pass them out."

"I suppose you got fired from Tut's?"

"Nah, I got two jobs. Working my way through law school. You still a blogger?"

"I run a legitimate news site!"

The fellow looked over the credentials laid out before him again. "Evidently not."

"I met the request deadline."

"Just because you made the request on time doesn't guarantee it will be granted. That's why it's called a request and not an order."

"Listen, guy, do me a favor…"

"Sure."

"Is Leo Kabler in there?"

It is rare that doing the right thing is so satisfying that it outweighs the desire to tell someone to go to hell. "Yes." he said, honestly.

"You've got to let me in."

"I don't."

"It's for the greater good of the country. You've got to get me inside."

He thought about this. "I've got to keep my job. The overhead on law school is a bit pricier than your blog."

The voice came from behind. "Excuse me, can I slip by?"

Teddy turned to see the diminutive glory of Lucy Burton of *The Brute*. "Why hello." he said in the voice he privately called *Quiet Thunder.*

"Oh… Good evening." Said Lucy, far more nervously. She turned back to the box office. "Lucy Burton – the *Daily Brute*. Ah, thank you." She took the credentials. "See ya inside." And off she went.

Inside the gala, the lighting was a cool and blue. Kenneth Macastle was swirling the remains of a martini and admiring what the light did to Anna Degrasse's well-preserved face. "Is that your Lucy Burton I see?"

"Yes, it is." Degrasse couldn't stand Macastle and had vowed never to sleep with him again. Again.

"She's had some fine coverage of that Mississippi senate race. Really good writing. Better than that lunatic she replaced." He hiccupped. "Hell, maybe I've had enough. You know a martini is like a breast: One isn't enough and three is too many."

"Charming. How many have you had?"

"Four." He signaled the bartender. "Five....and a Manhattan for the lady. Did I remember that correctly?"

"Yes. Perhaps you aren't a total loss."

"Let's finish these and head back to the office. Maybe you've got some samples of Smut Butter we can get into."

"Oh, don't you act so high and mighty, mister! That rag of yours flogs more ED pills and creams than a dockside cathouse. I'm not even sure what that stuff is. I don't get this generation – they're so touchy about sexual politics, then they go posting naked pictures of themselves and buying personal lubricants by the case. Good Lord, what's wrong with a glass of wine and candlelight? A little conversation. Even *you* have more sense than that, Kenneth."

"The lighting in here *is* nice tonight. Very forgiving."

"Not that forgiving, you ass. I know that look, what are you up to?"

"Anna, I'm afraid I've scooped you on the whole Southern political front."

"Oh really? How so?"

"I've got a man on the inside headed to that O'Conner dove shoot they throw every year down in the Delta. It's like the Iowa State Fair for the candidates but it's all closed door, back room... or barn... politics. That Betty Sue Wallace will be there. Man! She's like Daisy Duke was thrown into some of that toxic waste they store down in Alabama. Well, we're all doomed but at least she makes good copy."

"So who is your insider?"

Macastle handed Degrasse the manhattan with triumph, "Deke Kipling."

"You're poaching *my* writers?"

"He's freelance as I understand it."

Degrasse fumed. "So he is."

"And…"

"Damn. Deke is back *in print*. They'll be no living with him now."

"And…" Macastle took a whopping swallow of his martini. "…I'm getting the boy on the cheap, no expenses. Of course, how many hotels can there be in Clarksdale?"

"Well played, Macastle. Thanks for the drink. I have to go tell Lucy that she's been scooped."

Back in the lobby, Teddy had left the Will-Call muttering that he had to go to the restroom, then ducked around the corner, ninja-style, towards the kitchen. All of which was clearly visible from the box office window. The fellow in the Will-Call booth giggled to himself and returned to his law text.

Once in the kitchen, Teddy fairly melted into the hive of activity. He hadn't rented his tux, but he had bought it used from the rental place so it had the same affect. Since his poverty induced diet, it had started to hang badly on his frame with the end result that he looked like a temp agency waiter. Picking up a tray of stemware, he started towards the glittering gala on the other side of the swinging doors. "Hey you!" barked a harried woman, "Since when do you take a tray of empties *into* a party?!?" Teddy's eyes immediately focused on a half champagne glass with a well-chewed wad of gum floating in it. She handed him an empty tray. "Now go take a lap."

He dove into the party, scanning the room. Taxing his staggering talent for investigative journalism, Teddy saw Leo Kabler blinking about the place in his round, wire-rimmed glasses. Most of the working press referred to him as "the Congressman from Wenwipast" for his habit of answering every question from a reporter, accountant, or barista with a run-down of some semi-relevant points of his legislative CV:

"What sort of break would you like on these trousers, Sir?" a tailor might ask.

"When we past the Caterwauling Protection Act... " he might respond.

It would be a stretch to say that his coastal Mississippi constituency actually *liked* Kabler, but he was such a greasy self-promoter that it was generally considered prudent to have the little rube promoting them.

Standing next to Leo was a big, barrel chested dude who wearing pointy-toed cowboy boots with his tux and a string bolo tie. "That's a weird pair." Teddy said and longed for a vape to help him think. He eyed the two again. Missing was Leo's ever-present aide, Kelly, whose contortionist like figure had such a nasty habit of appearing out of the ether to block his master from unpleasantness. The congressman's flank was open! Time to mount the advance!

Then, through the blue pools of light came Lucy Burton of the *Brute*. No sour grapes for Teddy, though. It was hardly her fault that she'd been hired to replace him after he'd... left. She might prove a valuable ally and her hair, he'd noted, did smell faintly of cucumbers. He set down the tray and picked up an abandoned glass of wine. *Try to blend in.*

"Congressman Kabler." said Lucy beating him to the target.

"Not for long!" said Basco, "It's about to be Senator Kabler. Am I right! Hi there, little lady, Ronny Basco."

"Yes." She said, "There's been a shake-up, hasn't there! Now Mr. Basco, as CEO of Bayoil Energy, I didn't expect you to be chumming it up with such an ardent environmentalist."

"We're old pals, ain't that right. And we're off the clock, darlin'" Basco boomed. Leo looked uncomfortable. They weren't old pals and he was never really off the clock.

"Is the *current* congressman enjoying the party?" she asked.

"It's always great to support the arts, Lucy. When we passed the Early Education Arts bill, it was in the hopes that those kids would grow up to support places like this." Basco was grinning blankly and sweating into his bourbon. Then the tension melted suddenly away from Leo's face. "Mr. Basco and I are working to ensure the future with an environmentally conscious energy policy. Quite frankly, I don't know why we've waited so long to do it. After all, we are a nation of energy consumers, so we need to work together for sound policy and job creation."

Basco just kept grinning. He'd just made a perfectly legal donation to this tree-hugger's campaign on top of authorizing still another perfectly legal corporate contribution from Bayoil. That Ashley Kipling made sure it was all legal. What he hadn't told Ash about was the bets he'd placed down at the track. Also legal but he didn't want to explain why he was so confident. And there was Guillory showing up with a briefcase full of money. Nothing illegal you understand, but the timing was... Well he didn't want to know why that old lady Lemuex had been able to call that race, but he'd taken the money and didn't really want to rock the boat. These thought whirled around in his head and, instinctively, he swirled the bourbon in his glass.

"DAMMIT!" Leo barked suddenly. "How did that clod from SLAMNEWS! get media credentials?"

Teddy really thought that he'd been lurking well and inconspicuously until the trio turned *en masse* to look at him.

"I don't think that he did." Said Lucy turning back to Kabler. "Ten minutes ago he was busing tables. He had some trouble with Will-Call."

"Well that damned Betty Sue Wallace is in Jackson makin' deviled eggs and sweet tea, so I know who he's after tonight. Where is Kelly?"

As it happened, Kelly Makin had spied the irked presence of Dr. Blanche Barker earlier and had planted himself before her, snugly bound in a tuxedo that seemed ridiculously tight for even his spare frame. "I just want you to know that the congressman is still an ally to feminism. And so am I, for that matter."

Blanche fumed and scanned the room. "A curiously quiet ally since this Hell's Belles business."

"Well, the press cycle is a reality. It wouldn't hurt you to lay low, let it blow over…"

"Oh, just like a man! The uppity woman has spoken her mind so now she needs to go back in the kitchen!"

Kelly looked theatrically hurt with a slender hand covering his aghast mouth. "Dr. Barker, I'd never deny my white male privilege! The congressman is just focused on energy sector jobs as he makes the transition to the Senate. We'll be in a better position then, a better ally." Blanche was scanning the room. Kelly kept talking, "Is Summer with you?"

"No."

"She's such a strong, independent woman. Intellectually stimulating."

Blanche sniffed. "Easy on the eyes, too."

"I'd never objectify her like that. Look, the four of us need to meet. We'll have lunch after the election."

Across the room, Ronny Basco let out a big Louisiana Oil & Gas laugh and that's when Blanche saw Kabler. "What are you up to now, you little shit?" She growled.

"I'm sorry, what?"

"Kelly, I want you to set up that lunch. Call Summer. And I don't want you to wait until November either!"

"Yes Ma'am!" he yelped.

"Mark it on your calendar. Now!" As Kelly was struggling to get the phone out of his rubber tight tuxedo pants, Blanche Barker locked onto Leo Kabler like a heat-guided missile.

Something in Leo's political amygdala popped and hissed. He scanned the room and saw her coming. Visions of fearsome and savage violence that would erupt after Basco referred to Barker as "a little filly" or some such nonsense flashed across his mind. "Excuse me Ronny." Leo said and put as much distance between them as possible on such short legs. Barker saw the move and adjusted her laser-like course. Far distant Kelly Makin, encumbered by his stylish trousers, trotted to catch up.

"So, Mr. Basco," said Lucy, now that they were alone. "I'd love to talk more about this energy policy Bayoil is sponsoring."

"Would you?" he kept grinning. "That's great. I tell you I'm not really the fella to talk about environmental impact issues. Lemme give you my card, I'll hook you up with the right egghead." Basco patted his back pocket, "Hell! It seems I left my card in my blue jeans. I don't normally wear these monkey suits."

"You have no idea what Leo was saying just then do you?"

"Course I do. Now obviously, the employment and emissions protections are a little premature."

"But Congressman Kabler....?"

"Sheeiiittt..." Basco was shaking his head, "Look, completely off the record, that little fella is good for a sound bite, but that's about all he's good for."

Degrasse emerged from the dim lighting with a worryingly pleasant "Oh Lucy dear."

She jumped. "Sweet Jesus! You scared me!"

"Anna Degrasse." She extended her hand to Basco. "May I borrow my political correspondent for some housekeeping?"

"I think you need to buy her a drink." Said Basco, "She's a jumpy little thing."

They walked off. Degrasse was waving delightfully at someone when she said to Lucy, "We've got a problem with Clarksdale."

"No, I've already talked to Deke, he's set it all up." Lucy explained, "He told me where to stay in town. It's called the Sunflower Inn…."

"Well, that's the problem, isn't it? It's not like the old days when we had an endless expense account is it?"

"I'm not sure when those days were, Ms. Degrasse."

"Look, revenues are down. I can fly you down but we can't afford a hotel."

"Have the Smut Butter banner ads not panned out?"

"Oh shut up. Look, call Deke. Doesn't he 'booty call' at your apartment when he's in town?"

"The couch sleeps one, Ms. Degrasse. So does the bathtub."

"The bathtub?"

"He'd just flown in from North Africa. I think he still had a contact high."

"Yes… that Benghazi byline did have a strange flow to it. Regardless, I think he owes you."

"He's staying with his parents – it's a family thing."

"You know those Southerners. Aren't you from South Carolina? You people always going on about hospitality, fried chicken and cornbread. Surely, he won't make a pass at you in his parent's house. Anyway, this'll be great, you'll get some local color into how those bourbon-soaked aristocrats actually live down there."

There was a slight commotion across the room. Degrasse watched for a moment. "And there's that Teddy

Landry being man-handled by security. Why, that boy looks desperate to take any deal I offer."

From across the hall Teddy's voice cracked. "This is an outrage! The fake news and the politicos are in bed together, Citizens! Have we forgotten our American ideals? Where is the sanctity of a free and independent press?"

The doors swung shut and Lucy watched them for a long time. "Swell."

That was about the time that the men's rooms in the Nebraska Union at Burt Carlson's alma mater exploded.

THE EXPLOSION in Nebraska went largely unnoted on Frenchman's Street. The avenue that stuck out like a live wire from the New Orlean's French Quarter. Deke moved down the street past the people spilling out of the bars and falling into an impromptu parade, dancing behind a thrown together marching band. The music faded away behind him as Deke turned north onto Esplanade Avenue. The street ran like a darkened, muffled time out between the light and music and bustle of Frenchman's Street and the Quarter.

Deke stopped in front of the Harwell's well-preserved house, mopped his forehead with a handkerchief and stuck it back in his sport coat. The shades were drawn, but at the right angle, he could tell that lights were on, if only just, behind them. A wiry fellow in a badly cut black suit sat on the porch swing, smoking and reading a paper that turned out to be a racing form. Deke went through the little wrought iron gate and up the steps as the suit watched. "I'm a friend of Louis Guillory" Deke said it the old way: *Louie*. The suit scratched the back of his head, and through the gap in the collar, a circle of tattoos showed. Then he looked Deke over. "All right." He said, nodding to the door.

Deke stepped into the dimly lit foyer and almost immediately a waitress was in front of him. "Hey handsome, what'll you have?

"Bourbon and branch."

"Gotcha." She said with a wink, "You know that the minimum buy in is $1,000, sweetie. The fella over by the kitchen – his name is Pencil – he'll take your money I'm Moon."

"Of course you are." Deke looked over her head and – speak of the devil – there was Louis Guillory himself standing like a cavalier with two young ladies who most certainly did *not* look like strippers. "Swell." Deke made his way through the parlor. "Hey Louis, it's been awhile. What are you up to these days?"

Louis looked at him for a long moment, "Deke Kipling, sure. It has been a while. Have you heard much from ole Ferg? Heard Mr. O'Conner sold the firm."

"He's fine. What are you doing these days?"

"A consultant. A political strategist."

The waitress came back with the drink. "You gonna buy some chips?"

"How'd you find the game?" said Louis.

"Ha!" Deke laughed, "Funny story. I was looking for a private game and I just figured that you'd be in the know so I dropped your name. And here you are."

"Is that what you figured? Listen Deke if you are gonna drop my name around town, you'd better follow the rules. What are you doing these days, Deke? A reporter of some sort I heard. Well, you'd better watch that intrepid step of yours." Louis pointed to Pencil hulking over by the oak table. "For old time sake, I'm gonna warn you right now that vicious coon-ass called Pencil doesn't like writers."

"A guy called 'Pencil' doesn't like writers?"

"Do you know why they call him Pencil?"

"I didn't know they called him that."

"That's not the name his momma gave him. It's a nickname, cute right? When he was in fifth grade he stabbed a kid in the hand with a pencil – went right through it – over a chocodile."

"Well, that is a bit aggressive, but they were delicious. I'm assuming that age hasn't mellowed him too much."

"Nope. And if you use my name –"

"Louis!" one of the ladies flanking him said, "you *will* introduce us to your friend!"

"Deke Kipling, this is Mary Helen and Vivian. Ladies, this is an old friend of mine from W&L. He writes books so ... loose lips."

"How exciting!" said Vivian.

"I once ate a camel." Said Deke.

Guillory cleared his throat, "Deke you'll need to get some chips – they don't really like people standing around when there are games to be played." That charm was back.

"And there *are* games to be played." As if on cue, Claude Dechamp materialized out of the gloom. "Louis Guillory, I see you brought a friend."

"Claude Dechamp, this is Deke Kipling."

"And what do you do, Mr. Kipling?"

"Yes," said Louis, "What *do* you do?"

"I'm a comedy writer."

"Well isn't that funny." Said Claude and swatted his arm. "A friend of Louis is a friend of mine. Lets' get you some chips and into a game."

Pencil was less gregarious. With chips in his pocket, bourbon in hand, and a massive hole in his savings account, Deke moved back into the parlors as the Brothers Dechamp watched. "What'd he get?" Asked Claude.

"Minimum buy in." Pencil snarled.

"One of Louis' friends?" Claude sighed, "Said he was a comedy writer."

"Maybe these old-money folk aren't a rich as you think. Who cares about the age of the money, we need volume."

"Don't you start again." Said Claude and was about to launch into a lecture when a small, mousy hipster came through the front door. "Well who do we have here?"

Claude approached the girl but before he could say a word, she breathlessly said the same thing that she'd told the fella outside, "If I had *any* idea who invited me to these wonderful scenes, I'd kiss them on the mouth, but I just don't." It was a ridiculous thing to say, but Wendy had heard her sister use the line to create what she called *idiotic male confusion.* "I'm meeting Deke Kipling here. Oh, there he is!"

Claude watched her dive into the room. Perhaps she dressed like a hippie to piss off daddy: This high-end clientele really seemed to hate their parents. The more money they had the more they seemed to hate them. In general, Claude didn't enforce the minimum buy-in with ladies on the grounds that they were so good at standing behind these Southern gents and egging them on to drain their trust-funds. Then he noticed that the olives in Judge Avery's martini were sitting in the glass like two skewered testicles out for air. That wouldn't do.

Wendy X circled back around where Deke sat at the poker table in that same wrinkled sport coat, talking to some old guy who was obviously to another of *his* tribe. She watched, played a few hands and talked to the old guy beside her who was pretending that he didn't need glasses. She flirted and watched. Deke seemed to detach himself from the man with whom he'd been talking. She was about to make her move when she saw the fellow in the linen suit with some dolled-up glamorpuss on his side slide into the chair beside Deke.

Guillory leaned in, "I don't know what you are up to – but don't let Claude's prissy act fool you. He's colder and smarter than his big brother."

"Lord, those two are brothers? Did mom feed them toxic formula?"

"And don't go using my name anymore."

"Fair point. Sorry about that Louis. So, political strategist? How'd you get hooked up with these guys."

"I'm not. I'm just here for a private game. And no, it isn;'t like W&L. I'm retired from running the games now, I just enjoy them."

"I reckon that a lot of public figures like a more private game."

"I don't know anything about that."

"Well, Louis, don't worry about me, I'm off the clock."

"I have nothing to worry about. You on the other hand…"

"I think I'm gonna stop while I'm ahead."

Mary Helen leaned forward, "Ahh, Deke, you're on a roll! Play another hand while you're hot!"

Deke lost the next hand. "Damn it, woman, never call a streak!"

"Sweetie, how can I make it up to you?"

"I'm sure we'll think of *something*."

Louis still seemed agitated, "Well, I'm out."

"Let's have a drink at your house, Deke." Said Mary Helen, "Maybe your luck will improve."

"Sure, but I have to warn you that it is past my bartender's bedtime, and it's a school night." He signaled the waitress, "What where you drinking – a cosmo? Another one for the lady." And set a chip on Moon's tray.

While the nostalgic and half-blind old guy two tables over concentrated on his cards, Wendy slipped a few plops from an eye-dropper into his cocktail. She swept both drinks up quickly and came around the table.

"Deke Kipling! How are you?" She cried in that voice her sister used.

"Fine! How are you?"

"Wow! You don't even remember me, do you? Here, I bought you a drink." She handed him a martini.

Deke looked at the glass, Mary Helen looked at Wendy. "Well," Deke cleared his throat, "I am sorry, you got me this time...I'm drawing a blank on where we've met."

"Skinny-dipping....?" Said Wendy.

"Still drawing a blank. Which is weird because that sounds like something I'd remember."

Wendy could feel she was losing him. "Let's have a threesome!"

Mary Helen and Deke graciously recoiled. "Alright," Deke said and handed the martini to Guillory, "You're on your own, Louis. It was good to catch up."

"Deke, I got that for you!" yelped Wendy.

"Don't worry darlin' it won't go to waste."

Louis threw the drink back. "Dead men tell no tales, Deke."

Deke and Mary Helen walked back over to Pencil and cashed out about $300 richer than when he'd come. Which was good because, at the last one of these, before Louis Guillory knew his good name was being bandied about, Deke had slunk off $450 in the hole.

FIVE:
IMPROVING ONE'S AIM

IT WAS THURSDAY, and now the end of this awful week was in sight. Dr. Blanche Barker looked out of her window and longed for the students moving about below to clear out for the sort of a long weekend she tended to think of as a living monument to Rape Culture. Not even that grim thought was what really vexed her. She twisted up her face without turning around to her assistant. "Who told them to blow up the Nebraska Union men's rooms?"

"Well, Dr. Barker," Summer started, "Since ISOP isn't connected in any way to the OLA, I couldn't say. But no one was hurt." Blanche fumed and tried to tell Summer to jump off a cliff in sign language. "You aren't very good at charades, are you?" Summer noted. Before Blanche could use her mouth words, she asked, "They've released the security tape from Rock Ridge."

"I know that. I was just watching it." She replayed the clip on her computer. "Who is she?" Blanche was groping with her memory. Something nagged, somehow the mousy girl seemed familiar, perhaps a former student.

Summer had taken one look at the tape and, given Blanche's agitated state, decided that a pleasant, blank smile was in order. "I have no idea."

"Well stay on it. Until that Rock Ridge security guard was killed, OLA was considered a legitimate protest. Now even MSNBC has turned on us..." Summer sat smiling pleasantly until Blanche remembered to finish her thought. "...them. And we don't even have anything to do with it. What about *Tabula?*"

"I've been on the phone with the editor, but let's not give them anything yet. Since we – the ISOP – are clear, this will pass." said Summer. "If we condemn the OLA we are admitting that we think it was behind Rock Ridge. Which, in turn, admits a connection or at the very least some inside knowledge. Or do we stand behind the OLA and assume they weren't behind the fire?" The two women exchanged glances quickly. "Or not say anything and look like the movement is fractured?"

Blanche slammed her hands on the table. "First, the *Brute* runs that damn 'Hell's Belle's' story which makes a *speculative* connection between me and the OLA, and now the rest of the press has made a *speculative* connection between the OLA and this woman in Kentucky."

Summer was staring out the window. Things really had gotten out of hand. The only reason she'd been in Virginia for college in the first place was because she'd enrolled during the media cycle for a Thomas Jefferson biopic in which her mother had starred. The movie was universally panned, but mother was determined that if she could appear sincere enough about the role she might resurrect her career from the doldrums of a teenage sex comedy mainstay from the nineties. For her part, Summer had dropped acting in eighth grade because her mother felt having a teenage daughter made her look like someone's mother. In any event, Summer had stayed on for her masters and became Dr. Barker's assistant, thinking that was a good idea because mom had landed a role in a movie about a spunky young gal encountering America's corporate glass ceiling. Mom did not play the role of the spunky young gal.

"Well?" prodded Barker

Well, that movie had been panned too, in the end. Summer didn't really mind the ISOP or the hashtags – men really were awful at times. But now someone was dead.

"Summer…are you there?"

"I've got it!" Summer snapped, "We support the Nebraska Union bombing. Ignore Bardstown until asked. Then say there is no connection when they bring it up. If one emerges, we'll be shocked and condemn it. I'll draft a statement inviting the male student population into women's restrooms. Hash tag: Everyone pees."

Barker grimaced, "But *they* pee all over the place."

"I thought we were against bathroom segregation."

"Obviously, Summer, I'm all for equality but there is a hygiene issue isn't there?" she thought for a moment. "And a question of aim."

"Okay, treat them like barbarians." Summer sighed, "Hash tag: pee on a tree? That might blow back on us."

"Revolting visual, but I see your point." She sighed heavily. "Perception consumes 500 times it's own weight in reality."

"Pardon?"

"That's what that sawed-off runt Leo Kabler told me last night when I tried to talk to him. That was after he said he was glad the lighting was so dim because he didn't want to be seen with me. He claims to still be an ally to the cause, but it feels like we're alone, Summer."

"Possibly not…that Kelly Makin is pretty hot to set up a meeting…the four of us…"

"*After* the election. And Kabler is running against a woman!"

"We could force Leo's hand over the weekend. Force him to come out in support of ISOP, which, as you say, is in no way connected to OLA or any toilet bombs or dead security guards. Perception would move in our favor."

"And how would we do that?"

"Have you ever been to Clarksdale, Mississippi?"

"I haven't been to Hell either, but I'm not calling my travel agent!"

"Those don't exist anymore, Dr. Barker."

ABOUT THE SAME time, on Esplanade Street, Louis Guillory was waking up in Mr. and Mrs. Harwell's enormous bed with the marginally psychotic Harwell twins fuming at the foot of its gilded and silky expanse. Annaliese threw a shoe at him and Benjamin was going on about the Persian rug Guillory was going to pay for and if that smell coming from the between sheets was what they thought it was he was paying for that too. His head swam, it pounded, his tongue was swollen and chapped and his soul – what was left of it – called out for the sweet embrace of death.

He climbed out of bed, rubbed his eyes and slapped his face a couple of times. Naked he moved across the room to the twins when Benjamin snarled, "Just look at you. You're revolting!"

Taking the outside ear of either twin, Guillory boxed both their heads together. "Now get lost before I tell mommy and daddy what you've been up too."

"You shit the bed!" Screeched Annaliese, rubbing the side of her skull.

"Well look at that…" said Guillory. He turned back to the twins.

"Shit. The. Bed!"

"Will you pipe down!" Guillory rubbed his eyes again. "I can hear you." He moved into the bathroom and grabbed a bath sheet. "Nice towel. This thing is like a toga.

"You're gonna fix this." Said Annaliese, "Daddy is gonna –"

"Ahh, you two little trustifarians have mommy and daddy wrapped around your slender little fingers don't you? Of course, you do or would wouldn't be quite so useless. The real problem is the federal charges of racketeering. And this is where you say 'but there were judges and politicos here all week.' But you see, there weren't."

"What?" asked Benjamin.

"No one was here and if you try to prove all those mugwhumps *were* here... well, Daddy is done for, isn't he? And more than that, so are your trust funds. That's why we call them Ghost Casinos. Now, what kind of shower do mommy and daddy have?"

The Harwell twins watched him shuffle off into the shower. The only thing that Louis was certain of in this wrecked state was that someone had slipped him... something. That and he *had* fouled the bed pretty rotten.

LUCY MOVED through the long newsroom and plopped down at her beautifully clutter-free desk. Ms. Degrasse's open door was closed and her office empty. Lucy opened a drawer and found herself looking at pocketknife Deke had left in her desk when he was heading to the airport without a bag to check. It was sitting on a neatly folded and laundered gingham handkerchief that he'd given her in January when she was running to interview the drowsily alcoholic congresswoman from Oregon and had a head cold.

The phone rang. "Hey Lucy, this is Tim over in Congressman Carlson's office. Did you hear about the bombing last night in Nebraska? Carlson is going to make a statement at 10:00."

"No! Oh my God! What happened! Was anyone hurt?"

"Well, no. The men's rooms at the Nebraska Union were targeted last night. The place was empty."

"Oh." Lucy relaxed. "The OLA blew up bathroom again. Really Tim, you buried the lede on that one. I suppose we've got a histrionic press release about 'the revolution' somewhere."

"Yeah, the OLA statement is pretty heavy handed. #everyonepees is lighting up all over the place. And Hell's Belles has released a statement inviting enlightened men to improve their aim and share their welcoming, non-judgmental restrooms."

"Swell. Now I've lost the one refuge I've got in public." Lucy really was crestfallen.

"Anyway, I wanted to give you a heads up."

"Does Carlson know you're calling me personally?"

Tim cleared his throat. "I don't guess I mentioned it, no."

"I'll see you at ten. I've got some calls to make before then. Thanks for the FYI."

Then she was looking at the gingham again and picked up the phone.

DEKE'S BATTERED Land Cruiser barreled down past the causeway and down the lonely coast road into Mississippi with Ashley in the passenger seat. "So, Ash, what are we doing again?"

"We're getting flack from the union, our maintenance guys are claiming they are being forced on the road longer than the rules allow."

"Can't you just track the trucks down with GPS."

Ashely sighed. "The union contract states that GPS tracking can only be used for logistical purposes. Not for employee observation or evaluation."

"So you know these guys are dickin' around, you just can't call them on it through the GPS, right?"

"Makes me wiggly that I went into the law. Anyway, we have to be careful about how we handle that information. So we're heading out here with the camera."

"Where are we going again?"

"There is a gas station the truckers keep going to, a Digger Station near Waveland. The drivers are complaining about how long they are in the road, but they aren't making deliveries. Maintenance guys are always around too. This place is in the sticks, so thanks for driving, Deke, the Mercedes would have stuck out like a sore thumb out here."

"But Ash, it's so you."

Ashley looked around Deke's old Landcruiser. "Hell, *Front Street* is calling you these days, maybe it's time to retire this heap."

"Maybe not quite."

"Did they get a new editor? I thought the last guy pretty aggressively ignored you."

"No, it was the same guy. Claims to have been a fan all these years."

"But didn't they stiff you on that story they ran by accident?"

"They did." Said Deke. "Evidently, they liked the 'Hell's Belles' piece."

"Well, little brother, you have arrived. Congrats."

"Not there yet." Deke's cell rang. He looked down at the number and all sense of accomplishment went away. It wasn't from Macastle and suddenly that name didn't make him think about prestige, the portfolio or the damn expense account at *Front Street*. Once he saw the number he was thinking about Lucy Burton and how mad she was going to be when she realized that he'd agreed to write a piece for a rival magazine – in glorious, timeless print. A great opportunity sure, but as short as Lucy was, a savage groin punch couldn't be ruled out.

"Hey Lucy, what's up?"

"Tricks not so good. Deke, I have a favor to ask."

"Anything for you." At this point he almost meant it literally.

"Degrasse won't pay for the hotel in Clarksdale."

"The Sunflower? It's like a hundred bucks. Listen, no problem. Ashley and Peggy aren't going, so they'll be plenty of room at the Kipling Baronial Estate. We'll stick you in Jane's room. Hate to disappoint you, but Mom won't let us bunk up, I'm afraid."

"That's a naked pity."

"Interesting word choice."

"Well thank you. You're the best, Deke. I'll bring a cake. There is something else. Last night at a some fundraiser, Leo Kabler seemed pretty cozy with that fella from Bayoil – named Basco. Are they opening a faculty in his district or something?"

Deke looked over at his older brother, who was hugging himself and making uncalled for smoochie faces. "Let me ask my highly place source at Bayoil. Puttin' you on speaker – Hold on." He swatted Ashley's head. "Hey Ash, Lucy Burton of the *Brute* wants to ask you a question."

"Shoot."

"Are y'all opening some facility or something in Leo Kabler's district in Mississippi?"

"Nope."

"Then why are Kabler and Basco hanging out in Washington? Did Basco cut Kabler a campaign contribution? They seem like an odd pair."

"Well, completely off the record and a big guess is that the big guy likes to hedge his bets, I guess."

"You mean he's paying Kabler off."

"Couldn't say, Ask no questions, hear no lies."

"Lucy, did you hear that?"

"That's off the record." Ashley called.

"Did you hear *that?*"

"Yes." Said Lucy, "A highly placed source at Bayoil says that talk of facility employment numbers are premature."

"Exactly." Said Ashley. "I like her."

"Hey Lucy, send me your flight info. We'll pick you up in Memphis."

"Clarksdale doesn't have an airport?"

"Yeah, but it's for crop-dusters."

He hung up, but Ashley eyed him suspiciously as the Land Cruiser speed past an idling Prius on the side of the road. "You've invited the press to the Labor Day shoot? Does Mr. O'Conner know this?"

It really was a beautiful day, if you didn't mind the late August heat. Deke contemplating telling his brother that *a* Mr. O'Conner knew, just not *the* Mr. O'Conner. True, Ferg was about as discrete as an aneurysm, but the boy was also fully capable of pulling a fast one on his father. Ash had, to Deke's knowledge, never pulled a caper on anyone: His *métier* was legal ambiguity. White Bread was respectable, why involve him? "No, she's off the clock."

"Then she *is* a date. So why is she staying at a hotel?"

"She's not, she's staying in Jane's room."

"So why *was* she staying at the Sunflower?"

"I, uh, didn't want to get a bunch of flack from Mom."

"You were trying to *hide* your girlfriend – in Clarksdale?"

"Mom gave you a girl's name."

"I'll tell you what I was thinking of, Deke." Said Ashley, "That it might be fun to convert my carriage house into an art studio."

"For your collection of pen and ink renderings of 3D transparent boxes? It's a subtle genius you have."

"Alright, this is it. Pull in."

"I don't see a truck."

Ashley looked at his phone. "He's here, it's a maintenance van."

The Digger Station #27 was a big split-level cinderblock building that looked all the more isolated amid the scrub and the live oaks hung with sad Spanish moss. Deke pulled into the station.

"Go around back." Said Ash. There they found it. Hidden behind the upper level of the building was a Bayoil Company truck. Ashley gathered his camera. "Alright, you pull back around and get some gas. I'll take some pictures and meet you round front." Ashley climbed out of the Land Cruiser.

Deke pulled around front into one of the bays and went inside to pay. There was nothing remarkable about the station, other than its size. He passed through to buy some beef jerky went he looked at the sales counter and saw, standing in the door of a back office, Pencil Dechamp, looking a lot more at home in jeans and a black tee shirt. He was nodding grimly to weather-beaten man in a black leather vest that said Rebel Yell MC on the back around a death's head with a confederate flag. The man lifted a tattooed arm and waved some money. Pencil shrugged his shoulders and pressed a button by the door. Rebel Yell stomped over to an unmarked door as a faint buzzer sounded and disappeared inside. And then Pencil looked up and focused on Deke. Their eyes met as Deke's went wide and Pencil's narrowed. Deke turned to the beef jerky.

The bell tinkled and Ash came in, took a leisurely lap around the aisles and stood by Deke. "Well, the truck is ours, but I can't find him. I'd like to get a picture. I know he's on the premises. Maybe he's in the can."

"How do you know?"

"The union also got company smartphones from us. I know he's on the premises. At least his phone is."

"He may not be in the can. That nasty looking fella behind the counter is the muscle for an illegal casino in town. He just buzzed some biker into that door." Deke nodded discretely.

"That one?" said Ashley, pointing across the store much less discreetly.

Pencil was starting at them arms folded across his chest. "Can I help you fellas find anything?" He said it in the most unhelpful way possible.

"Just a fill up and this jerky." Said Deke.

Five minutes later the brothers were heading back the way they came with an almost full tank. "He stabbed him with a what?" Ash asked.

"A pencil. That's why they call him Pencil."

"Over a chocodile?"

"In fifth grade."

"Well, they were delicious."

"I know, right?"

The Land Cruiser rambled back towards Louisiana, passing the Prius pulled on the side of the road. It quietly hummed to life.

"So where is your maintenance guy supposed to be, if not here playing craps with the Dechamp brothers?"

"We had a call about a pig-launcher on one of the natural gas lines."

"The what?"

"Deke, settle down, you can only get to it with an air boat."

"We're are clearly going on an airboat."

"We aren't."

"TEDDY." Said Danny Spewe, "Ballyhoo need your talents. You endured the fistbath and kept your head about you. You'll of course have noticed that your initiation video has not been posted. There is a reason for this."

"Yes." Said Teddy. He was sitting in a both at Milo's Greek Restaurant staring a Danny and Trevor. Danny smoothed his shiny hair, just yesterday he'd gone to the barber to get his "fashy" haircut trimmed and picked up his new "TV Suit" from the tailor, a snug three piece dark blue with a bold pinstripe.

"Ballyhoo needs your membership, your induction, to stay quiet for now, just a little longer. We have an assignment, and open collaboration wouldn't be a good idea."

"Do I get my gun?"

"What? We're a patriot militia, not the army. We can't issue weapons. But you are required to supply an AR15 for the bugaloo."

"Is that like a New Year's Eve party?"

"The looming race war, Teddy."

"Oh."

"You'll need to get a weapon though, it's in the by-laws. But listen, this is important: Ballyhoo isn't starting anything. We are protectors. That's why we're going down to the Presidential Library of Jefferson Davis in Biloxi, Mississippi."

"Which one was he?" Asked Teddy.

"The Confederate one." Said Trevor. "Keep up."

"We're gathering there to protest the left's suppression of free speech of white males in this country."

"Isn't Jeff Davis kind of a slavery thing?"

"It's history. White people – white man's history being erased. Now we don't want any violence but we will stand our ground. Sometime revolution needs violence. But we won't fire the first shot."

"That's good."

"You see," Danny Spewe continued, "'A well regulated Militia, being necessary to the security of a free state, the right of the people to keep and bear arms, shall not be infringed.' That's the second amendment, Teddy."

Teddy knew that, but he thought the 'well regulated' bit might be a bit rich. "What do you want me to do?" he asked.

Danny took and deep breath, "Well, as you know that the mainstream media is against us."

"Tell me about it."

"That story that ran in the *Daily Brute* made us look like fools."

"You mean 'We're Not Wankers'? Weren't you called the Hard Boys back them?"

Danny took another deep breath. "I remember the title, thank you. So we rebranded." Danny said a little too quickly, "Gotta stay hip and edgy in this game. That Kipling fella did a total hack job of course."

"Total hack job." echoed Trevor. *Well*, he thought to himself, *not a TOTAL hack*. Trevor had been there when they'd met that writer in the all-night café – he'd even picked out the black turtlenecks they wore for the meeting. He remembered that Danny had in fact started the interview by leaning in and saying, "The first thing you need to know, Mr. Kipling, is that we're not a bunch of wankers." Trevor didn't think much of the comment because it did sound like something Danny would say, but then he saw the smile spread across the writer's face like a man who'd figured out a hilarious punchline before delivery.

"He was totally fixated on the masturbation thing." Said Danny. "Probably a fag. Did you know him at the *Brute*?"

"Not well, he is freelance."

"We want SLAMNEWS! to cover the rally without the liberal spin." Said Trevor.

"Yes." Said Danny, "We need an embedded journo who will just tell the truth. Teddy, it should be the easiest thing in the world. But we can't be *seen* as colluding. That's why your membership must remain secret for the moment. SLAMNEWS! has credibility after you broke the story about that establishment patsy David Davison and the casino lobbyist. You need to keep that credibility when you tell our story. The saga of Ballyhoo. After you break the story, the press will have a field day, just like with Davison."

Teddy swelled with pride. The pain of the fistbath had been worth it.

"Now," Spewe continued. "We've booked a block of rooms at the Magnolia Coast Motor Lodge down in Biloxi, but it would be better if you didn't stay there."

"I thought I was embedded."

"Not *that* embedded. And you can't ride with us either. You'll have to make your own way."

"Geez, that sounds expensive."

Trevor placed an envelope on the tabletop between them. "We've raised some money for your expenses." He said. "But it has to be in cash. No electric trail."

"Okay." Said Teddy, "Say, how'd y'all raise the money?"

"Ballyhoo has its ways."

"I thought I was Ballyhoo. I mean, just cause I'm a secret operative and all that."

"Mr. Androlakis is a fascist." said Trevor.

"Shut up you!" hissed Danny.

"Who?"

"My boss." said Trevor.

"What? He took the fistbath?"

Danny motioned with his wide palms for calm. "We know it's a sacrifice, Teddy. But perhaps this will help."

He pulled a stiff mailer envelope from his computer bag and set it on the table. "As I've said, Ballyhoo has its ways. We happen to know that Leo Kabler took bribes from an off-shore gaming company called Corsair to ensure their license. In this envelope is the smoking gun. We want you to run it at the same time as your coverage of our rally. Got it?"

"Where'd you get it?"

"Hey!" came the booming voice or Mr. Androlakis from across the dining room, "Trevor, get back to work! Your break was over ten minutes ago!"

"HEEEEELLLLLLL yeeeeaaaahhh!" Deke hollered into the air as Ashley pushed forward the throttle on the airboat.

"Listen Hee-haw." came the voice through the headset. "Get a hold of yourself! And quit yelling into the microphone." The launching station rose out of the black water before them: a thick section of pipe that arched out of the water and was surrounded by a metal grate platform. Ashley slowed the boat down on the approach and Deke stood on the edge to moor the airboat as they climbed up on the station. "This thing has missed its last maintenance call." Ashley started taking pictures of the stamp on the lock.

Deke looked around. "Can you duck hunt out here?"

"That's all we need... the animal rights crowd joining up with the environmentalists. Speaking of, thanks for taking the boys up for the shoot."

"Glad to do it. We'll get the little fellas away from the video games and make outdoorsmen out of them yet."

"Good luck." Ashley said, shaking his head, "It's not like it used to be. They might be tarred and feathered if they talk about it at school. Take Margo for example, she's told every day to be strong and empowered, which is a great thing to tell a child – boy *or* a girl. But Peter and Derrick are constantly told they're the bad guys. Not because they've done anything wrong, but that they will, or we that did, or Dad did. Peter isn't any more rambunctious than I was. Now Derrick – I love him, but the boy is a spaz. Reminds me of you."

"Me?"

"The teachers want to dope him up on Ritalin. Like being a boy is a disorder to be treated. The kid just needs to burn off some energy, but PE has been replaced with Wellness and I don't even know what that is. Hell, I remember what those pills did to you."

"I don't."

"You were just, weird. Like a zombie but a really focused one. I felt so sorry for you I declared a wedgie hiatus."

"I'm still grateful, Ash. I mean that."

"Mom took you off the stuff and Dad forced you to join the wrestling team and sent you hunting all winter. I was the only kid in the state sick of eating wild game."

"It wasn't all fun and games." Deke said, "He made me refurb all the duck blinds and deer stands in the summer. They were like bucolic living rooms."

Ashley laughed, "Yeah, and Dad and Mr. O'Neal had to go out there and rebuild the damn things after all your 'innovative improvements.'"

"Really? Wait, was all that manual labor just busy work because that Mom and Dad thought I was a spaz?"

"*Everyone* thought you were a spaz, Deke! Anyway, I told Derrick's teacher the boy didn't need to be doped up, he just needed to run around after lunch. Boys are just like that, I said. God that was the wrong thing to say. She started going on about that damn congressman elk penis and toxic masculinity and how I'm excusing some future rape conspiracy. She only settled down when I pointed out that I paid her salary. And she's no fan of yours, Deke..."

"Oh, for the love of... don't *you* start!"

"Seriously, how the hell did she make that leap? Sure, that congressman is a sleaze, and he deserves whatever happens to him – but you know – there are crazy, violent women out in the world too!"

The signal light exploded with the first burst of machine gun fire. The next burst ran along over their heads, then lower, along the pipe. Ashley leapt forward into the shallow black water while Deke fled along the catwalk until his ankle turned and he fell hard into the grating. Shots ricocheted of the metalwork as Deke rolled off the six-foot drop into the water.

Above them, on a man-made ridge badly constructed at the height of the Huey Long administration, Wendy X watched Deke go down on the catwalk and his body roll off into the swamp. That was enough. She folded down the tripod under the Barrett M82 .50 caliber she'd mounted on the tail of the Prius and covered it with an unbleached and organically grown hemp blanket from Colorado. Closing the hatchback, she jumped behind the wheel, pulled her beret down, hit the gas.

The report of the .50 caliber report was still ringing in her ears when below the ridge, Deke and Ashley paddled to the far side of the pig launcher and climbed out of the water. They stayed low behind the cover of the metalwork.

"This camera is toast." Ashley said, "Eight hundred dollars! I'll bet I can expense it."

"Damn, Ash. That Save the Earth crowd is really playing for keeps. That was a turd in the punchbowl."

SIX:
AN EVENTFUL JOURNEY TO NOWHERE

TEDDY WAS CONFLICTED about a lot of things. Some were big constitutional issues like where one citizen's rights ended and another's begins – in this case violently illustrated by the passenger in front of Teddy dropping his seat back into Teddy's lap. "Metaphors suck." he mumbled. There were other conflicts vexing him as well. The big envelope Danny Spewe had given him was less 'smoking gun' than he'd imagined: A few spreadsheets from Corsair, a receipt for a BMW 7 Series Hybrid, what looked like a pair of quarterly shareholder's reports from Bayoil Energy. Whatever it was, it looked like it might lead to something mildly embarrassing for the Congressman Kabler, but Teddy failed to see any dramatic punch. A politician took campaign money from big oil, don't they all? Nothing SLAM! about that. The car was a bit much, but he had to at least try to connect the dots. He needed something truly awful, the sort of real-time developing click-bait you can flog about fifteen times a day. While the plane was still at the gate, he tapped out:

SLAMNEWS!

Leo Kabler bombshell – Details tomorrow! @SLAMNEWS!

The very name of the man who'd had him thrown out of the gala made his pale skin bloom red. Of course, it wasn't revenge for Teddy, it was uncovering the truth – but it would be sweet.

Lucy Burton spotted Teddy's blaze red hair as she moved past the first class seats into economy. Immediately she began to study the seat number printed on her ticket with a concentration not generally afforded to 18B. Two rows short of his, she could feel him watching as she stopped and asked the man in 18A to help stow her bag overhead. She slipped into the seat without looking back. Teddy cleared his throat and said the back of the seat two rows up and across the aisle: "I see you are headed to Atlanta as well." No response. Perhaps that his opening line was a little vague in an airplane bound for Atlanta. He cleared his throat. "Ehem!" Still no good.

The plane had barely climbed to cruising altitude when the pressure in Lucy's bladder began to grow. When the TSA agent had told her that she couldn't take her water bottle on board, Lucy had downed the whole thing because, well, aqua pure is a girl's best friend. Now she was thinking she hadn't actually won the encounter after all. She got up and, looking straight ahead , over and beyond the blazing mop of hair, marched herself to the restroom.

When she slid the door back open, she was confronted with the weirdly childlike face of Teddy Landry staring down at her. "Sweet Jesus!" she staggered back into the head. Teddy, his arm propped comfortably up on the wall, ignored it. "Well hey! Lucy Burton of *The Brute* is it?"

"Teddy, right? Did you ever get that press credential business straightened out?" She didn't have the heart to tell him she'd witnessed his lively exit as well. "They can be a pain sometimes."

"All part of the game, Lucy. All part of the game. I guess that's happened to you to before?"

"Not yet. Well, I'm sure you'd like to get in the restroom. And I'd like to get out of it. So…"

"Are you headed to Atlanta?"

She looked down the cabin. "We all are." Please don't say you're flying to Memphis. Please don't say you're flying to Memphis…

"Ho! Oh yes. I mean, is that your final destination?"

"I think people are waiting." They weren't but when Teddy made a head check she slipped past him. A few minutes later he was standing over her again, arm causally on the back of the seat in front of her. He let the *Quiet Thunder* roll. "I really liked 'elk penis'. It happens I'm working on a big one too." As an icebreaker, it had really sounded less awkward in his head. He cleared his throat. "A big story, I mean. Obviously. Not a big…"

"Hey!" said 18A, "pump the breaks, fella!"

"Yes, I'm heading down to Biloxi to cover the Ballyhoo White Voices rally."

"The what?" asked Lucy, "You mean that screeching white men's rights group?"

"Ahh. Well, there is more to them than that, I think. There is talk of armed protest. That's what I'm going to find out. I'm also digging into some leads on Leo Kabler's campaign. Big story."

"That sounds great!" said Lucy, "Good luck with that!"

"I saw *you* talking to Leo Kabler at the gala."

"Yeah. Sorta my job."

"There is a lot of corruption down there in Biloxi. It needs to be exposed."

"That's what you said. Good luck!"

"Yup. Gonna hit 'em pretty hard. Hit hard and expose…things." Teddy continued as Lucy's copy of *Vanity Fair* rose ever so slowly from her lap upward to eye level. "Don't get me wrong, I loved working at the *Brute*, learned a lot, made some good friends. Those were good years…good years."

The top bleed of the magazine was now about nose level. "Yeah. It's swell."

"So where are you off to?" He leaned in, "What are you going to expose?"

"Hey buddy!" barked 18A. "Don't ask her a thing like that! What in the hell is wrong with you?"

"I'm not… exposing…anything really." Lucy said. "I'm just…I'm going hunting…"

"Really? You don't strike me as a… wait… The O'Conner hunt?" Now he wasn't looking at Lucy, *per say* so much as at the charming, agreeable face of Will Smith.

From behind Teddy a stewardess cleared her throat. "Sir? I've got to get by."

"Nothing like that." Said Lucy, now looking at a picture of a handcrafted Teddy Bear that inexplicably sold for £135 at Harrod's. "I'm hunting… bear."

"Sir?" came the stewardess's voice again.

"Oh, I get it."

Lucy peeked over the top of the magazine to see Teddy touch the side of his nose. "Wait…*what* do you get?"

The drinks trolley nudged his ankles. "Sir! Please get to your seat. I'll have to call the captain."

"Fascist!" Teddy snapped and returned to his seat more intrigued than anything else.

Of course, she was hunting *bear*, the Old Bear of the Senate, Aubrey Laudermilk. That fat bastard had spent 30 years on the Hill claiming to be a Republican but, in reality he'd been "reaching across the aisle" and selling the country out to the liberals. Teddy looked over to Lucy. She had ambition, he had to give her that. They were hot on the same story, really. That they were kindred spirits only proved why she'd done so well in the post he'd been… he'd retired from at the *Brute*. They could work together on the story and make it bigger together. *SLAMNEWS!* in partnership with the *Daily Brute*. Any bad blood would be washed away with the light of the truth and justice. Together they would expose – no, scratch that – they would work together. The idea had legs. He smiled and slipped the envelope from Spewe back into his carry on and began to listen to some seriously vintage Duran Duran.

WENDY SAT in the little coffee shop around the corner from the house on Magazine Street. She was scowling. After losing the beret, she had her hair pulled up into a ponytail and was wearing simple pink shorts and a sleeveless top of the sort she'd seen sorority girls wear. She was looking at the television high up on the wall, where the news was playing the security tape from the Rock Ridge. She felt more preppy and land-rapey than sustainably sourced, but her revolutionary beret and smock were certainly all over the national news by now. The change in wardrobe seemed prudent.

But she'd done it! Goddess Dammit, She'd done it! Wendy X of the Ovarian Liberation Army was fired the first shot of the revolution and was now *underground* and how Days of Rage was that? The rickhouse fire had simply been the unfortunate dark cloud of a gathering storm. She looked at her laptop and began typing:

The opening salvo of the war has been fired and the OLA has hit its mark! Other pawns of the patriarchy beware, you can run but you can't hide. Men of the world, your oppressive domination of our gender is over! We will win because eventually, you're gonna have to take a shit!

Outside a siren wailed and she scrunched down a bit. Reading that last line, it did sound a bit vulgar. She listened as the siren faded into the distance. She was still in New Orleans because she assumed that with the ensuing manhunt after the assassination of damn deke, the pigs would assume that the assassin would be fleeing town. She'd out think the testosterone-soaked police by staying put and leaving with the hordes on Monday after a holiday weekend.

The wide flat screen up on the wall showed a lighthearted teaser for the early news: Activists were gathering to counter-protest the Ballyhoo rally in Biloxi, *and* how to make the perfect Labor Day burger. Details at Six!

Wendy glowered. *That* was the teaser? What about some misogynist prick being gunned down? Or the OLA strikes a blow against the patriarchy, or how the future is female. Maybe they hadn't found the body and it hadn't been long enough to file a missing persons report. Then she looked at her phone in horror. The she just decided, hoped, it was wrong. But how? She'd intended to wipe and destroy her phone as soon as feasible, but then she checked the GPS, the blue dot... *his* dot...was moving again.

Okay, she thought, he left his phone in the airboat. Bayoil has found the boat and hasn't reported it to the police. No, they'd jump at the chance to be victims. If the police have the phone, they'll search the area and find the bodies. So they have the bodies and aren't releasing the information for some reason. "No...."

She kept scowling at the phone, zoomed in on the blue dot moving along I-55 North. *If the police had the phone, it would still be downtown.* "Goddess damn it." *That little fucker was still alive.* Where the hell was he heading? She looked at the map; I-55 would take him through Jackson and into Memphis. She enlarged the image and a tiny line emerged into a squiggle of letters she could barely read to the east. She enlarged it again. Clarksdale. Clarksdale? Something clicked.

Quickly she switched targets and looked for the little red dot. It pulsed without moving for a long time before going dead. She touched her head but the beret wasn't there. She quietly left the coffee shop with a righteous scowl.

COAHOMA COUNTY, Mississippi − home-turf of the town of Clarksdale and not much else − was once one of the wealthiest counties in the nation. The post-Civil War years, however, have been touch and go. Mostly go. It was the birthplace of Rhythm & Blues and Rock & Roll and therefore − by the Transitive Property of Societal Algebra − largely responsible for the American Teenager. It is the place where poor ole Robert Johnson went down the crossroads of fabled Highways 61 and 49 to hitch a ride out of there and got posthumously labeled a witch. Teenagers can be cruel that way. Unfortunately for Clarksdale, there is no equity in legend. The town is surrounded by the low, flat Mississippi Delta that stretches in a nearly unbroken horizon of plowed fields along a quiet, unstoppable river. This largely explains the drinking.

Located about 18 miles outside the town in that alluvial expanse was a white Greek revival house built in the 1950's that, from the two-lane road passing before it, was doing a fair to middling job of looking like it had been built a century earlier. Several houses had occupied the site over the years. The first structure built by a white man was typical dogtrot cabin had been occupied by Benjamin Laudermilk, who would go on to build a grand mansion there in 1850. The Federal government, underlying its lively political point regarding secession and the institution of slavery, had burned the house down during the long summer that Ulysses S. Grant spent making himself so obvious in the area. The next house on the site was less grand. It was so second string that it hadn't passed to a male heir but to Benjamin's granddaughter, Eunice Laudermilk, who was clever and ruthless enough to exploit the hand she'd been dealt. She sat on the purse-strings of her reduced fortune like a determined honey-badger. The fellas used to tease her husband, Timothy O'Conner, about this. The bottom line was that Tim was never able to actually lose the farm at the poker table despite it being common knowledge around the hunt club that he had the skill-set to do it. By the time the New Deal programs had affectively made the Mississippi Delta planters rich again, Eunice and Tim's eldest son, who'd inherited the pile, deemed the sad old house unlivable. In 1958, he built what he was certain an exact reproduction of the old grand mansion General Grant had reimagined with such fiery gusto. Or at least that's what he told everyone. Regardless, it was certainly what he thought the old place *should* have looked like.

Now Beau O'Conner, the barrel-chested grandson of Eunice Laudermilk O'Conner, strode the back gallery looking over the folding tables and chairs lined up across the back lawn. Yes yes. Copper dog baths sat waiting to be filled with iced down bottled water. Yes yes. But people hadn't been coming to this shoot for more than a generation for the ice water. No no. On either end of the gallery two tables were set up that would soon be transformed into glittering bars that were still mere accents to the real center piece of the shoot's traditional refreshment. In the middle of the gallery was a low empty table, just waiting for its half whiskey barrel filled with Haint Punch.

He turned back to the lawn and eyed the smallish fellow assembling the oil drum smoker as the anchor of the eating area. "Not too close to the house, son." Beau bellowed, "The misses will have my hide if the smoke smudges the paint."

"I haven't moved it since you told me where you wanted it." The boy said.

"Well, watch the smoke anyhow." Beau said brusquely. The boy continued to read the directions and scratch his head. "Good Lord, son! Do you even know what you are doing?"

"It's a new model, Sir."

"I know it's a new model. It's the latest. That's why I bought it! This is very important. If Wilson Hardware can't handle the job then I'll get someone else to do this and I'll send it back with you! What's your name, son?"

"Hank." said Hank as he stared at the half-constructed smoker. "We'll get it right, Mr. O'Conner. If you'll just let me finish putting it together, we can wheel it wherever you want."

"It's where it's exactly where it's supposed to be, *Hank*! I just told you to mind the smoke so I expect you to do it!"

Hank had no reply that. He had no charcoal or wood with him and he certainly wasn't starting a fire before he'd put the thing together. "Yes, sir."

Beau eyed the boy suspiciously and decided that he didn't like the upstart's tone. No no, it wasn't going to dampen his mood though. For Beau, the annual shoot was all very comforting. It reeked of tradition and that was comforting after a financial hiccup had managed to swallow his commodities trading firm, O'Conner & Locke, up in Memphis. After selling out, his old partner Jim Locke had skedaddled off to Venice, Louisiana to spend his early retirement wingshooting and fishing and eating well. Which he chronicled in a self-published book called *Wingshooting and Fishing and Eating Well*. O'Conner thought that Locke lacked vigor.

As for Beau, he still had some life left in him. He'd returned to the house in Clarksdale where all things were as they had ever been since he was a boy. The opening day of dove season was a hallowed tradition Beau kept sacred, except that the Confederate flag bunting his father had hung had morphed – sometime in the nineties and at the insistence of his distant cousin Aubrey – to the current flag of the Republic. It was a small concession to make to the modern world, Beau thought. As Senator Laudermilk recalled it, at the time, that had not been Beau's reaction at all.

He did an about face and strode once more the length of the gallery, elbows out, chest forward. "Beau!" came the voice of Mrs. O'Conner. It was the spine-gripping Texas twang that got Beau every time. The first Mrs. O'Conner had possessed such a honey-sweet, whiskey-cured drawl so common of Delta girls of a certain generation. If only she'd been a better sport about the whole "what happens in Atlanta, stays in Atlanta" dictum they'd probably still be married to her and not facing fatherhood again at the age of 62. "Beau!" the voice split the humid air and ricocheted against his medulla. Despite her regrettable accent, he was very nearly certain that he loved the young Darla.

The fact that he called her Darla (not what her parents christened her at all) was quietly resented by the new Mrs. O'Conner. Back when she was his secretary, Beau decided he didn't like the name Darlene. She let it slide while in his employ, but on their wedding night - basking the tender afterglow of things matrimonial - she'd asked him to start calling her Darlene because they were married now and that *was* her name. "Yes yes. Anything for the new Mrs. O'Conner." He said and drifted off to sleep, forgetting forever that the request was ever made. She never brought it up again. Darlene Tick was no Eunice Laudermilk.

Ten months later a baby girl showed up while Beau was away on a hunting trip with Aubrey and the congressman from the great state of Nebraska. Darlene had gotten her revenge my naming the girl after *her* grandmother – Mavis. Beau called the child Molly.

In his customary take-charge manner, Beau strode into the kitchen where Darla was standing before a cookbook. "What do you want to eat tonight?" she asked, "Eunice will be here for dinner, right?"

"Lawd Woman!" Beau bellowed, "Have I got to think of everything? I'm dealing with every detail of this dove shoot and now I've got to create tonight's menu too!"

"The shoot never changes, besides, they're your kids, Mavis is still on mashed peas. I thought you might have some ideas. I see Eunice once a year. Is she a vegan again?"

"Probably!" he sighed. "But I'm not going hungry because of her. It's my house!"

"That's okay. I'll do a pork tenderloin with lots of vegetables."

"Make it an English roast, mid-rare, with asparagus and roasted potatoes."

"I'm not sure I've got all that, Beau. We *do* have a tenderloin."

A crackling voice came over the baby monitor that was sitting on the counter. "Hey there, this Johnny Torch. I'm headed up to Memphis. I'm looking for some friendly company! Over."

They stared at the baby monitor. "Hey," said Darla. "You said buy the best and the salesman said this was the best, most powerful baby monitor on the market."

"I'll say. Those truckers are a randy lot, aren't they?" said Beau before focusing again on subject at hand. "No no. Eunice is a vegan. We'll have the English roast. Yes yes. Where's Ferg? Is he in the mudroom?" Beau ducked around a corner and poked his head into the mudroom. It was an enormous closet with a gun safe, hooks along the walls, a deep sink and a tile floor with a drain in the middle. Sitting on a stool before a whiskey barrel that had been sawn in half was Ferg, applying more concentration than he'd ever shown in his career into measuring and mixing large quantities of bourbon, fruit, and wine. "Hello, My boy. How's the haint punch coming?"

"Very carefully." Ferg, a long and thin man topped with thin blonde hair, was consulting and old yellowed typewritten recipe originally invented, it was said, by Timothy O'Conner, lo these many years past.

"Yes yes. Your twin is flying in to join us. Into Memphis, I believe. Are you going to go up in the puddle-jumper to pick her up?"

Ferg looked up from the punch, "Daddy, you know that she only makes the trip down here and sneer at us for the weekend and then go home and tell all her friends what unenlightened hicks we are."

"Don't say that, Ferg. You know how much joy sneering brings to Eunice. Besides, she's family. I'm just glad to have everyone around. Sorry Missy couldn't make it."

"Yeah. I know. Not much for country life, that one. Deke's in town, his gal is flying into Memphis too so we're gonna fly up together." Ferg dipped a coffee cup into the punch and took a healthy slurp.

"Good good. Well, don't do too much testing of that punch if you're going to fly."

"Right-o."

"Beau!" Both O'Connors grimaced. Darla appeared at the door. "You – good Lord – you're making that hoochy in the barrel again? Last year there were splinters in it!"

"There are splinters every year, Darla." Said Ferg, resuming his focus on thoroughly juicing a grapefruit. "It's tradition."

"That's right. Yes yes." Said Beau. "Tradition."

"It's dangerous! Shug. Do you think that cousin of yours is gonna put you up for a job in Washington if he's got splinters in his mouth?"

"The whiskey retards infection." Said Ferg.

Beau grumbled. "This is a family tradition. Let's not be vulgar and talk about networking. No no. We're just having fun." He never really meant to talk to Darla like she was one of Eunice's friends, but he did have about twenty years on her.

"Well, a little networking wouldn't hurt Ferg here." Said Darla. "His only marketable skill is making that damn haint punch with splinters."

"I'm changing tack, Darla. I'm putting Missy and the kids to the curb and finding a fortune to marry. It's worked so well for you."

"Quit antagonizing your step-mother, boy!"

"Don't you start with me, Ferguson Beaumont!" Darla started, planting her fists into her hips, "Go ahead and joke but we need to support your father and make a good impression. It isn't just Senator Laudermilk – he's almost family. But didn't you say you invited Betty Sue Wallace? Why, this is real national politics. That Betty Sue, I'd vote for her for President! Bet I will too, one day. Now I've got to go into town and pick up a roast for tonight and *while I'm out,* do you need anything for this boffo concoction?"

"Please. Another sack of oranges would be helpful." Ferg had dipped the dainty cup into the whiskey barrel and took a taste.

"Can I just get a gallon of juice?"

The O'Conner's grimaced again.

"No no. It's a sack of oranges or nothing. So, you've decided on an English roast, eh? That's fine Darla. Couldn't do it without you. If you're heading into town, I think my suits are ready from the cleaners."

Darla sighed. "Lemme make a list, Beau. Is everyone coming here Sunday after church?"

There was a knock on the open door and in came Deke. "Hey Mr. O'Conner, Mrs. O'Conner."

Darla turned and sized the intruder up. "Oh, Deke. So good of you to come and take care of Ferg. Please call me Darla…or Darlene even." She gave Deke a long hug and her hand lingered in his hair. "It makes me feel old when a handsome man calls me Mrs. O'Conner." Both O'Conners grimaced yet again. Deke grimaced in his soul, where it really counts.

EUNICE O'CONNER shared her brother's thin blonde hair but not his lanky frame. She had inherited what her father called his "squatty body" on which she wore the latest granola-hipster styles to the worst possible effect. She was wearing skinny jeans and a blousy artist-smock that, on her heavy bosom, made her look like a ball of twine atop two pipe cleaners. Her adornments were of natural, sustainable material and appeared somewhat hand made by clearly impoverished children. Her scent was a fashionable BO. The only glitter in her appearance was a small glinting diamond stud in her nose. Unlike her brother, who seemed content going to work for Daddy to rape Mother Earth – or whatever it was that a commodity trading firm did – Eunice had fled the Mississippi Delta as fast as she could. At first to an exclusive all-female boarding school where she found a small but vocal tribe of girls with which she could sneer at the rest of the student body. It was little much for the local high school boys so Eunice was something of a dateless wonder.

On graduation, she got into UC Berkley where she thought her tribe would be bigger. It was. She even toyed with changing her name to free herself from its patriarchal roots until she realized that in a place like Berkley, California the name Eunice was about as far out as they came. She took to the place like a duck to water. By her senior year, her roommate managed to convince Eunice that she was both a lesbian and a witch. After a semester of honest effort, she decided that, while it was all great fun, she was neither. There was an emptiness in that little slice of paradise as well. At Berkley, while she had very many people with whom she could sneer, there were precious few worthy of really righteous contempt. So, she moved to Knoxville where she found both a loud tribe at the local university and lots of unenlightened locals who didn't know what to make of them. She made it a point never to miss the annual O'Conner Labor Day dove shoot.

Eunice walked into the small private terminal behind the Memphis International Airport and scanned the room. Behind her she dragged an enormous wheelie bag with another, slightly smaller case strapped to the top of it. She'd never met the woman she for whom she was looking, but had looked her up online after dragging the name out of her brother. Then she saw her.

During her layover in the Atlanta airport earlier, Lucy had been cornered into a coffee kiosk by Teddy, who made several jokes about changing his flight from Biloxi to Memphis. When got up to go to the restroom, Lucy made her escape. Now she sat in the private terminal in Memphis mercifully alone. Until she felt some approaching menace vibrating up her amygdala and turned to watch, with growing discomfort, the determined looking hippy lock in on her and begin an enthusiastic approach.

"Burton of the *Brute?*" She roared.

"Yes."

"Eunice O'Conner. My brother and your boyfriend are flying in on the family jet to pick us up." The little six seat Cessna was called the puddle-jumper by everyone accept Darla and Eunice. They both referred to it as "the family jet" despite its obvious propellers. Darla thought "family jet" sounded so much grander and therefore more wonderful, and Eunice because it sounded so much grander and therefore so much more awful.

"My boyfriend? Deke and I...yes...."

"Oh, I get it. I used to date my professors too. Just not to get good grades – that would be unethical."

"I don't think that you get it at all."

Outside the Cessna was taxing in. "See," Ferg was saying. "I told you not to worry about the haint punch – which you'll agree is gonna be great this year – take off is easy. And a little coffee bean brew and a half hour flight, wham-o, I'm good to land. Speaking of unfortunate drinking though, you know who called me yesterday? Louis Guillory... remember him from W&L? He was actually looking for your phone number."

"Really? I hadn't seen him in ten years until the other night at some casino house party."

"Yeah, Louis did like the cards. He didn't go to jail for running those books in Charlottesville did he?"

"No. That was after college. Securities fraud. I dropped his name to get into an illegal game."

"I know, he was pretty steamed about it. How'd you know it would work?"

"I knew he was back in New Orleans. Seemed like an educated guess, all things considered."

"You don't gamble."

"True. I'm working on a story but for God's sake don't tell him that. He has no idea what terrible habits I've picked up since college."

"He thinks you poisoned him."

"What?"

"Apparently, you spiked his drink and he woke up in his host's master bedroom, having used the bed for all the things regular people used the toilet for."

"That's a hell of a thing... I didn't give him a drink... oh wait a minute, some hippie gal bought me a drink on the way out and I handed it to him. It was a martini."

"The hippy girl was trying to date rape *you*?"

"She was probably more interested in my wallet. Tell me you didn't give Guillory my number?"

"Who loves ya, Deke?"

Inside the terminal Lucy was asking what she thought was a simple question. "What do you do, Eunice?"

"What do I do? I'm the director of University of Tennessee chapter of ISOP – the Institute for Sexual Ownership and Parity."

"Oh, a professor. That's interesting. What do you teach?"

"No, sweetie, I'm an activist." Eunice corrected.

"I see. So, what's your *job*?"

After a long moment, with both gals exploring a mighty awkward silence between them, Eunice cried, "Deke! Ferg!"

The boys came into the terminal as Eunice popped up and theatrically hugged them both. "Don't feel bad, Lucy, we grew up together." Then she took Lucy's hand, "Ferg, this is Deke's girlfriend Lucy Burton of the *Daily Brute*. We've been getting to know each other. Lucy, this is my twin brother Ferg O'Conner"

"Pleased to meet you, Lucy." He slapped Deke on the shoulder, "Good news travels fast. The entire state wants to celebrate your engagement."

"Easy big fella." Said Deke.

"I've simply got to tweet about this!" screeched Eunice.

"I've simply got to file some forms and we'll be off." said Ferg and shuffled off to the desk, sipping his thermos of coffee.

Deke reached for Lucy's bag and Eunice cried, "He's always been such a gentleman!" and left hers too as she breezed out into the tarmac hammering away at her smartphone. "Hashtag: *damndeke!*" She called cheerily, "Everyone still hates you, *dhaaling!*"

Surrendering to the inevitable, Deke picked up Eunice's massive wheelie bag set as well. "How was your flight, Lucy?"

"I was accosted by Teddy Landry on the Atlanta leg. Do you know him?"

"The SLAMNEWS! fella? He's not coming too is he?"

"Not for a lack of trying. I *think* he made his connection to Biloxi. Sorry about Mrs. Degrasse making me bunk with your parents."

"Glad to have you. I owe you a few. I drove my nephews up this morning so it's a full house. Mom likes a full house."

"And Poppa Kipling?"

"He likes a nap. Be warned, in the last 24 hours you've gone from *just-a-friend* date to girlfriend to pinned."

"I'm getting that impression from Eunice."

Eunice was waving from one of the rear seats of the Cessna. "Lucy! I've saved a seat for you..." she called. "We'll let the boys ride up front."

"Enjoy..." said Deke, "she's a live one." He climbed up front and put on a headset.

As the little plane moved upward, Eunice let out a groaning, weary sigh. "It's so nice to relax after a hectic summer. But, no rest for the weary, there is a lot to do."

Lucy asked again, "So what do you do for a living, Eunice?"

"Activism. Haven't we talked about this?"

"They pay you?"

"Oh, that... well no. I'm very educated, I have a Masters degree. It is *so* hard to find the right fit, isn't it? Especially being a modern, educated and sexually aware woman."

"Jesus, Sis!" said Ferg and flicked a switch near his leg.

"I think male bosses are scared of me, and female bosses are intimidated. It's because I'm educated and completely own my sexuality. Sorry Ferg."

"I can see how that limits your options." said Lucy.

"I wouldn't worry about it, Eunice. The gender spectrum is wide and varied." Said Deke.

"Listen to him. Isn't he just a dear! I have to admit that I was miffed when he wrote that 'Hell's Belles' hack job. Nice title though. I think our Deke was having a little flirt with yours truly, I mean, it's part of our history, really."

"..." said Lucy.

Eunice grabbed her hand again, "This is so much more fun that first class *commercial*. The cabin was full of industrialist one percenters. I tried talking to the lady next to me about this but she was just a prude. Very repressed. Probably constipated too. The two are connected."

"..." Lucy continued along the same theme.

"You know, the people in coach are just so much more real... I really should start flying with them." She trailed off. "Lucy, I hope you aren't the jealous type, and I'm glad we can talk like modern women, but your Deke was one of the reasons that I own my sexuality so completely."

"I really don't think that I am." Said Deke, toying with the headphones.

"We went skinny dipping together."

"Hey Ferg," said Deke, "You got any more of that haint punch? Ferg?"

Ferg didn't answer.

Eunice squeezed Lucy's hand. "Don't be jealous Lucy, it was ages ago. Right Deke?"

"Eunice, we were six!"

"I was very precocious."

"I wasn't. I was hot... it was July."

Eunice's voice got uncharacteristically soft. "In an innocent way, yes it was... *hot.*"

"It was hot in a July sort of way!" said Deke, "It was hundred degrees! I wanted to go swimming!"

Eunice rolled her eyes. "I hope my sister, Molly... Mavis... whatever her name is... will grow up owning her sexuality. But it's not likely in that house. Am I right Ferg?"

Ferg didn't answer but leaned into the center of the console to get a reading as Deke picked up faint traces of Wagner coming from his headset. Ferg loved his twin sister the best he could and a pillar of that family understanding was a slightly out of character fondness on Ferg's part for classical music. "It drowns out the sound of her voice and I know that it's the one style of music she'll never ask to sit and listen to with me." Ferg had told Deke many years ago. "Too patriarchal and land-rapey."

Ferg looked up and gave Deke a swell smile and a thumbs-up. In the rear, Lucy was still smiling in horror and thinking that she'd read somewhere that the best way to survive quicksand was to go limp. "Lucy, I've made you jealous. Don't be." Eunice said calmly and with entirely too much eye-contact. "What we had was beautiful, but it's long over. So how'd you two meet?"

"We work together."

"Ah. Are you writing a story about Uncle Aubrey too?"

"Deke?" Lucy asked.

"What?" Deke said a little too quickly. "I've yet to write a story about Laudermilk and I'm not starting this weekend. He's almost family."

"Yeah, but he's never run for president either."

"He is?" asked Deke.

"Care about the country's future much, Deke?" said Eunice and squeezed Lucy's hand again. "I'm very politically minded. We should talk. I could give some advice about your column."

"I'm not a columnist."

"It wouldn't hurt the *Brute* to focus on the new political reality of this country – we won't be in the fringe for long. Despite what Deke writes about us. Right Deke?

He didn't answer.

"Isn't he dear?" Eunice said. "We go way back."

From the front seat, Lucy was vaguely aware of the rising crescendo of *Siegfried's Entrance into Valhalla* from *Götterdämmerung* coming from both headsets.

SEVEN:

TEAM COLORS

WHEN THE TWO white men in suits – Guillory
thought they were lawyers downtown – emerged from
the forgettable door and onto the street, he got up and
paid for the coffee. Outside, he crossed from the dark
shade, into the bright, hot street and then into the shade
of the far side where he used his own key to open the
door and head into the courtyard.

In her junky room, Madame Lemuex was speaking
to her daughter, the camp creole gone from her accent.
She turned to Guillory, "Those two, did they come from
the casino?"

"No." He was still rubbing his stomach.

"You look terrible. Did someone put a hex on
you?"Lemuex laughed.

"I think a mickey is a better word for it. Listen, that
Basco fella I brought is pleased with his winnings."

"I do good work." Said her daughter, Tamara.

"Well, you've got to calm him down." Said Lemuex,
"Look, horseraces, basketball, we can even – ehem –
throw a curse on a boxing match with enough time. But
you have to get football out of Basco's head."

"You told him you could."

"Well I can hardly admit that *Le Grand Zombi* can't
throw a hex, can I? But I think I've put him off, but you
got to explain the limits of the magic."

"What'd you tell him?"

She laughed again, "That I put a hex on Colin Kaepernick and he's never quite come back."

Guillory burst out laughing. "That's brilliant."

"I learned from the best." Said Tamara.

"Ok, Madame Lemuex, lemme talk to Basco. He laughed, "I may have some leverage. Now, let's talk mixed martial arts."

PASS CHRISTIAN, Mississippi is one of those gulf towns that started life as Louisiana and never received the memo of a transfer. The entire peninsula, wedged between Biloxi and New Orleans was owned by one Widow Asmard who, upon her death in 1799, bequeathed most of what is now downtown to a *gens de couleur* libre – free person of color - because that would really chap the neighbors. By 1801 they were all Americans, but there was no telling them that. The booming upper class of New Orleans began to build summer mansions along the coast.

This was not one of them. True, the mansion looked antebellum – and it was built in 1925 and therefore before *a* war – but like the O'Conner property, not as "ante" as it let on. It had been a nice house, but then battered by hurricanes and floods and only marginally maintained by a succession of owners. The last of that line loved the place and bought it on the cheap. Then came the monumental expense of restoration, along with, and this is what surprised the current owners, the Kafkaesque labyrinth of red tape required to get anything done with an historic house.

Then a prissy, charming man named Claude Dechamp showed up and offered the shell-shocked couple a possible solution. He hosted an honest, friendly, admittedly tax-free but mostly private game for those who liked to gamble but preferred something more discreet than the clanging casinos. The Lady of the Manor was horrified. The Lord had decided he'd better be as well, but his heart wasn't in his indignation. Then suddenly some of the permit hassles freed up and, lo and behold, their new friend Claude reappeared seeming to know something about it. He again mentioned the private game, and what they'd take as a cut. And that cut just might help with the costs of the renovation. It was temporary, you understand. Host a few nights, then they'd be on their way. Might call again in the spring. That was, of course, up to them.

The Lady was much less horrified the second time around. As it turned out, a game in New Orleans had ended abruptly and no one wanted to know more than that. So Claude took over the house and began to fuss up the parlors – still in the midst of renovation – with a decaying opulence. Claude had a touch for that kind of thing.

An hour after leaving Madam Lemuex's, Guillory pulled up in front of the house and still felt like rot. Whatever Deke or that hippie had slipped him was taking its time to get out of the system. He painfully climbed the steps to the house and looked around the entrance hall. "Like what you've done with the place, Claude."

Claude caught sight of him. "Louis, how good of you to come. I hope you are feeling better?"

"That was low, Claude."

Claude fussed with a pocket square. "What do you mean? You're the one who vomited on the floor and shit the master bedroom. We took care of you. You need to remember who your friends are, Louis. And you pays you. Those sadistic twins won't have us back. And the Harwell's go abroad *every summer.* You've caused a lot of trouble for us."

"One of your truck stop whores poisoned me."

"Let's not make accusations we can't take back, Louis."

"And let's not get ahead of ourselves, *Claudel*, your precious clients don't come to your games for the gamble or the whores –"

"Sure about that?"

"They come for Lemuex."

"Oh please, they don't believe in that voodoo."

"They believe that she can fix a game. And having a judge in your pocket isn't going to do much good there. Vegas can outspend you.

Claude drifted off. His eyes were still looking at Guillory but his mind had moved beyond him. Trying to unravel some idea that was like mastering one of those metal ring games: he almost had it, but not quite. "How's she do it?"

"Voodoo, Claudel, I told you."

"Uh huh." Claude said, still working the ring trick in his head.

"You don't wanna fuck with that. Or me. One of you truck stop whore poisoned me!"

"Louis…"

"Claude, I don't care who you've bought off! I can take them out of office as easy as I can put them in. So, don't fuck with me, I *know* where the bodies are buried."

By now Pencil had come out of the back of the house and was standing with them. Claude cut him a quick glance and said, "Interesting word choice. I'm not so sure it was one of my girls, Louis. There were a lot of people, shall we say, out of place the other night. Your friend, the mousy little hippie, stole two martinis from Mr. Macbee. And he's a very good guest. And then you were drinking them, with *your* hippie friend."

"I don't know who the hell that was!" said Louis. Pencil quietly began examining his fingernails. "She wasn't *my* friend. I'd never seen her before in my life."

"Well, she did seem to know your chum, Deke Kipling was it? He was there on your recommendation, was he not?"

"I hadn't seen that guy in ten years."

"And yet there he was, using your name to get in. He's been playing a lot lately. Came by the truck stop yesterday. With friends like that…"

He looked at Pencil again. "You can't strong arm me. One phone call will bust this place wide open."

Claude smiled warmly. Pencil maintained something cold and inhuman. "Well," said Claude, "Let me save you the trouble. Judge Able will be here opening night, along with the chief of police. Shall I let them know your grievance?" Claude let that sink in. "And your friend, Deke Kipling. Silly name if you ask me but I'm Claudel Dechamp so what can I say? Turns out he's a journalist. Not a comedy writer at all. You, Louis Guillory, invited a reporter into this private game. That really will get everyone thrown out of office. And what do you think these esteemed guests would think about that? They have voters to think about. Can your Madam Lemuex put the mojo on an election?"

Pencil's iron like arm fell around Guillory's shoulders. "Don't worry about it Louis. Your credit is still good. Let's go get some chips." Pencil walked him through the kitchen and onto the back porch where they were alone. The first punch hit him like a hammer and knocked his head back against a column. The second hit to his solar plexus, dropped him to his knees. Pencil pulled him back to his unsteady feet and delivered another crashing punch to his ribs. He sank back against the column and turned to steady himself on the railing with his left hand. Then man born Clement Dechamp pulled the pencil from behind his ear and jabbed it into flesh between the pointer and index finger.

"Pencil!" came Claude's voice coming out on the porch. "Clean him up! This is why we can't find good help!"

Pencil picked up Guillory and walked him into the kitchen, splashed some vodka on the wound and padded it with some paper towels. "Jesus Guillory," he muttered, "You make a mess everywhere you go."

Claude sucked his teeth. "Also, the judge said he heard, – God only knows from who – that we have a bookie with some, let's say interesting odds. So get yourself fixed up, Guillory – you're on.

"And be careful who you drink with. We're all guilty of something, right?"

"MOM, DAD, this is Lucy Burton. Lucy, this is Army and Booey Kipling." The Kiplings lived in a large and well-maintained old house that certainly would be gutted and modernized by the next owners as the only war it predated was the second French Indo-China one

Booey Kipling was a tall, elegant woman in pearls. She had a warm smile that said she wasn't terribly concerned with being perceived as a tall, elegant woman in pearls. "It's so nice to meet you. How are you? I understand you flew in with Ferg and Eunice."

"Yes ma'am."

"Oh Lawd!" roared Army. "Let me take your bags, Lucy. It's off the kitchen if you need to powder your nose. Deke and I will take the bags up and then we'll talk about what you want on your ice."

Booey continued to smile at Lucy, who finally blurted out, "Eunice is terrifying."

"Did she tell the…"

"Sexual awakening at the fishin' hole story?" Lucy finished. "I'm afraid so."

"I wish she wouldn't do that." Booey said calmly. "So how long have you and Deke…"

"Worked together? Oh, I don't know. About year, when I came on at *The Daily Brute*. We knew each other in college. Or I knew *him*. He was a couple of years ahead of me...may not have know I existed." Booey maintained a smile that expected more. "I'm from South Carolina, originally."

Feet thundered down the steps from above and suddenly there were two boys and a pair of Brittanys standing on either side of their grandmother. "Aunty Suitcase!" said Peter with relish.

"Beg pardon?"

"I expected you to be taller." Said Derrick. Booey cuffed the boy gently on the head.

"Everyone does." sighed Lucy.

"Boys, this is Uncle Deke's...friend... Lucy Burton." They were shaking hands when Army and Deke came back down. "The pups are Linus and Maxine."

"Lucy...gin or bourbon?" Army said on the way to the butler's pantry.

Booey said quietly. "We have wine as well, dear."

"What are you having, Mrs. Kipling?"

"A martini with more vermouth that you children like these days."

"I'll have what Mrs. Kipling is having!" she called.

Dinner at the Kipling's was a long, lingering affair terminating in pecan pie and the ice cream. Army was feeling expansive and looked around the old house from the head of the table. "Ah, nothing lasts forever. The kids left; Ash is in New Orleans, Jane is in Memphis, Deke every other place in the world... I can't say that I blame them. No one was too keen on the family business. Not sure that I'd have been if I'd thought I'd had a choice in the matter." He laughed, "Ole Deke here couldn't get out fast enough."

"C'mon, Pop. It's not like that..."

Booey picked up, "After W&L... Lucy, is that where did you two meet?"

"No ma'am. I went to Hollins. My roommate was sweet on your boy here until he disappeared."

"After W&L, Deke joined the Navy." Booey said.

"Mom, I'm right here."

"I thought he was crazy but he spent five years writing for their paper and has been doing it ever since. So I guess he knew what he was doing."

Lucy looked across the dinner table, "I didn't know you were in the Navy. I never heard what happened to you. Nancy Adams never spoke your name again. She told people you'd been eaten by lions."

HANK WALKED into the Wilson hardware Store early Saturday morning thinking that all was well. It was shaping up to be a beautiful day, if a little hot, and air and sky were clean and clear. He had forgotten O'Conner's strange nitpicking yesterday about the placement of the smoker when old man Wilson hung up the phone behind the counter and peered over the top of his readers. He hated it when Mr. Wilson did that. "Hank! I've already got a complaint about you from Mr. O'Conner!"

"What did I do?" He said, pushing back the foam fronted trucker's cap bearing the Wilson Hardware & Sport logo. "It's 7:00 am."

"You got smoke in his house!"

"How? I never lit the grill!"

"Well," said Wilson softening a bit, "Mr. O'Conner did mention that. Where ever the hell you left that thing, it has potential to smoke up the house." The boss was never inclined to argue with a good customer – the sort of customer who, like Beau O'Conner bought the latest and greatest of everything.

"I see. Well, I wouldn't worry about it boss. That new model is basically a wheel barrow and a smokestack."

"Well, Mr. O'Conner is worried about it so I'm worried about it so – ergo – you are worried about it. Understand? That hat you're wearing is a scared trust."

Hank reached up and scratched under his sacred trust. "Okay, then. You want me to go out there and wheel the thing someplace else?"

"No. O'Conner doesn't want to see you again this early. Go out this afternoon. Right now, I need you to go make room in inventory for new insulated coveralls we're getting in for deer season."

"Really? *Dove* season doesn't start for another day and a half. It's 98^0 outside. Who'd buy an insulated jumpsuit this week?"

"Look you clod, you've got to stay ahead of demand. Everyone in the county will be shooting off their guns this week and they'll be thinking about fall hunts to come. Then they'll put on their camo coveralls, discover they've gotten fat and they'll be back here. It's been a long, gun free summer and we've got get rid of those discontinued coveralls to make room for the new line."

"New line? Does it make you look like a different kind of tree?"

"It's got a new, micro-thin space age insulation. Developed by NASA or some R&B artist – from Norway or someplace – for dance sequences. I don't know. I can't remember what the fella said. But it keeps you extra warm with no added weight."

"We live in a steaming swamp." Hank pointed out.

"Oh it's cold enough during deer season. Now quit yammering and work on moving that discontinued merchandise. But first I need you to take these faucet handles down to the Sunflower."

The Sunflower Inn was a quaint twelve-room bed and breakfast located in downtown Clarksdale, half a block from Wilson's hardware. Its proprietress was none other than Mrs. Wilson. Which was a matter, Hank thought, between the Wilsons. Yet it had consumed him as well, as they both seemed to think he was an employee of either concern. Hank had been hired when the Wilson's son had moved out of town. Looking back, that should have been the red flag, as Wilson Junior had opened a restaurant in French Polynesia because – and Hank remembered the Junior's explanation clearly: "Bora Bora is the furthest you can get from Clarksdale without coming back."

Despite the slow trickle of European guests seeking the birthplace of Rock N' Roll or Robert Johnson's portal to Hell, The Sunflower rarely hit half capacity. Then, during music and art festivals the dozen were booked and the staff (the Wilson's quaint nickname for Hank) found himself sorely taxed. Exactly why the place was full this week Hank didn't know but suspected it had something to do with the O'Conners. When he walked into the small lobby with a box of faucet handles, Mrs. Wilson was in a tizzy. "Hank, we've almost got a full house this weekend. I think that's ten for breakfast."

"Mrs. Wilson, you know I can't cook."

"No, I need you to open up the front desk at five tomorrow morning. I'll handle the kitchen. Five o'clock sharp."

"Geez! Five – but it's Sunday! Why so early?"

"These are important guests! Did you know we've got Betty Sue Wallace and her husband in 31 and Leo Kabler across the hall? Think about that. It's pure power politics! Something like that could put the Sunflower on the map! We need everything to be perfect. And I'll need some help in the back."

"Yes, ma'am."

"And take that ridiculous hat off."

AT THE MAGNOLIA COAST Motor Inn, it was just starting to get muggy when Teddy shuffled back to the car he'd slept in and changed from standard Ballyhoo aloha shirts to one of those where the long sleeves are kept up with tabs like he'd seen real war correspondents wear.

He'd spent the night in a truck stop parking lot, and driven back to the Magnolia Coast ahead of the White Voices rally. Up in his room, Danny was standing tall in his red and white aloha shirt and pressed olive cargo pants. Trevor was giving him a last roll with the lint brush. He looked sharp, but Danny was giving the evil eye to a smudge he'd spied on one of his black Doc Martins.

Teddy was tucking his shirt in when he heard the first thunderous rumble of the motorcycles down the road. Quickly he made sure his camera and notebook were handy. Images of Hunter S. Thompson's cigarette holder flashed through his head, and he retrieved the big orange vaporizer. He was climbing the stairs when what sounded like Attila's motorized hordes arrived with Confederate and Nazi flags flying from their bikes. Teddy snapped a few shots and stepped knocked on Danny's door. Trevor answered, "Who is it?"

"It's Teddy, Trevor. I just went down to change my shirt. Now open up."

Trevor opened up. Danny was standing in the middle of the room, looking crisp and bland at the same time. He smoothed his hair. "Trevor," Danny barked, "his voice could have been faked. We can't be too cautious."

"Who'd pretend to be Teddy?" asked Trevor.

"Danny," Teddy stepped inside. "the Hell's Angels are here."

"Oh no." corrected Danny, "What you see here is not the Hell's Angles, but the Rebel Yell Motorcycle Club. They will be our color guard for the procession to the Jefferson Davis Presidential Library."

"I know where the rally is, Danny," Said Teddy, "but do they know that they are merely a color guard? I mean, they look like they mean business."

The Rebel Yells were doing wheelies in the parking lot and hollering to the skies.

"And they *do* mean business. You have to admire their spirit, brutish though it might be. Real fighters. They'll stand up to the liberal mob."

"Yeah," said Teddy, eyeballing his rented Chevy Spark. "I didn't opt for the rental insurance, so I hope they steer clear of my car."

"They'll fall into formation when they need to…"

"Are you sure they're gonna take orders from you?"

"Why wouldn't they?" Said Danny Spewe, licking his thumb and attacking the smudge on his shiny boots. "I'm a militia commander."

Down in the parking lot, Teddy could see one of the Rebel Yell old ladies was doing a handstand on a bike while taking a pull on a bottle of tequila. "No reason."

"Look, you're the journalist, Teddy. You need to go talk to them."

"Now?"

"They seem to be in a loquacious mood."

"Is that what you'd call it?"

As it was, Teddy's attempt to get a quote from J.E.B., the Rebel Yell president, resulted in a fearsome atomic wedgie which he was trying to dislodge in the rental car when two white rental vans pulled up. Out poured the black-clad protestors waving placards reading "Abide No Hate!" while others threw smoke bombs and other swung baseball bats at random cars. The chaos was short lived when the counter-protestors caught sight of the

Rebel Yell bikers. The two gangs stared at each other for a few seconds until the cyclists let out what Teddy assumed was the original rebel yell and roared into the counter-protesters, who went screaming back into the vans or into a nearby drainage ditch.

Trevor and Danny Spewe watched from the motel window. "I'm not sure this is going to be as non-violent we wanted." Trevor offered before slapping Danny on the back, "Well, *Commandante* time to address the troops."

Spewe scrunched up his face, "Maybe we should let them calm down a bit. Looks like their blood is up."

"No sir." Said Trevor, putting a hand of Spewe's narrow shoulder. "This is the time. Don't be afraid, this is your destiny to be a leader of men. You founded Ballyhoo for the Bugaloo. To put men, white men, back in their rightful place in society. It is time to step into your destiny, sir."

Danny Spewe took a deep breath and stepped onto the balcony. Behind him the door swung shut and the lock was thrown. He took another deep breath and one long step to the balcony overlooking the melee and tried to strike a Benito Mussolini pose. Despite having watched hours of the man online it is very hard to achieve that coveted *Il Duce* vibe being a skinny dweeb in an aloha shirt. Danny cleared his throat, "Gentleman," he called. Nothing. "Warriors to the Cause!" still nothing but eventually one of the riders, a shaggy man who looked like a cave-bear, looked up and called, "Hey, Are you Spewe? Yeah you! The skinny fella…"

"Yes, I'm Daniel Spewe, founder of the-"

"Sppeeewwweeee!!!!" they called sounding like a chorus of lowing cattle.

"Yes, that's me." He finally said, "and this is –" he noticed that Trevor had not joined him on the balcony. "Yes, thank you for coming this morning to this crucial rally for White Voices."

"Spppeewwee!" They were still having fun with it.

"Yes, thank you." Danny tugged at his shirt, "For today to work, we have to work like a well-organized machine. Military precision. You see all around us — DEAR GOD! Did you take a prisoner!"

Down near the drainage ditch, some of the old ladies had separated a black-clad protestor from the herd and were force feeding the kid tequila. "Hey J.E.B.," said one of the women, "Can we keep him, the girls think he's sorta cute."

"He's a little fella, like a pocket friend!"

"Okay," Said J.E.B., "but *not* across state lines, that got us in trouble last time!"

Upstairs Danny smoothed his hair again. "We can't take prisoners!" he screeched.

"Spppeeewwweee!" the club lowed.

The huge, shaggy cave-bear stared at Spewe. "Hey, you want us to take you to your little pep rally or not?"

DEKE SAT at his parent's kitchen counter, watching his mother on the landline with Ashley, "Well I don't care what the rules are in your house, Ashley... humph... so you *don't* let him drink his morning juice out a martini glass? Well, he just seems fascinated by it."

Finally, Deke had enough. "Alright Mom, I need to talk to Ash." He took the phone away and readied his notebook. "Okay, did you find out who owns that Digger Station?"

"Honestly, I'd always thought it was corporate owned, but looking of on the vendor agreement it is Chad Wallace."

"The owner of the company?"

"No, that's Casper Wallace. Listen Deke, these Digger Stations are just vendors. Now if they're breaking the law-"

"They may not be. It just looks strange. Can you tell me how much gas they buy?" Deke scratched in his notebook. "How old is the station?"

"About five years."

"Do you know what Chad Wallace is paying the company in francise fees."

"That's not filled out."

"Ashley isn't it your job to see these contracts are filled out correctly?"

"I'll tell you what isn't my job, Deke, is talking to you about it. Anyway. that's between franchisee and owner – legally. Again, that's got nothing to do with Bayoil. Look Deke, do me a favor, let me know what you find before you run a story."

"Will do." Deke hung up and wandered into the library to find Lucy and young Derrick sitting in a pair of easy chairs. She sipping a cup of coffee and he nursing milk from a martini glass.

Derrick sipped his *martini leche*, "Well that's interesting, Miss Lucy, so what happens when a source doesn't want to talk?"

"You keep on asking."

He pondered this, "Hmmm. Interesting. That's exactly what Mom and Dad tell me *not* to do. Imean, they really get riled about it." He turned to Deke, "Ahh, Uncle Suitcase, so glad you could join us."

"Young Derrick was just telling me his plans to join the Foreign Legion and have an affair with penniless baroness." said Lucy.

"Can't you just watch *Star Wars* like everyone else?"

Lucy was still looking at Derrick with the *martini leche* but speaking to Deke "It's like looking into your past." she said.

"Yeah, well… listen you know something about Betty Sue Wallace –"

"I've got here cornbread recipe."

"Wait, what? Never mind. Who is Chad Wallace, is that her father-in-law?

"Son."

"But the Bioy was named after her father-in-law, correct?"

"No. Betty Sue's father was Chad. The kid is named after him. Casper is a junior."

"Huh. Does Casper have any siblings?"

"Only child." Said Lucy, "I think Betty Sue likes it that way. She pretty much dominates Casper from what I'm told."

Deke leaned against the book case. Derrick got up and poured out another milk into a cocktail glass from the silver shaker. "Shaken, not stirred." He said and handed his uncle the glass. "Thanks. So why would the boy own a gas station on the coast? Wouldn't it be simpler for the corporation to own it?"

"Maybe it's got something to do with a family trust?" offered Lucy.

"Perhaps our friend Chad is the pawn of darker forces." Said young Derrick as he sipped his *martini leche*. Lucy and Deke stared at the kid. "What? It happens?"

ON THE WALL of Casper Wallace's maroon and white man cave hung a not inexpensive portrait of Bully, the Mississippi State mascot, as if it were a family heirloom. Surrounding Bully were fraternity composites, hunting trophies, and a photo of a younger Casper gazing enthusiastically up the skirt of the cheerleader he held aloft along on the sidelines of the football field. Betty Sue hated that picture, hated Mary Katherine Shanks and her backside too. For his part, Casper maintained that it was only wholesome school spirit the photo captured in his wide smile and nothing else. The room was dark and muted save for the cold and white half bath – a more sterile and down to business toilet couldn't be found in a hospital or a monastery. It was his favorite room in the house.

He was sitting on the maroon leather sofa, following his Saturday routine of doing largely nothing. He sipped his coffee and, with one week to go until football season started, sat watching the sports channels discuss that there was week left until the season started. The phone rang.

"Hey Mr. Wallace, It's Theodore Landry. Listen, I hate to tell you but the White Voices Rally in Biloxi isn't going to happen."

"Praise Jesus. I told Betty Sue to steer clear of that Confederate foolishness. We're not gonna cotton to that crew. So how can I help you?"

"Listen, you want me to go after Kabler, leave the establishment alone until after the elections, and frankly Mr. Wallace, I couldn't agree more with your instincts…"

Despite still being in his comfy maroon and white pajama bottoms, Casper was scowling.

"…and I think I need to be in Clarksdale."

"I wouldn't bother with that, Teddy."

"I'm just down the road. Really Mr. Wallace it wouldn't be a problem. They're processing my bail right now."

"Bail?" Are you in jail?"

"Well, evidently the Ballyhoo color guard had some simmering feud with a Mexican motorcycle gang called 'Q'. They attacked us on the procession to the library. I'm telling you, this is why immigration is a hot topic issue."

"Color Guard?"

"A stout rally of patriots called the Rebel Yell."

Now Casper was sitting straight up. "The motorcycle gang? They're drug dealers you fool! So are the Q! Wait, why they'd arrest *you*? Aren't you pretending to be a journo?"

"Well, the police arrested everyone – including the hostage."

"Who took a dad-burn hostage?"

"The Rebel Yell. Then the Q made off with him. Anyway, eventually the cops came and they put the guy in the drunk tank."

"So there was no drama at the Jeff Davis Library?"

"Not exactly. The toilets in the men's rooms *did* blow up. What are you gonna do? Nothing to do with us. Crazy liberals. Anyway, I should be in Clarksdale this afternoon."

"Teddy, I don't want to see you anywhere near that shoot. Understand? You need to be finding what you can about Leo Kabler! You said you had a lead."

"Oh it is the smoking gun, sir."

"Well, what is it?"

"It's all a bit boring. I mean it's a bunch of spreadsheets. It's very thorough, very compelling, just not very SLAM if you see what I mean."

"I don't."

"But don't you worry, Mr. Wallace, my sources tell me that Leo Kabler is going to be at the O'Conner shoot in Clarksdale."

"*I* told you that."

Teddy was up against the wall. "Leo is taking kickbacks to approve business licenses."

Casper stopped. "Okay, that's not really what congressmen do, but alright. Whose paying him off and can you prove it?

"Sure, it's all in the spread sheets."

"Where did you get the spread sheets?"

"I have my sources. Look, Mr. Wallace, this shoot in Clarksdale is an *event*. I need to be there. Whatever is in those spreadsheets still be there next week. We don't want to drop the bombshell too early, Mr. Wallace. They voters will forget about it by November. Wednesday night I was at a gala society event and saw Mr. Environmental himself being chummy with the CEO of Bayoil. I'm telling you, Mr. Wallace, Leo Kabler has gone over to the dark side. This story is going to be hot. A perfect example of Washington's liberal hypocrisy. Very SLAM!"

"You son of a buck! I own 150 Digger gas stations and truck stops! I'm a Bayoil Gold Club Vendor and have the dab burn trophy to prove it! They are NOT the dark side! Now I don't want to see your flaming red behind this weekend!" When Casper had the man-cave installed, he'd had the builders sound proof the ceiling because baby Chad was born with lungs like pair of bagpipes. As a result, he didn't hear his wife's brand new boots come down the stairs.

Suddenly Betty Sue Wallace stood before him looking like something out of central casting for a mid-sixties T&A safari movie: Tall brown boots, olive pants, slightly flared at the hips, a matching shirt, rolled up sleeves secured with tabs. A kerchief around her neck and her hair, as always, immobile.

"Are you looking for the source of the Nile?" Casper asked. He was still worked up.

"Don't be an idiot. We've got -"

Casper motioned to the phone with a helpless face. "Look. Betty Sue just came in. She's been shopping. Listen, you get back on that plane to D.C. or stay in Biloxi - at this point I don't care. Understand?" He hung up and looked his wife over. "You forgot your pith helmet."

"I couldn't find one that wouldn't muss my hair. There is going to be media all over this hunt."

"It's a shoot and no, there isn't. When I talked to Ashley Kipling, he said media is *never* there. That's why it's such a hot ticket. How much did that get-up cost?"

"Let's not talk about that right now." Whenever Betty Sue said that, Casper felt a great disturbance in the universe terminating in his wallet. "Look, we need to go to that *shoot*. The media may not be there, but Aubrey, excuse me, Senator Laudermilk will. I'm going to Washington, Casper, I've got to meet the movers and shakers in this state. There is even a rumor that the Old Bear is looking into a presidential run. We've got to get in good with the man before everyone wants a piece of him."

"That's some anti-establishment platform, Honey. Your little Teddy is very disappointed."

"Oh, quit whining. Was that him you were talking to? We really can't have that goon showing up at the O'Conner's. He's too seedy. Too small fry. Hey, they can't trace the money you've sent him to us, can they?"

"No. I sent...you don't want to know. Teddy is in Biloxi – that damn White Voices rally got sidelined by a gang war –"

"Babe I can't help it if the far right loves me!"

"Dab burn it! Steer clear of them!"

"Well, they vote too."

"Biker gangs? I don't think that they do."

"Either way, that Teddy better not come to the hunt! I can't have that vaping buffoon hanging around after I – we – win. We'll have national press then."

Casper leaned forward. "We haven't won yet, Dear."

"You think the state is going to vote for that sleaze Leo Kabler?"

"He's been a congressman for years – he has a base."

"Yeah in *Biloxi*."

"Your only experience is running the Lady's Guild at a church in Jackson. That's the political reality. No offense, dear."

Offense was taken. Badly. Part of what made Betty Sue Wallace an excellent politician, she had told herself every morning since the gals at the Lady's Guild had talked her into running for Senate, was her ability to respond in the right way, even if it galled her. What she wanted to do was reach over and brain her husband with that grinning photo of Mary Katherine Shanks' spectacular rear end. Had Casper seen what the intervening 20 years had done to that ass? Rough…but no…instead, she smiled and leaned forward over the couch, "But I ran it like queen, didn't I?"

"Yes."

"I knocked out the incumbent, didn't I?"

He swallowed. "Yes."

"Now let's go shopping."

"You don't expect me to dress like that, do you?"

"You can't wear those awful patched up trousers out to the O'Connor hunt."

"Shoot. Yes, dear."

"HELL FIRE!" grumbled Danny Basco from his perch and the end of Galitoire's upstairs bar. It was a hushed, paneled room, and he scratched his upper arm under his peach polo. "You look grim, Louis. D'ju get into a fight? What'd you do to your hand?"

"*I* didn't do anything to it."

"Hell of a shiner too." Basco said before losing interest. So why couldn't this wait until Monday? I got games to watch."

"I'm about to head out of town." Guillory said and ordered a bourbon – a George Stagg. He looked at his taped-up hand, and softened. "This… I had a disagreement with the Dechamp brothers."

"Who?"

He leaned in, just a bit, and lowered his voice. "The fellas that host that private game you like…"

Basco made a motion with his hand to speak lower. Guillory's voice was barely above a murmur, and that's when he knew that the hook was set. "What about?" Basco speaking in hushed tones was more heavy air that articulation.

"Well," said Guillory leaning in closer, "That's what I need to talk to you about." The bartender brought the dark bourbon with a single ice cube, and set it down. "There was a nanny cam at the Harwell's..." Basco said nothing to this, had no reaction on that fleshy face. "... upstairs."

"I heard ya."

"I've got the file, sir. Took it out of the camera myself. Dechamps aren't happy about it, though." He padded the wrapped hand on the bar.

Now he was looking at Guillory's black eye with greater interest. "The footage, do I need to see it?"

"Depends, are you a mirror over the bed type guy?"

"Son, I am a lot of things, but that ain't one of them."

"Then no. It never streamed and I've got the only copy."

"Can you destroy it?"

Guillory slid the thumb drive over to Basco. "You can."

He palmed the drive, slid it into his pants pocket and ordered another round even though Guillory had barely touched his drink. "Who else?" he huffed.

"Only copy. The Dechamps have seen it though. So... no blood no foul."

"Fuck that! This was a foul if I ever saw one. Shiieet." They touched glasses and Guillory nearly polished his off. "Well, son, you might want to get outta bed those two, but much obliged."

"Well, there is one thing."

"MY GODDESS!" said Blanche to no one in particular, although Summer was standing right there. "Even *Tabula* has turned on me!"

"Well..." said Summer, who Blanche thought looked a little too perfect for a hot Saturday afternoon. "There *is* a national man – or woman – hunt for the operative who killed a guy using OLA's MO."

"Operative... MO... who are you, Joe Friday? And why are we meeting here?" The two were sitting in a charmingly shabby student bar near campus.

"It's across the street from my apartment."

"Really? You live there? Why didn't you come to my office?"

"Dr. Barker, It's Saturday, I've got a date tonight."

"*I've got a date!*" she mocked, "With a man?"

"Well, yes." Summer said pleasantly, "I can only be me."

"I can only be me!"

"All right, Dr. Barker, what seems to be the problem? Someone at *Tabula* wrote something condemning the toilet protests that have become fatal. You can't expect them to support a protest after it turns fatal. But as you keep telling me, *you have nothing to do with the OLA.*"

"Keep your voice down."

"It's a shame the Nebraska chapter pulled their protest when they did. That really caused too much attention at the wrong time. As it stands, the world has forgotten – somehow – about the elk penis. Which is a shame because *that* was a gold mine. And then there is Biloxi."

"I'd have thought the that ridiculous white men's rights rally would have illustrated the need for everything that I do."

"Well, it didn't happen and the toilets blew up anyway – as a counter-protest against a rally that never happened. On the bright side, no fatalities. I've issued the press release praising Nebraska Union, I'll send one out for Biloxi so we'll be allies against racism. And we'll continue to ignore Kentucky.

"Sure, let's all slink off into oblivion. The battle is lost."

Summer smiled at the bartender, "She'll have another cosmo." She turned to her boss, "Now, Dr. barker, I'm gonna get you girl drink drunk."

"What would Helen Gurley Brown think of me?"

"She'd think you're a hero. But like the good editor, I too need to get some lovin', Dr. Barker, so let's wrap this up. Hashtag *everybodypees*, is going well. The problem is that Hashtag *peeonatree* is also circulating. I ran the analytics, it seems to have started with the OLA, but was adopted by Ballyhoo and some other 'men's rights' groups. Apparently, they are calling for men stop using exploding bathrooms altogether and go urinate outdoors as a primal manhood form of protest against our protest against their protest."

"Isn't that what they do normally?"

"Yeah... I don't think it's made much of an impact except with the environmentalists. They say all the urine is killing the urban treescape."

"There's an urban treescape? Well, no matter, surely the environmentalists will line up against some chauvinistic men's groups, right?"

Summer looked at her watch as the bartender set a wildly garnished and bright red cosmo before Blanche, "Well, actually the environmentalists are blaming the OLA for blowing up the toilets."

"Huh..."

"Look, Dr. Barker, if we don't want the Justice Department crawling its way from the OLA to us, we need to get the heavy guns on our side... and I don't mean another social media slapfight. We need someone on the Hill who is staring down the barrel of an election.

Now we know where that oily Leo Kabler is going to be, we can get to him *without* the press around and explain to him that he's either for us or against us. If he's against us it's back to the private sector with him and if he's for us, he's going to make sure all of this legal trouble stops with the OLA. Got it? Now I'm going to book us two seats on the first flight I can find to Memphis. So, don't get *too* girl drink drunk on that thing. Just enough to be less...*you*."

"Are you canceling *your date*?"

"No ma'am, I've got time. I'm on a mission." Summer got up and walked out of the bar. Blanche and the bartender both watched her leave, but for entirely different reasons.

Then there was something warm and wet on her leg. Snapping around she saw a vividly hammered undergraduate with the same Greek letters Blanche had accused of gang rape last spring was relieving himself under the bar. "Hey Dr. Barker," he laughed, "Everyone pees." On his young face hung the vision of smug adolescent triumph until the bartender leapt across two and a half feet of polished wood and began to pummel the boy about the face and shoulders.

EIGHT:
WELL BALANCED HONKEYS AT THE
CROSSROADS

THE GIRLISH SQUEAL Mrs. Wilson let fly on seeing Betty Sue Wallace promenade into the Sunflower Inn was perhaps the first girlish thing she'd done since Jimmy Carter had left office. Mr. Wilson's tittering was only marginally less so. "Oh Mrs. Betty Sue Wallace – we are so honored!" she oozed.

"Really very honored." said he, "We've set y'all up in our best room! Great view of downtown. Can we get your bags?"

"That would be lovely!" Betty Sue gushed as Casper fumbled for his wallet.

"Hank!" Mr. Wilson roared, "Bags!"

Hank appeared and took up the bags, "Room?"

"We're putting them in *31*." Mrs. Wilson said in such a silky voice that Hank thought she was referring to an entirely different Room 31, presumably not at the Sunflower. She led the way up the steps with such spirit that Hank was afeared the old bird would hurt herself.

Mr. Wilson was still sitting behind the desk, grinning to himself when in walked a tall, unfamous man with a seriously blacked eye and a bandaged hand. "Can I help you?"

"Louis Guillory, I have a reservation."

"Son, you got a shiner."

"I know. Do you have my reservation?"

As Hank came down the steps, Mr. Wilson called, "Hey, did you deliver those bags to Room 31?"

"Where else would I have put them?"

"That's enough out of you!" Mr. Wilson looked at Guillory, "Want somethin' done right... geez." He came around the desk looking almost giddy. "Hank, check Mr. Guillory in."

"Okay, here Mr....Guillory... yes, here we are."

"Who is room 31?"

"Betty Sue Wallace – dang! I'm not supposed to say that."

Louis took out a hundred dollar bill and laid in on the counter.

"Aren't ya payin' with the card on file?"

"I am. That's so you don't feel bad about the Room 31 nonsense. Listen, has a fella named Teddy Landry checked in yet?"

"We aren't supposed to give out information on other guests."

"Ahh, don't feel so bad about it." He tapped the bill.

"Huh... Well, no sir. I see he made a reservation earlier today, but he hasn't checked in yet. The desk closes at seven."

Guillory looked at his watch, "Lucky me, it's only five. Let me know when he gets here, will you?

DEKE AND LUCY pulled around to the back of the O'Conner's house to see Ferg climbing out of the Porsche 911 he'd never been able to bring himself to unload since the selling of O'Conner & Locke Commodities. "Had to run the to the liquor and the grocery store for more ingredients." Ferg was saying as he unlocked the back door, "There is a helluva lot of evaporation in that punch." They stepped inside around the wooden half-barrel that did look a little low. "Oh, and Daddy'll get on me if I say anything around him, but you can stand easy. Some college friend of Eunice's showed up and they've gone out."

"Oh," Lucy said, "I hate to miss her."

"You're a dear." He took the teacup and ladled out a juice glass and handed it to her.

"Is it supposed to have splinters in it?"

"Just drink around it." said Deke, "if you get poked, the whiskey retards infection."

"He's right, you know." said Ferg and nodded back into the house. "Laudermilk is here, but he's got company."

"Hey Lucy, have you ever met the Old Bear?"

"Once, briefly."

"Well, that's not nearly enough. C'mon."

They drifted into a suspiciously well-appointed study where Laudermilk roared, "Deke mah boy! I was hoping you'd drop by... and with Ms. Burton of *The Brute?*" That twinkling eye dug into Deke.

"What is *she* doing here?" spat Congressman Carlson. "Beau, I thought there was no press allowed."

"Oh, settle down, Carlson." said Deke, "I haven't missed a hunt since I was twelve."

"I'm not talking about you!"

"I know who you're talking about! Lucy is my date, not the press. So she slapped you around a little bit about the elk knob, you have to admit you were asking for it. We're off the clock."

"Deke," said Laudermilk, "Be nice."

"One of these days I'd like to sit down with you, Senator." Said Lucy.

"I'm sittin' down now, Ms. Burton of the *Brute.*"

"Well," Beau announced mightily, "Actually, there is a precedent mentioned in your piece on the congressman, Lucy, about the traditional gift of a walking stick made from a bull… uhm… member. I've got one upstairs, would you like me to bring it out?"

"No!" everyone in the room shouted.

Everyone except Carlson to be precise. He angrily muttered that he *would* like to see the thing. The Texas twang of Darla came from the kitchen and pierced the room. "You are NOT bringing that awful thing out!"

Carlson cleared his throat. "All right, Miss Burton, if you're down here on vacation with your new boyfriend, then why aren't you getting to know your soon to be in-laws?"

"Well, Congressman," said Lucy "If you must know, we are waiting for his parents to fall asleep so we can make sweet, nasty love in his sister's bed."

The change of tack baffled the congressman. "Huh?"

"That walking stick, beautiful craftsmanship…very traditional." Beau purposely strode out of the room. "Here, let me go get it."

"Beau…NO…" came the voice from the kitchen.

"So." said Carlson, pinching up his face, "If you two are so tight, then why were you accepting dates with my aide Tim this week."

"Congressman, that was clearly professional." said Lucy, "There weren't going to be any genitals involved – mine, Tim's or any other poor mammals."

"Chilrun'" muttered Laudermilk.

"Huh," Deke knit his brow, "you didn't tell me that Tim was *still* in the picture."

"What?"

"Why, here I've brought you down to meet my parent's, Pet," Deke rubbed his hair in frustration, "… and you're still talking to that Lothario Tim!"

"Deke…it's not what you think…"

"I feel blue."

"Let's have some haint punch, Deke." Said Ferg and handed a glass over. "Always good for a broken heart."

"Deke…" said Lucy, "… sugar loaf… let's talk about this at home. Then you can give me a good rogering after your parents fall asleep."

"Well, that *is* something."

Carlson was eyeing them suspiciously. "I don't like it."

"Well," said Lucy, "the way I see it, you've told the world you are in Nebraska, and with a phone call the said world can know you are here."

"Now c'mon Miss Burton." Said Laudermilk a little louder. "I thought we were off the clock."

"Well, sir." She said, "it's just a hypothetical."

"And it is an interesting one," said Laudermilk, "wouldn't you say, Carlson?"

"I don't like it."

"Well, it's getting late, you might want to head back to the Sunflower, then."

Beau appeared with a highly-shellacked walking stick in hand. "If you check out the end, you can tell it's a real bull penis."

"Let's have another round." Said Lucy.

And then another.

The House of Kipling was dark when they returned. Lucy was concerned with the staircase. "Those look steep. By the way, that haint punch really sneeks up on you."

"I've done this before." Said Deke, "Old house, don't use the railing as support, put your fingertips on the wall, but avoid the picture frames. That's the trick. I'm pretty sure Mom hung them on straight pins – not hooks, mind you – so she could hear when we came home drunk."

"Smart woman, that Booey. Hey Deke, what kind of name is Booey?"

"A silly one. Now if we lean on each other we can avoid the rail *and* the wall."

"Okay. I think." Eventually the pair reached the top of the stairs. "Which one is your sister's room again?" she asked in an incredibly loud whisper. They shuffled to what was still being called Jane's room. The drapes were open and the room flooded with moonlight. "Hey thanks for throwing me under the bus about Tim."

"At least we can make-up. You know, work through our relationship problems."

"What can a girl say? If it weren't for this damn headache coming on." She kicked off her shoes and laid down. Deke sat on the edge of the bed and began to take the pearls out of her ears. "Navy huh?" she said, "Is that why you and Laudermilk are so close? Y'all are Navy men!" she pulled a strand of hair under her nose like a mustache. "Do y'all have matching tattoos?"

"You're gassed." He pulled out the second pearl.

"I'm gonna call you, *you*, Popeye the Sailor man."

"I'm gonna call you Drinky McGee. You joke, but that was the last honest job I ever had."

"It shows. Hey Deke, why do you want to work for Degrasse so bad?"

"Stability I guess. Health insurance. Gimme your phone." He put it on the bedside table.

"Deke, if you had that kind of stability, you'd be bored to tears. If you were bored you'd be deprusss... you'd be blue."

"Why do you say that? You have a staff job and you aren't bored."

"But I'm not you." She closed one eye to focus, "Booey told me embarrassing stuff about your childhood over coffee this morning. Then so did Senator Laudermilk tonight told me too."

"Swell sentence structure."

"Apparently, Eunice wasn't the only little girl to see your little nekkid fanny."

"She's the only one who took it personally."

"Nancy…"

"Who?"

"Nancy Adams, from Hollins. She prolly saw you nekkid too. Before you were eaten by… the… lions."

"I do love haint punch. Enough about my nudity, let's talk about your policy…"

"Nope. Nope. Nope. Now *that's* boring. Booey just wants you the find a nice girl and settle down. She worries."

"Focus all my nudity of one poor girl?"

"Well, she didn't say it like *that*."

"I knew I shouldn't have left you two alone."

"You're a good boy Deke Kipling." She kissed him on the cheek and flopped back down on the bed. "Thanks for everything."

Deke shuffled back to the room he'd always had. He sat down and looked at his phone. There was a voicemail from Kenneth Macastle. "Ahh, Hell. Deke what have you gotten yourself into?" He laid down without kicking off his shoes. "Nothing. Nothing at all. We're all being completely professional."

How long Deke lay in bed before something rapped against his window he couldn't say, other than not nearly long enough. Then another. Then another followed by a Eunice-like screech. "Hey Deke! You up!"

"Oh good Lord." He rolled out of bed and opened the window. Eunice was about eighteen inches away, squatting on the overhang of the back porch. "I forgot about that trick."

Eunice pushed him out of the way and climbed into the room. "How's your night been?"

"Ferg said you were out with a friend. I didn't think that you had any friends in town."

"Deke, I'm bored."

"Well, I'm pie-eyed. I've got to get some sleep. I'll come over to the house tomorrow, we can be bored then."

"C'mon, I'm bored! NOW!"

"What time is it?" He tried to focus on his watch. "It's 1:30."

"C'mon, let's go for a drive, or will your *girlfriend* get jealous?"

"Eunice, go away."

"Derrick Armstrong Kipling, a lady needs an escort for a midnight drive and you're going to let her face the darkness alone."

"Where's the lady?"

She playfully swatted him on the chest. "Okay, a fallen lady. Remember that time that your mom caught me in your bed without a stitch of clothing on?"

"I do not."

"Well let's make some memories, then." She hopped on the bed and the springs of the mattress screeched in protest.

"Alright, Mrs. Dubois. My parents are down the hall. Where do you want to go?"

She threw him the key fob. "Eunice, I may be a gentleman, but I've a very drunk one." He tossed the keys back.

They climbed out the window and tried not to die. Eunice drove the Porsche with gusto through the deserted streets telling Deke everything that she hated about the South and more specifically Mississippi and more specifically still, the Delta and, with laser like focus, the area currently under the rape and pillage by her family. She reached behind her and grabbed an orange from the open sack in the backseat. Deke thought the breeze felt nice on his face. "Hell, Eunice, you cash those farm checks don't you."

"But that gives me the ability to protest against it. Can you peel this for me?"

"Sure." He threw it out the window. "Someone had to rape the desert or the seafloor to make the gasoline we're zipping around on."

"You're just a stooge of the capitalist industrial complex." Eunice said, "And, really, it's just like Ferg to buy a car like this. Am I right?"

"Small, efficient. What's the problem? You came here in a private airplane."

"Not the whole way." They crossed over the over river into what was called downtown, and Eunice pointed the car to the worn brick façade of the Crossroads Blues Club. They pulled ferociously into a parking spot as the air that had been whipping around his face and keeping him awake was replaced with hot, stagnate breath. Inside, the Crossroads was a cavernous place with neon beer signs on the exposed brick. On the stage a trio belted out twanging, bluesy tunes. "I love this place, it's so real." Eunice cooed. "Look, you can get moonshine!"

"No!" Deke said. "Coffee."

Eunice climbed up onto a tall barstool and leaned in, hoisting her cleavage onto the bar. "Moonshine."

"How you like it, Miss?" the bartender asked.

"How do real people drink it. *Your* people."

"My people? I'll just get you a ginger ale. How about that?"

"Moonshine!" screeched Eunice. "And I can take it straight up."

"Yeah, but that's a tall stool you're sittin' on and it's a long way to a hard floor." He looked at Deke and pointed.

"That ginger ale sounds about right."

The bartender gave Eunice the heavy shot glass of moonshine and opened a bottle of orange soda. "That's about as old school as you can get." And slid Deke his ginger ale.

"So, what's the story with you and Lucy?" Eunice asked as she sniffed the shot and grimaced – it smelled like a mixture of ammonia and rubbing alcohol.

"I owe her a favor. Hold on!" Deke got up off the stool walked across the dim, sparsely crowded bar to where Leo Kabler was dancing, badly, before a table of three black couples entirely overdressed for a place like the Crossroads. Leo was dancing with one of the wives, much to the amusement of the others. She'd shake her hips and he'd answer in unintentional three-quarter time as his head sort of bobbed to the beat and his tiny round glasses shimmied down to the end of his button nose. Next to the table, but not sitting was the wispy figure of his assistant, Kelly Makin, in snug khakis and a blue blazer.

Deke slid next to the man in a blue pinstripe suit. "Hey Mr. Mayor, Deke Kipling, Army's boy."

"Oh Hey!" roared the mayor, "How're you?"

Leo's eye's popped open and spun around at the voices. He was never exactly sure how much whiteness black voters around here would put up with, but he was pretty sure that he was just the right amount. There was Kelly, of course, but he was so inoffensive and forgettable that he probably didn't register. This fella, and he looked familiar, seemed to have a personality and Leo didn't need some local yob upsetting the gathering's finely calibrated dose of honkey. Leo grabbed the hand of his dancing partner gallantly and she patted his bald head. The table laughed. At the bar, Eunice pinched her nose and threw back the entire slug of moonshine. She coughed and grabbed for the orange soda. "Hit me again."

"You sure about that?"

"Yes." She gasped.

"Well...sip it this time." He shook his head, "That's how *my* people do it."

"Hey, who is that little fella with the funny glasses?"

Across the room, Leo stuck his hand out accusingly at Deke, "Leo Kabler, running for *your* Senate."

"Deke Kipling – somewhat fatigued."

"I'd appreciate your vote on-"

"Sorry Kabler, I live in New Orleans."

The cloud of distrust circled again. The mayor laughed loudly. "Deke here is a local boy. I've known him since he was in short pants. In Clarksdale he's world famous. He's a –"

"A Writer." Said Kelly, suddenly close. "You wrote that hatchet piece on the Dr. Barker."

"Yeah," said Leo as the gears clicked, "You were pretty harsh on the women's movement, don't you think?"

"Don't see how. I was harsh on some people falsifying police reports on four drunk morons for the sake of symbolic gesture."

"What they symbolized is pretty awful."

"Fair point. That dove shoot I'm gonna see you at on Monday, what do you think that symbolizes? I'll bring my camera."

"What shoot?" Leo demanded indignantly.

"Oh Lord!" the mayor laughed. "Stop it Deke, you're stepping on all my lines." The table exploded with laughter.

Leo threw his shoulders back, "I'm here the meet my future constituents. To see how I can be of service. Why, when we passed-"

Deke was no longer looking at Leo, but beyond him. This, Leo took from years of Machiavellian political experience, to mean that Deke was working out the finer machinations of some political skullduggery. Leo was mistaken. In fact, Deke was merely watching Eunice heading their way with an unsettling determination. Kelly saw her as well and tried to run block, almost skipping in front of her way with an enthusiastic "Hey girl! It's been awhile!"

"Congressman Kabler!" Eunice squealed, pushing Kelly aside. "It's Eunice O'Conner! I organized a demonstration for that Pay Equality Bill you co-sponsored with Congressman –"

Leo sat transfixed and said "...". Which isn't to say that the man wasn't thinking. Oh, for cryin' out loud! Now the whitey ratio is really out of whack! If anymore white people show up at the Mayor's table he's libel to throw his support behind...well surely not that Wallace wing-nut, she's got a Scarlett O'Hara fetish. Perhaps some independent African-American candidate. Are the Black Panthers still a thing over here? You never can tell in the Delta. "So nice to meet you." Was what he eventually said, leaning in close enough for his glasses to fog with Eunice's moonshine and orange Ne-Hi breath. She wanted to dance. "You're with the University of Mississippi?"

"University of Tennessee." Said Eunice, "But you know Congressman, social justice is a right in any state."

"Oh...yes. I suppose." *And why are these voteless out-of-staters hanging around?* The congressman was there to collect votes. He was on the clock.

The mayor leaned into Deke, "That buffoon thinks that if he admits he's going to that damn shoot he'll lose the black vote."

"Why? Aren't all of you gonna be there?"

"You know I will, boy! I limit out every year." While not remotely true, Deke thought that it was nice the mayor thought so. "Don't tell Leo, though. We've been stirring him all night. He's nervous as hell." He giggled, "If one more soda cracker comes in he's gonna pop."

Outside the bar, the blue lights of a police cruiser flashed. The bartender went around the to the front door to find a short police officer, her hair in a tight bun, standing beside a Chevy Spark, peering in with a flashlight. "Hey André" she called to him, "Is this one of yours?"

"No. He ain't drunk." said André. "He sat in here for three hours drinking water and I told him to go home."

She shrugged and rapped on the window. From the fetal position in the cramped back seat, Teddy looked up to see a bright white light in front of flashing blue. "Step outside the car, please." she ordered.

"Dammit." He opened the door, "Yes, Officer?" he squinted at the name badge, "...Crenshaw."

"You can't sleep here. Go home."

"So you would prefer me to drive home rather that sleep it off? That hardly seems compatible with public safety."

"Alright, get out." Crenshaw ordered. Teddy climbed out of the car in jeans and a rumpled tee-shirt. "André says you're not drunk, so why don't you go home? Are you homeless?"

"I am not! Do I look homeless?"

"Sleepin' in your car you do."

"I'm a reporter. I got into town after that hotel down the street closed its front desk." Teddy retrieved his apparatus and started vaping greedily.

"Jesus. You're a mess. Look, there's a Bargain Inn out on the highway, you need a bed, go there. But you can't sleep here."

"I have reservations at the Sunflower Inn. Those boobs closed the front desk before I could get into town. I *have* to be at the center of the action."

Crenshaw looked at André with an unblinking stare that said *White People.* André shrugged and went inside. "I don't care where you go, but you can't sleep on a public street."

"I was in my car."

"On a public street."

"That's right and I'm the public! This is reverse racism!"

Crenshaw scratched her head. "Now I can take you down to county and get you a comfy cot with a dozen of your best friends if you want."

"Yes' ma'am." Teddy trudged into the smoky bowels of the Crossroads and headed for an empty padded booth in the back. Eunice had dragged Leo over to the bar as Kelly trotted behind. She ordered another round of moonshine and a couple of orange sodas.

"Listen Eunice," Leo was saying, "Thank you, but I don't think so."

Kelly was trying to fill the space between the two with his narrow frame, "Eunice, so great to see you again! You know, we're both allies to feminism. I've got a protest project you might like."

"Congressman Kabler," Eunice was saying, "if you want to serve these people, you must be like them. We have too much privilege to understand where they came from, but we must have empathy."

André set three more bottles of orange soda out, mumbling, "These people... Jesus." Then he looked over their heads. "Hey!" he called spotting Teddy's disheveled mop slipping into an out of the way booth, causing Eunice to snort moonshine up her nose. "Two drink minimum fella! And you can't sit back there and go to sleep. This place is for paying customers."

Teddy shuffled to the bar, ordered a beer and watched that bastard Leo Kabler try to force some orange soda into the coughing Eunice. She'd sneezed into the glass sending it all over their faces. Kelly watched Teddy move to the bar, and while a devoted aide to the congressman, was he not also a man? He saw his chance to both relieve his boss of Eunice and have a little face time with her as well. "Congressman?" Kelly said, nodding to Teddy.

"Hell!" Leo said when he saw the dejected figure at the end of the bar. "There's that troglodyte from SLAMNEWS! Is he stalking me?"

Eunice snapped around and screeched from the end of the bar. "Hey! Shithead!" She climbed off the barstool unsteadily. André rolled his eyes and Leo made a quick dash across the room to hide at the Mayor's table.

Kelly stood alone at the bar. "Damn."

Teddy blew a long plume of vapor into Eunice's approaching face, "Can I help you?" he said calmly.

"Yeah you can shut down that rightwing Nazi propaganda blog you call a news site!"

"Oh good, one more screeching progressive. Here, let me buy you some birth control, you Godless Harlot."

"Oh, no, fella! It's go time!" boomed Eunice, "Scared of a woman who owns her sexuality, you repressed infant! You think that you're a big man hiding behind that misogynistic blog! I'll tell you who a big man is... Leo Kabler!" she stopped and considered the man. "Well, not physically, but he's always been a firm supporter of ISOP. He's done more to fight the war on women than any of you GOP goons ever have!"

"By supporting the domestic terrorism of a bunch of toilet bombers?"

"We are the Ovarian Liberation Army and we will blow your teeny balls off! Poor baby! Are your scared?!" Teddy wouldn't have phrased it that way, but that was the nut of it. Eunice was prancing about, sticking her breasts out in a general air of what she intended to be of savage mockery. Teddy, however, had led a life sadly devoid of breasts – prancing or no – and took the whole opera in an entirely different light.

On the other side of the place, Leo was trying to wedge himself out of sight mainly by hiding behind Deke. "Stop it, Kabler" Deke struggled out of his seat. "this is shameful!"

"She's terrifying!"

"Don't I know it. Kabler! Be a man, for God's sake!" Deke crossed back over to the bar about the time she stopped prancing and caught Teddy looking at her heaving cleavage.

"Good Goddess, you rapist!" she yelped. "You do *not* have a right to look at my breasts! Even if I show them to you! I own my sexuality, not you. I'll tell you something else, chubby! I'm here to make sure big business can't pull an enviro-rape in Mississippi. That Leo Kabler is gonna win the election and he'll make sure to put an end to that gulf coast drilling!"

That last statement, coming over the room as it did during a bluesy lull, made Leo visibly nervous.

"That's right, run off all the businesses." belched Teddy, "Who's gonna pay for your welfare state and birth control then?"

André looked at Deke and sighed. "I'm gonna have to throw your friends out."

"If you throw her out," declared Kelly, "you'll have to throw me out too!"

"Suit yourself."

"I only know Eunice here." said Deke, "And for that I do apologize. I'll clear her out."

"Oh hell, that's Eunice O'Conner, iddn't it? Now I'm puttin' it together. She almost raped my brother Marvin one Christmas. Momma still talks about it."

"Mine too."

"Why'd you have to bring her in here? You tappin' that?"

"I'm not that brave, I only work in war zones. You're Marvin Thomas's brother? I'm Deke Kipling, tell him I said 'Hi.' I heard you opened a place." He looked at Teddy "I don't know that guy... you do whatever's right."

"I'm gonna grab carrot-top, then. You take care of Eunice – I don't wanna mess with that." He looked at Kelly, "That little Congressman is already headin' for the door." Kelly did the same in tight-pants double time.

Deke grabbed Eunice's purse and retrieved the car keys as Leo disappeared out into the night, heading down the sidewalk towards the Sunflower Inn at an excitable shuffle. André came around the bar, grabbed Teddy by the twisted tee-shirt where he struggled enough to pull it over his head and lead him outside. Eunice, sensing her sparring partner impaired, followed him to the door to finish the job and shouted. "This is OUR country! WE want it back you land-raping war monger!"

"All right, Eunice." Deke was saying, "C'mon, we're thrown out too."

"What did *we* do?"

They climbed into the Porsche and Eunice started scrounging around in the back seat. Deke headed down the street with one hand over his eye to keep his focus. On the sidewalk that Deke was praying he'd miss, Teddy was walking quickly down to the Sunflower Inn, straightening out his rumpled tee-shirt. Further down the sidewalk, Kelly was using the guest key to get both he and Leo in the front door and disappear inside. Teddy made a dash to the door as it swung shut. He was so close that he heard the lock click as he reached out for the handle. He stood with palms on the doors as he watched Kelly's shape disappear up the steps. Eunice grabbed an orange from the back seat, squeezed it once, and hurled it at the unsuspecting Teddy, getting him squarely in the side of the head. "War is not the answer you fascist!" she screamed.

"Lord Eunice! Settle down! Is he okay?"

She slid into the seat and lit a cigarette. "Well, that was fun." She said wistfully and without a hint of sarcasm. "You know, it really is good to see you. Oh Deke, why didn't we ever hook up?"

"Hard to say, really."

Within the quiet safety of the Sunflower Inn up on the top floor, Betty Sue Wallace examined herself in the bathroom mirror. She looked good, she thought. She went over her talking points again and told herself that she needed some sleep. In the bed, Casper slept soundly in his silk sleep mask and earplugs. Blues music drifted down the street from a spot called the Crossroads, but that wasn't what was keeping her up. Feet were moving quickly down the hallway, but that wasn't it either. It was nerves. Her nerves were what would keep Casper up too, for that matter. For all her love of competition and performing, she always got violent jitters the night before. Her mother had always told her – even back in the days of the Little Miss Beauty Pageant – the jitters gave her an edge. Casper recommended medicine, or at least more wine. He slept in the guest room quite a bit these days. So much so that he'd originally booked two rooms but Betty Sue decided that if the press found out, there would be an empty marriage sort of scandal. Casper pointed out that once the press got to know Betty Sue, they'd understand. She canceled the second room anyway.

This was her moment to shine. She'd hob-knob with the people who made things happen. And as long as that dweeb Teddy Landry did his homework on whatever that Guillory guy dug up – and kept his distance – they'd have Leo Kabler by the short hairs. After a couple of deep breaths, she turned off the bathroom light and slipped into bed. A few more deep breaths. Then, outside her window, came an awful voice shrieking something about fascists from a car speeding off into the night.

Now she was wide awake again. She nudged Casper. Then she poked him. Then poked him hard. "Ow! What's wrong with you, woman?"

"Can't sleep."

"I see." Casper rolled over to competently and confidently service his wife without ever removing the sleep mask or the ear-plugs.

NINE:
THE LORD FORGIVES AND ANGLES DRINK

It was daybreak when Teddy pulled his little rental Spark up in front of the Sunflower Inn – again. After that maniac had brained him with an orange, he'd headed to the bus station to wash the citrus bits out of his hair and hopefully grab a nap before another cop threatened him with jail. When the janitor nudged him awake and warned him to scoot, the sun was breaking on a steamy Sunday morning. He drove back to the Sunflower where the front door opened and a bell tinkled overhead.

Hank was opening a sack of grits in the kitchen when he heard the fearsome buzzer. "We've got people coming in already." chirped Mrs. Wilson. "Hank, you go see what they want, Sweetie." Mrs. Wilson was a morning person.

Grumbling something about how sweet it would be to still be in bed, Hank shambled out the kitchen and heard the metallic desk bell ding. By the time he'd reached the front desk, it had rung out twice more the red head was bringing his hand down on the bell a fourth time. "Alright, I'm here. How can I help you? Checking in?"

Teddy rolled his eyes dramatically, "Why else would I be here?"

"Great." Hank started fumbling with the keyboard, "...and your name?"

"Landry, Theodore Landry."

"Got it. You're here awful early Mr. Landry, did you just drive in?"

"No! I did *not* just drive in! If you'll check you records I reserved a room last night but the front desk was closed when I got here! I won't pay for last night!"

"Of course not, sir. Mrs. Wilson closes up at seven unless someone's coming in late."

"I was coming in late."

"Did you call to let us know? We recommend that on the website."

"Just how far out in the sticks is this place that I have to call and tell Ma Kettle I'll be in after sundown?"

"Hey, Mister, people are trying to sleep upstairs. Try to keep it down, please. Ahh, here... we've put you in number 21."

"Great! Is it a bed or just a hay bail?"

"I'll need to see a credit card."

Then the voice came from the staircase – sort of a magnolia drawl subjected to electro-shock therapy. "What are *you* doing here!?!" Betty Sue Wallace stood on the landing wearing black yoga pants and a synthetic weave golf shirt calculated to make her look active and vital.

"Mrs. Wallace! Great news!" said Teddy.

"There is nothing great about you being here, Teddy!" I thought that you were covering that oppressed men's rally in Biloxi! You were told –" she stopped and eyeballed Hank, who was aggressively eyeballing the computer monitor in an effort to steer clear of the storm.

"There we are, all approved." Hank handed the card back to Teddy. "Now you said something about a hay bail? There might be an additional charge for that. I'll ask Ma Kettle."

"Don't be funny. Good to know you peckerwoods have started taking Federal money again." Teddy sniffed.

"Now how do you think that makes me feel, mister?"

Betty Sue stared at Hank and smiled graciously. "Gosh. Durn. Yankees! I apologize for this red-headed buffoon, I really do. I need to talk to him about his manners." She cuffed Teddy across the back of the head. "Now, Hank is it? Could you be a shug and bring us some coffee in the dining room?"

On some level Hank didn't quite understand, the honey drawl and the matronly curve beneath the formfitting clothes told him that all would be well. "Yes ma'am." Hank disappeared into the back and Betty Sue dragged Teddy into the empty dining room by the arm.

"Mrs. Wallace, I need to get my bags!"

Hank watched the pair disappear into the dining room and picked up the phone. "Hey Mr. Guillory. Mr. Landry Just checked in. We've got him in 21 but 31 doesn't seem too glad to see him…. Well that's very generous, sir. Oh what the hell, you know Leo Kabler's in 34. No need, sir, that one is on the house."

In the dining room, Betty Sue pushed Teddy into a chair at an out of the way table while he swatted at her deceptively strong hands. She dropped into a chair opposite, "Teddy, now what are you doing here?"

"I thought you wanted me to dig up dirt on Kabler? That's why your husband sent-"

Teddy learned very quickly that Betty Sue slapped much harder than Danny Spewe. "I don't know what you are up to, but that little dweeb is too shifty to *do* anything unsavory this weekend. He's staying here for Pete's sake! Waddaya think he's gonna do?"

"I know he's staying here! Look Mrs. Wallace, I'm working with Lucy Burton over at the *Daily Brute*, we're gonna break the story together."

Betty Sue looked the boy over. Well, that does change things. "Isn't she the one who took your job?"

"She filled the position I left, yes. Listen, Mrs. Wallace-"

"Shut up, Tubby. I'm thinking. Look, this may have legs, you and Burton of the *Brute* working together. We'd certainly get more traction than it being a SLAMNEWS! exclusive. Where is she?"

"She's going to the O'Conner hunt. She's working on an exposé of Aubrey Laudermilk. She's going to screw him to the wall."

"WHAT!" Betty Sue almost screamed as Mrs. Wilson came in with two cups of coffee. "Oh, pardon me." Betty Sue drawled to the old lady and watched her retreat back into the kitchen. "You dumb Yankee!" She hissed, "Laudermilk is our best ally right now. You can't go freaking out the establishment before the election! Those are primary tactics! Kabler is the opposition!"

"Mrs. Wallace, this weekend needs to be live tweeted."

"What this weekend does not need is your hysterics. Don't you worry about Leo. That boy couldn't hit a barn door painted red. Casper and I have that covered. *I'll* be live tweeting the event. What you need to do is get that Lucy Burton off Laudermilk's back, okay? Can you *not* mess that up?"

"Yes ma'am."

Mrs. Wilson came back out, "Are y'all ready for breakfast?"

"I am." Said Betty Sue. "This one's going to his room."

"Yes ma'am." Said Teddy and lumbered out of the dining room.

At the table, both heard Casper's voice from the lobby bark "Landry, you son of a buck! What in the tarnation are *you* doing here?"

Betty Sue looked at Mrs. Wilson, "That'll be my hubby right now!" She said delightfully. "He'll order eggs and bacon, but oatmeal and fruit will be fine."

THE PAIR STOPPED for coffee on their way out of the terminal of the Memphis International Airport. On the television screen above them was the weirdly goateed face of Mark Pratt of *Here's the News!* – the self-proclaimed leader of the Sunday morning political shows. "Let's do a walk over to the social media kiosk." offered Mark and the camera obeyed. At a screen that looked like an enormous smartphone he began to swipe at graphics, revealing the top trending stories. "Well, it isn't dignified, but it is the top trending news – hashtag: *everybodypees*. No matter where you stand on the issues, there is an undeniable truth to that statement. But it begs a larger national question: Does one group have the right to destroy the restroom facilities of another and call it legitimate protest?"

Blanche groaned into her macchiato. "I called the producer over at this damn show – offered to give her the leading voice of the women's movement and the ISOP – and you know what they said? And I say 'they' because I didn't actually speak to the producer, but her assistant. The assistant said that I was too hot for the show. Can you believe that?"

"Actually," said Summer, "I can't."

"What?"

"Too hot for the news? I called ABC last week and they told me that after the rape story, you weren't credible."

"You mean after 'Hell's Belles'."

"I'm just telling you what they told me." Summer cleared her throat, "Of course, I disagreed."

"Yeah, the little shit said that too."

On the screen a serious looking, ghastly white woman in a black pant suit was talking, "Well, obviously there needs to be a national moratorium on the War against Women, and anyone who thinks legitimate protest should be banned is part of the oppressive patriarchy."

"We should also point out," said Pratt, "that hashtag: *peeonatree*, which started out coming from the OLA, now better known as Hell's Belles, has largely been co-opted by Ballyhoo and the so-called 'White Men's Rights' movement."

"Wait a minute!" said Danny Spewe's head against the back drop of downtown Biloxi. "Why are we 'so-called'?"

"Him…" Blanche growled.

"And joining the conversation from Bilox-"

"Because men have all the oppressive rights they need in the patriarchy." The woman barreled on.

Blanche stared fiercely at the screen. "Agatha, you wiry bitch! Summer, will you just listen to her?"

"I thought she sounded good, Dr. Barker." Said Summer, flipping through a copy of *Tabula*. "I mean, it's pretty much your position, isn't it?"

"Yes, so *I* should be saying it. Agatha plays it safe, keeps her hands clean and gets all the press. While those of us rolling up our sleeves for sexual equality and ownership are called 'too hot.'"

"Did they actually call you that?"

"You know one of those little brats from that damn frat house urinated on me at that bar you picked out."

Summer looked up, trying not to laugh, "I did not know that."

"On. My. Leg. Just because those little shits didn't actually do anything. Not that night at any rate. Just peed on me. That's the patriarchy for you."

"Wow. What happened to him?"

"Nothing. Total impunity! Male privilege."

"Really? Tommy didn't do anything?"

"Who the hell is Tommy?"

Summer was pulling her phone out of her purse. "The bartender."

"Not. A. Thing.'

"Summer was scrolling through her contacts,

"Summer, are you calling him?"

"Of course! And I'd better do it now before we start driving down through radio free Mississippi. Really, Tommy just let that happen?"

Blanche could remember, quite clearly, the boy called Tommy pummeling the boy before turning him around and literally – not figuratively – throwing the kid out of the bar Western style. Something Blanche had only seen in movies. "Well," she sniffed, "he may have said something to the boy. Really, there is no reason to call the ape. He's probably asleep." Blanche looked dramatically back to the television screen. "What's this little twerp going on about now?"

"Peaceful protest!" said Spewe pointing a long finger at the camera. "The radical Ovarian Liberation Army blew up the toilets in the Nebraska Student Union, and the Jefferson Davis Presidential Library.

"Jefferson Davis? Why does *that* guy get a Presidential library?" said Dr. Shondra Wilmont, an African-American professor of African American History. Dr. Wilmont had heretofore been sitting at the *Here's the Press!* roundtable in dumbfounded silence.

"Men only pay attention when their genitals are on the line." said Agatha.

"That's my line!" Blanche screamed at the television.

"Seriously, Jeff Davis...?" said the Dr. Wilmont. "... *of the Confederacy*, has a presidential library?"

"The OLA killed a man in Kentucky! Congressman Carlson is in hiding for his life!" screeched Spewe. "This is not peaceful protest! A man is dead!"

Pratt leapt in from the Social Media Kiosk, "Speaking of, hashtag: *notyourpenis* has dropped out of the top ten trending topics this week!"

Agatha primly cleared her throat. "Correct me if I'm wrong, didn't the congressman just go home to his constituents in Nebraska."

"Well, no one has seen him there!" said Spewe.

"Really? No one is gonna touch that? Jeff Davis?"

"Is that because he's holded up objectifying some innocent woman with a bear @&*!%!"

A wide eyed Mark Pratt breathed a sigh of relief. "I'd like to thank Jim in production for catching that one! And just in time, too! This is network, folks, try to remember that. I have a feeling we're going to see that again as next week's top hashtag."

In the Memphis airport, Blanche turned to Summer, "I thought you said Carlson was in Clarksdale."

"He is."

"But Agatha said-"

Summer smiled as she flipped through *Tabula*. "Agatha is wrong."

DEKE WOKE to a sharp pain in his leg. He snapped awake to find his mother standing calmly at the foot of his bed as if she hadn't just pulled the hair on his exposed calf. "Damn Mom!"

"Language. Did I hear correctly, did you go out *after* Lucy went to bed?"

"Well, yeah, I guess."

"Would that explain why the picture framed in the stairwell are all hung catawampus this morning?"

"It might. Look, it was Eunice, she climbed up through the window."

"And she carried you back out, I suppose? A retired naval officer?"

He really hated when she said that. "No ma'am. I climbed out myself."

"You woke your father. You know how he has trouble getting back to sleep."

"If I woke Dad, how did *you* hear it?"

Booey pinched his leg again. "Deke, don't be an idiot. That girl down the hall is precious! What is wrong with you?"

"I agree, Mom, but we aren't actually dating."

"Who would date you? You smell like a distillery. She's weighing better options! Now get in the shower and come downstairs. We're going to church at 10. I don't want an argument."

He put his hands up. "I know when I'm outgunned."

The headache was terrifying. He stood under the scalding water until it ran cold. Deke put on a seersucker suit and came downstairs to see Lucy sitting at the breakfast room in a Lily Pulitzer sundress. She was flacked by the twins in khakis and sport coats. "Nice threads." said Deke.

"Uncle Suitcase, you don't look so hot." said Peter.

"Jet lagged, my boys. Just need some coffee." He shuffled into the kitchen and poured himself a cup and saw what looked to be a final dram of haint punch in the bottom of the mason jar. He checked the door, filled a juice glass and wolfed it down.

"Eh hem."

"It's not what you think."

Lucy leaned against the kitchen counter. "Good. Because it *looks* like you're wolfing down some weapons grade eye-opener just to make it to make it to church with your parents and innocent little nephews."

"Easy mistake to make. But don't let those two half pint scalawags out there fool you. They're both dope fiends – just like their grandmother."

"Well, I wouldn't have guessed that."

"No one ever does. That vamp Eunice climbed up on the porch overhang and came in my window."

"Another fishin' hole incident?"

"I was honestly trying to avoid one. She threatened nudity so we went out to the Crossroads so she'd keep her clothes on. Theoretically. That reminds me, that goofy SLAMNEWS! fella is here in town. Eunice tried to eat him last night. I think he's staying at the Sunflower. At least that's where he was heading when Miss Free Love '08 beamed him with an orange. But enough about me... how's *your* helmet?"

"I've had better mornings. You are jabbering like a lunatic. What's in that stuff?"

"Some ancient recipe. Ferg'll never tell me. I feel rotten. You, on the other hand.... How'd you know to pack church clothes?"

"Educated guess."

"Mom's mad at me. She thinks I stepped out on you."

"You did. Glad she's got my back. Is this about Tim? Because we can work through this, Honey bear."

"How do I look?" It was Derrick straightening out his jacket that was still a bit big.

"Like a brown noser!" screamed Peter from the other room.

"You look wonderful." Said Lucy and kissed the top of his head. "I'll just bet you never get as ugly as your Uncle over here."

Deke and Lucy followed his parents and the boys to the All Saints Episcopal Church where they parked next to the O'Conner's gleaming silver Range Rover, out of which climbed Beau and Darla with Ferg, expertly handling his infant half-sister. "What, no Eunice?" asked Lucy.

Ferg cooed at his half sister, "Last time Eunice set foot into a church she turned into a pile of dried bones."

They all congregated before the open front doors where a bombastic priest, sweating mightily under heavy robes, was greeting parishioners and moping his large, pale head. "Hey Deke," Ferg said, "I heard Eunice was headed your way last night."

"Can't you give that woman a sedative?"

Which was about the time Ferg heard a familiar sound coming down the street. "I've really got to hide my car keys from Sis." The Porsche came roaring down the street and came to a stop on the curb opposite the church. Out popped Eunice in a black leather cat suit and pulled out a hand lettered sign that read: *I'm Protesting The Churches War on Sex.*

"Eunice..." growled Booey.

"That slogan could use some work." said Deke as the entire congregation heaved in a determined but polite retreat into the sanctuary from whatever devilment the catsuit was unleashing before them. Darla snatched up wee Mavis.

"Boys!" said Booey, "look away!"

Ferg grabbed Lucy's arm, "Y'all better get in quick before they bar the doors."

"Aw Lawd!" roared Beau, as he descended the steps toward his eldest daughter. "Eunice, Princess, that's the Catholic Church down the street you want to protest. These people are Episcopalians, they're chock-full of lady priests and queers. They don't believe in unpleasantness."

"The church has been squeezing women's ovaries for centuries!" Eunice fairly screamed.

"It's too hot for mental picture like that." said Lucy and went inside.

And yet Eunice stood her ground, flashing the placard at any car that passed. Beau was coming dejectedly back up the steps. "Deke," he moaned, "where did I go wrong?"

They walked into the sanctuary where two ushers actually did rush to shut the doors. "Well, sir, did you drop her on her head?"

"Not enough times to matter I shouldn't think. Surely not. No no. She used to be so sweet."

"When was that exactly, Mr. O'Conner?"

"Maybe you're right. I hope Molly grows up a little more agreeable."

"Who?"

"The baby, Deke. Keep up."

"I thought her name was Mavis?"

Through the small window set into the heavy oak door of the church, Beau looked at Eunice across the street. "Iddn't it too hot to be out in that get up? Will she get heat stroke?"

"Don't worry about it Mr. O'Conner, without an audience she'll go home in about ten minutes."

"Thanks for talking Deke. Yes yes." Beau said and drifted off into the sanctuary to find a seat next to his current wife.

Deke padded in and slid into the pew next to Lucy. She pointed across the aisle and a few rows up where, seated underneath her enormous Kentucky Derby style hat was none other than Betty Sue Wallace seated primly next to her husband. Casper was uncomfortable, thinking that all this Episcopalian pageantry looked dangerously Catholic. "God almighty. I think I'm going to throw up."

"Well, Deke, it's a silly hat, granted. But it's not *that* bad." Lucy whispered, "I could have sworn she was a Methodist."

"It's not the hat…entirely. Need more haint punch. Must maintain."

"More of that concoction is *not* what you need." she whispered. "That stuff is liquid Eunice."

The weather and the unusually large crowd quickly overwhelmed the church's air conditioning system. Deke felt an oily slick of toxins oozing over his face. Somewhere he was aware of a church service going on, and then, Oh Lord, the priest was fondling that big smoking orb. "Why would he pick today for High Church?"

"Deke, stop it."

Father Mike lit the pulpit and told a joke. Being Episcopalians, there wasn't so much fire and brimstone as a polite euphemism that if we sinners didn't do right, we'd all go to Hell. Then came another joke and the polite inference that Father Mike was probably not going to join them in Hades after all. Although he had it on good authority, from some theologian that no one in the room had ever heard of save himself, that no one would really like it there because the level of service in Hell is really just awful. The turn down service was a cosmic joke. Eventually the man tired of his sermon and the communion procession started and Lucy leaned over. "Can't join you…I'm Catholic."

"Whatever's right. I need a drink." The physics of how his mother's arm reached over Peter's head and past Lucy's shoulders to pull the hair at the back of his neck, Deke never understood. After going up to the altar rail, and not getting nearly enough wine to fix the problem, he came back down the aisle, passed the pew and headed out to the narthex. He stopped at the baptismal font and considered dunking his face into the cool, pristine holy waters. While never exactly sure how much of that afterlife business he actually believed, Deke thought that seemed a pretty profane.

At the heavy oaken doors, he gazed out the little window in the door and was almost certain he saw black-clad figure of Eunice O'Conner laying spread eagle on the shoulder of the road. The placard had tumbled down the road. He went back inside the sanctuary and tapped Ferg on the shoulder and whispered. "God just smote your Eunice."

"Again?"

The two went outside, pulled the girl to her feet, walked her back into the narthex and set her down on a bench. "Don't we need to give her some water?" asked Ferg.

Deke was again considering the baptismal font. "If we give her holy water she might melt. Is there a secular water fountain somewhere?"

Ferg dashed off as Eunice slid over on the bench and Deke tried to see how one loosened a leather cat suit without the occupant popping completely out of it and turning the congregation into well-dressed pillars of salt.

"Wow." said Little Derrick, "Miss Eunice is curvy." He was standing transfixed by said curves.

"Right you are."

"How'd she get that space suit on over her clothes?"

"She didn't."

His transfixed eyes widened. "You mean she's....nekkid!"

"Well, underneath the suit, yeah."

The kid swallowed. "How can you tell?"

"No lumps." Now the boy's eyes seemed dangerously wide. "Hey Derrick, you can't faint too. Only one is allowed. Why aren't you inside with Booey and Granddaddy?"

"I have to go to the bathroom."

"Then get."

Eunice shifted against Deke. "Where am I?" she mumbled.

"In church."

"The fuck why?"

"God's idea of a joke, I reckon."

Ferg came back with a cup of water. "We've got to get her home."

"We? She's *your* sister."

"C'mon man. She needs to stretch out in your truck, I'll drive my car home.... Keep an eye on the keys."

Deke turned to his nephew, still struck catatonic by a curvy Miss Eunice with no skivvies. "Derrick, listen to m: I want you to tell Miss Lucy to ride with the O'Conner's back to *their* house. Not Booey and Granddaddy's. Got that?"

He swallowed hard. "Can I help carry her?"

"No." Said Ferg. "No, you may not."

The two poured Eunice into the back of the Land Cruiser drove out to the farm. At the O'Conner's, Deke wrestled with the semi-conscious Eunice in the back seat as Ferg fumbled with the keys. "Hurry up man! Are you drunk again!"

"Again?" Ferg got them through the door and together they walked Eunice up to her room and dumped her on the bed. "Eunice!" Ferg said, "Get out of that damn thing."

She mumbled something incoherently.

Her brother yanked off one boot. "We've got to get her out of that get-up. Deke, you do that while I get some water, or something."

"Hold on Spanky." Said Deke, pulling off the other boot. "You're family. *You* do it."

"I'm her brother, that's just creepy. Don't worry about it Deke – just pretend you're six again."

Ferg disappeared down the stairs and was back up with a bottle of Gatorade and back out again just as quickly before Deke could make a tackle. So there Deke stood trying to figure out how she'd gotten into the thing and how he was going to get her out of it. There was a heavy-duty brass zipper hidden under what looked like a seam following the contour of her back. "Hey Eunice. Can you hear me?"

"Let's go swimming, it'll be fun." she mumbled.

"Swell." Deke rolled her onto her belly, turned her head to the side so she could breath. He stood as far away as possible and still hold onto the zipper, and gave it a pull. Once going, the brass teeth released a lot of glistening flesh quickly. He pulled at the arms and the top half of the suit rolled down easily. Downstairs, there was some commotion as Deke grabbed hold of more slick, sweaty folds of leather. After a few tugs, the whole thing just slid down her legs quickly, sending Deke stumbling backwards. The interior of the suit slapped him in the face. "Jesus, Eunice, is this baby oil?" He threw to suit to the side and climbed to his feet only to see to see the heaving figure of Beau O'Conner standing in the doorway looking between Deke and the oiled, semi-conscious, Rubenesque body of Eunice laying face down on her bed and dressed exactly the way she'd come into the world.

"For the record, Mr. O'Conner," sputtered Deke, "I wanted Ferg to handle this part of the rescue."

"For God's sake, Man! Cover her up!" roared Beau.

"Can we get a female relation to hose her off? She's slick."

Darla's twang came from the hall. "Don't look at me! I'm just the step-mother."

Beau was flipping the duvet over onto Eunice. "C'mon Princess. Drink something."

"You're always trying to control me you land-raping bastard." She cooed.

"I love you too, Princess."

"I'm not sure what the washing instructions are." Deke said as he handed the suit off to Darla in the hallway and made a quick retreat downstairs. He had polished off a bottle of water by the time he found Ferg in the mudroom, quietly contemplating the level of the haint punch barrels. "The angels have gotten their share." said Ferg.

"You're no angel."

"A host of angles, Deke. A host of angels have been through here." Ferg dipped the tea cup into the punch. "Still good though."

Deke took the cup to see for himself.

"Boys, boys!" said Aubrey as he came into the mud room. "It's the Lord's day!"

"Sorry."

"You must share."

"Right-o."

Deke drained the cup and handed it over. "Hey, Uncle Aubrey, did Lucy ride with you?"

FASCINATED BY the notion that grown-ups could go about without any underwear and not get yelled at, young Derrick had returned to the pew intrigued by the question of who else was going commando in the house of the Lord. The lady in the massive hat, he guessed, might give it a whirl. Then there was that loud priest, if he wasn't probably ought to consider it because he was sweating like a pig. But then, God would know. Then again God had made Adam and Eve nekkid in the first place... hmmmm. Derrick was always prided himself for thinking about the big theological questions during church. He looked at Miss Lucy. There was something he was supposed to tell her, but then he was suddenly wondering about her underwear policy and that was that.

With the service over, he filed out and saw that the Uncle Suitcase's truck and the Porsche were gone. He came within a hare's breath of remembering his Uncle's message. Ultimately the synapse was blocked by the image of black leather stretched to distraction. He was looking at Lucy's sundress until Peter cuffed the back of his head.

At the Kipling's, Lucy went up to her room to change and to call Deke when she saw the text from Mrs. Degrasse asking for a field report. The phone rang again.

"Lucy dear, how's farm life?"

"Actually, it's lovely. It's nice to be out of D.C. for a bit."

"Good. Where's Deke?"

"Well, he's not here."

"Where are you?"

"At the Mr. and Mrs. Kipling's house."

"So where is Deke?"

"I'm not sure…."

"Well, he better not be over at the O'Conners with possibly the next President and the next junior Senator while you're having tea with Mrs. Kipling! Good Lord, Lucy! The reason you are staying with Deke is to keep an eye on him!"

"Pardon?"

"He's covering the hunt for that smarmy Ken Macastle over at *Front Street*."

"But Deke said he was just down here for the shoot."

"Well, Deke lied then, didn't he?"

"Are you sure?"

"Of course, I'm sure. Macastle can't hold his liquor to save his life, he was bragging about the other night."

"Why didn't you tell me?"

"I thought that you'd stick close to him – he's your inside source! Now he's off conducting exclusive interviews for *Front Street* while you're sitting at home with your future in-laws. Keep up, Lucy…I guess feminism really is dead. Just shove it down a toilet and light the fuse. You know how Deke got the last time they published that alcoholic clown story. In print! Listen, if you can't do it for your gender –"

"Sex."

"Thanks for the grammar lesson. If you won't do it for your *sex*, do it for me. Now get that story first!"

"Are you sure about this?"

"Lucy Burton – if you let that freelancer scoop you while you're having chicken salad with your in-laws – or whatever it is you people eat down their... I swear to God –"

Lucy hung up and tossed the phone on the bed, quickly changing into a pair of jeans and a button down. She took a deep breath. *Mustn't be rude. It's not the Kipling's fault they raised a back-stabbing ass.* She didn't want to face Booey; that woman seemed to know things. She went downstairs, avoiding the kitchen and found Army throwing a ball to the boys in the yard. He looked up, "Hey Lucy. You want me to drive you out to the O'Conners?"

"No sir. Can you take me to the Sunflower Inn?"

"Sure. The mattress too hard in Jane's room?"

"No sir. I have to meet someone." She held up a notebook, "Duty calls."

TEN:
THICK AS A JUNE BUG IN AUGUST

LOUIS GUILLORY was having coffee in his room checking the results of the yesterday's races. He smiled, Ronny Basco had paid through the nose for Madame Lemuex's hex and the hex had worked. The filly Steako darlin had placed. Lemuex had told Basco that Steako wouldn't win – but the favorite, slappychappy, had come in a disappointing sixth along with a comically sluggish run by Chinadoll baby. He'd spread around some other bets on Basco's hex while he was at it. Not bad, Madame Lemuex, He thought, your otherworldly bullshit managed to push Steako darlin into second place. "The old gal certainly knows how to managed expectations."

He looked out over what Clarksdale was calling downtown, glancing at his watch and his bandaged hand. *Well,* he thought, *the kid had slept in long enough.* Guillory got up and pulled the thick manila envelope from his brief bag. He opened it and looked and the lease agreement from Grande Terre and Digger Stations Corp., then flipped through the attached bank statements and spread sheets. He slid the sheath back into the envelope and was going to put them back into the brief bag when a sharp bolt of pain went from his bandaged hand like an electric current. "Fuck 'em." He groaned, tucked the envelope under his arm, slipped a small leather wallet into his pocket and opened the door.

He peered out into the hallway before quietly making his way down hall to Teddy's room. The handle was locked and he rapped on the door. He heard Mrs. Wilson sing out "Good morning, Mr. Landry!" and the bell over the door rang out without a reply. Louis retrieved the wallet and set to work quickly on the old-fashioned lock, padded lightly into the room and slipped the envelope into Teddy's briefcase.

Then it caught his eye, the other envelope in the computer bag. It was still crisp, as if it had only been opened once. Louis looked inside to see what appeared to be a bill of sale for a BMW purchased by a company called Corsair and now registered to one Leo Kabler. "Is it possible the little dweed is smarter than he looks?" He said to himself.

THE HAND LETTERED sign on the front door of Wilson Hardware read: *OPEN THIS SUNDAY! GET READY FOR DOVE SEASON!* The problem was, Hank thought as he sat behind the counter, bored stiff, was that Mr. Wilson had been too cheap to advertise the extended hours so the only way to know the store was open was to go and stand before the front door of a business district that everyone in town assumed was closed on Sunday.

Inside, Hank sat reading the comics trying to forget about Mr. Wilson's deranged order to sell insulated coveralls when it was steamy 95^0 outside. The bell above the door tinkled and he looked up from the antics of Snuffy Smith to see that damn Yankee from the Sunflower come in the store and look helplessly around. They caught sight of each other.

"You work here too?"

"Yes sir. How can I help you?"

"I've been invited to the O'Conner's dove hunt, all rather last minute I'm afraid. I need some hunting gear."

"Ok then."

"I'm not really a hunter, so I don't need any of that top dollar Kevlar stuff."

"We don't sell Kevlar here, sir."

"Well, that's good, because I'm not buying it. I'm sure you people would love to fleece the 'Damn Yankee'" Teddy made air quotes. "but it ain't me Bubba. I'm on to you."

In fact, it had not occurred to Hank to fleece the damn Yankee in any way until both the idea and Teddy were standing right in front of him. "Well, sir." Hank said, folding the paper closed so that it would look like he'd been reading the sports section. "That's not the way we do business here at Wilson Hardware and Sport. I've got a discontinued line of field clothes – marked cheap – that you might like." Hank went and fetched a pair of coveralls. "Sir, you're going to like these – you only need to buy one piece."

"I don't know." Said Teddy, feeling the material, "It looks pretty thick. It's like Africa hot outside."

"Well sir, the material *absorbs* the body heat. It's made of an entirely different fabric than the padding that keeps you warm."

"Really?" Teddy was dubious. "It seems pretty thick."

"Well, yeah. We'd all die of heat stroke if it wasn't. Hadn't you ever heard the expression 'thick as a June bug in August.'?"

"No."

No one had. Hank had just made it up. "Well, that's where that sayin' comes from."

"I see." He didn't. "I guess there is some down-home wisdom to that."

"Like granmaw's cornbread."

"Is it bulletproof?"

"Granmaw's cornbread? Well, I reckon it is a bit dry."

"What? No! The jumpsuit – is it bullet proof? You know against hunters with bad aim?"

The polite *No, sir* that had formed in Hank's head simply could not make it to his lips. Being Sunday, Hank's soul was really rooting for an honest response, but ultimately the words that he heard coming out of his mouths were, "Oh, you want the *bullet proof* line... Lemme see."

Hank took the coveralls into the storeroom, took the tag off a second pair and printed out a replacement tag marked BLLTPRF, doubled the price and reattached it. He walked back to the counter and laid the suit out.

"This is double the price of the other one!"

"It's bulletproof, Mister. Whaddaya expect?"

That did make a certain free-market sense and there was something very SLAM! about going into the field wearing bulletproof gear. "Okay, I'll take it."

"Ok." Said Hank, then stopped before the cash register. "You'll need a hunting license."

"Quite right." Said Teddy, who was doing the math in his head, reconciling the Greek fascist's 'donation' to SLAMNEWS! and how much all of this was costing him. Hank pulled out the forms and slid it to Teddy.

While Teddy was filling out the hunting license form, Hank leaned forward and said firmly, "Now, what are you shooting?"

"Dove, I guess."

"I guessed that, sir. What I was asking was with what weapon are you to shoot the doves out of the sky?" Hank could have gotten the guns out and suggested something suitable, but decided it was just easier to have this know-it-all just tell him what he wanted.

Which presented a bit of a problem. What little Teddy knew about firearms came from Trevor, currently preparing for the looming race war that Ballyhoo referred to "the bugaloo" after some 1980s break dancing movie. Honestly, Teddy didn't know much about dancing either, but seemed to recall that break dancing had been a black thing. Which meant that someone in the chat room bowels of the white oppression movement had really stepped on their metaphors.

"What'll you be shooting?" Hank prompted Teddy.

"Ah..." he said, coming back to earth. If he was going to have to buy a gun, he'd better make it count. "An AR15."

Hank was now genuinely tickled.

Ten minutes later Teddy was walking along the sidewalk with an enormous puffy bag from Wilson's Hardware in his hand, a pair of green rubber wellie boots in the other and an AR-15 Bushmaster − the civilian version of the military M-16 − slung over his shoulder. He stepping into the lobby of the Sunflower Inn and walked past Mrs. Wilson. She was impressed with young Hank. Ever since those AR-15 had become the weapon of choice for mass shootings they'd been a hard sell. The boy showed promise.

Outside, Army pulled the car to a stop and said, "Here we are. Just give me a holler if you need a ride back. Deke ought to be back in a few."

"Thanks Mr. Kipling." Said Lucy and hopped out, went inside and asked Mrs. Wilson if they had a guest named Teddy Landry.

Mrs. Wilson was more than a little taken back. "The chubby red-headed boy?"

"Yes."

"Sure. He just came in."

"Would you mind terribly ringing his room and telling him that Lucy Burton of the *Daily Brute* is here to see him?"

Mrs. Wilson rang the room. "Mr. Landry, can you come to the lobby? You have a visitor... well, that's a terrible thing to say on a Sunday... coverall's?... how would I know that? No, Her name is Lucy Burton...." She put the receiver back on the hook. "He hung up."

There was a frantic rush of feet descending the old wooden stairs that stopped out of sight. Teddy came into view on the stairs at a leisurely pace and leaned onto the bannister, "Well hello there, Lucy." He let the *Quiet Thunder* roll.

Both she and Mrs. Wilson cringed.

"We're going to lunch." Commanded Lucy.

Teddy cringed; both his debit and credit cards were, essentially, toast.

"The *Brute* is buying. Grab your notebook."

Teddy smiled again. "Great, I'll grab my notebook. It's in my room. C'mon up."

"I'll wait here, thanks."

Mrs. Wilson leaned over the counter and whispered, "I don't know how well you know Mr. Landry, but I thought I'd tell you he's got an assault rifle up in his room. It's really none of my business, but I don't think he knows how to use it."

"Gosh. That's terrifying."

"Well, that's why I'm telling you, Sweetheart."

The rush of steps came again and stopped just out of eyesight. "Where is a good place for lunch." Lucy asked Mrs. Wilson.

"For Sunday Lunch? Or just lunch that's open on Sunday."

"Curtain number two, please."

A few feet away in the dining room, Guillory mostly overheard Lucy and Mrs. Wilson. He looked up from his table to see the pair walking out the door. Rising to follow he spotted the small, mousey girl who pressed somehow in his memory. Wendy X was looking over a selection of fruit on the salad bar. Guillory approached, "Excuse me, but you look very familiar –"

Wendy turned with a shock of recognition as she looked at the man who'd quaffed Deke's spiked martini. "I don't think so." she stammered nervously.

For Guillory, the connection still floated behind a deep fog, but he did know something about fear. This girl was suddenly very frightened. "A mutual friend perhaps?" Louis asked as he scanned Wendy, catching sight of the number on her room key as he stepped back.

"I don't think so." She stammered again.

He smiled. "My mistake. Sorry to have bothered you." He returned to his table as Wendy quickly picked up some fruit and retreated upstairs. After she'd left, Guillory went outside and around to count the windows. The girl's curtains were drawn tight so he went into the Sunflower's small guest lot and then his eyes fell onto the Prius. He couldn't say why he connected the car with the girl, but in the back of the mental fog a distant shape was forming and somehow the two went together. He approached to see something large and covered with a hemp cloth in the back. Louis checked the window again, went to his car and retrieved the slim-jim from his trunk and popped the lock on the Prius, and looked under the hemp.

While the .50 caliber machine gun was something to behold, it didn't actually jog his memory.

DEKE, FERG and Laudermilk sat in rocking chairs on the long back gallery as the ceiling fans churned the still air. They passed a mason jar of haint punch between them. "Did'ju see Betty Sue Wallace's hat?" said the Old Bear. "Lawd in Heaven! She really cocked up my plans whupin' ole Davison like she did. He wasn't so smart but he was reliable. The problem with these freshman, Kabler, Wallace, or any of them, is that they're gonna be impressed with themselves for winning the seat and think they deserve to be big-leagued. Which wouldn't be too much of a problem except somebody is gonna see the low hanging fruit and indulge 'em. Both of 'em are media hounds, and they'll want to make some splash in their first year: Wallace is gonna start on tossin' the immigrants out, and Kabler is gonna work some wildly expensive education bill that makes the teachers happy but doesn't do the chilrun' any good. Some rascal is gonna take them out to dinner in a D.C. inner circle restaurant and tell them they can do it. That's how you get politicians bought." He took a sip and handed the jar to Deke. "I mean what the hell? Gambling along the Mississippi River was supposed to give the state the money to update our school system at least to the *last* century. It just didn't happen and no one running the show can tell you why. Just a little peck here, and little there. All the money just got…skimmed to death. If I had one legacy, it'd be to route that bullshit out." Aubrey shook his head, "Well, I reckon the people have spoken."

"Legacy?" said Ferg, "you hadn't even started on that. I thought you were thinking about a White House run?"

Deke was somewhat aware of his phone vibrating in his coat pocket. Laudermilk looked over and smiled. He'd heard it too. "Say, Ferg, what are you doing these days?"

"Geez, Uncle Aubrey, not much. After Daddy sold the firm, I flogged insurance for a while, then worked for a tech start up in Memphis, but that didn't pan out…."

"Tech entrepreneur… huh?"

"Well, I wouldn't go that far…"

"I would. That's got me thinking."

"You're always thinking." laughed Deke.

Laudermilk craned his thick neck around to look squarely at Ferg, "How about *you* run for Senate. As an independent?"

"…"

"Whaddaya say?" Laudermilk laughed and slapped Ferg's knee.

"I don't think I'm qualified."

"Good Lawd! You can sell can't ya? If you can move something as abstract as commodities, then you can work a crowd for votes. How old are you? Thirty five? Hell son, that's old enough."

"Really?"

"Why not? The parties are comin' apart at the seams because of the Internet. Poor ole Carlson, he's got people sending models of his John Thomas around the world on an hashbrown."

"Hashtag?"

"Yeah right!" roared Aubrey, snatched the jar from Deke and pressed it into Ferg. "Deke here knows all about hashtags. Those Hell's Belles he pissed off would like to kill him, I hear. Now look, I'll throw my support behind you. That'll really piss off the White House. Well good. I'll show him who's the Chief." He took the jar from Ferg. "Boy you need to slow down. Save some for the rest of us." He took a swig. "Gad man! This stuff gets pretty fierce when it's hot!"

"So how does this work," Asked Ferg, "running for the Senate?"

"Get your name on the ballot and kiss every baby in sight. Go back to Jackson, sell that Porsche and buy an American made SUV."

"What about Daddy?" asked Ferg. "He's angling for some political appointment. He won't say it, though–"

"He'll sure as shit say it to me. Naw, this'll only help. You know how this country likes its political dynasties!" now the Old Bear was laughing now. "We're at the start of sumthin' big boys! The Roosevelt's! The Kennedy's! The Bushes, Clintons and now the O'Connor's of Mississippi."

"Wow." Said both Ferg and Deke for wholly different reasons. The latter reached for the jar from Aubrey.

"Deke, now you listen up, this'll be a helluva feature in *Front Street*." At that Deke fished his cellphone out of his pocket. There was a voicemail from Kenneth Macastle. He took an unseemly slug from the jar.

Beau came out of the house leaning on the bull penis walking stick and being very Lord o' the Manor about it. "That's where all my haint punch is going!" he laughed heartily.

"Beau, that thing is gonna have to go back in your closet." said Aubrey. "We gotta talk." He whispered to Ferg, "Why don't you let me take the lead on this one."

Deke stepped off the gallery and into the back lawn. He took a long look at the voicemail icon on his phone and started to feel sick. Where was Lucy? And how the hell did Laudermilk know about *Front Street*?

LUCY AND TEDDY sat in a booth at Collie's Catfish Cabin. "You're distracted...I can tell." Teddy asked with a hair too much compassion to be taken seriously.

"Yes."

"You want to talk about it?"

"I wanna talk about the senate race. Waddaya got?"

"Oh I've got a thick file on Leo Kabler. It's pretty damning too. Mr. Environmentalism is pretty corrupt."

"Right. I spoke with him and Basco at the opera party. They seemed pretty chummy. What've you got on it?"

Teddy paused. "He, uh, he's in the pocket of those oil companies down in the gulf."

"Okay. Not really breaking news. How so? What's in your file? What do we know?"

"The smoking gun." Said Teddy with just a trace of *QT*, "that's what's in the file."

"So there *is* some documentation?" Lucy was looking down at her notepad. There was a clear 3D box, a daisy, and an elephant with a bowler hat.

Teddy was frantically trying to get the attention of the waitress. "You draw very well."

"I'd rather be writing. What's the smoking gun Teddy? Sorry, Theodore."

"Oh, here comes the waitress." he said.

The waitress was about eighteen, "Looks like y'all are ready to order. What can I get ya?"

"I'll have the catfish plate and a Yolabusha beer." said Lucy.

"That's what we're famous for." She turned to Teddy, "How about you darlin'?"

"I'll have the same. Listen, what wine to you recommend?"

The waitress smiled. "With fried catfish? Well gosh, we've got a chardonnay. That might work. It's pretty terrible but then again… we are a catfish joint."

Teddy looked desperately to Lucy who was smiling for the first time in five hours. "What'll it be, Johnny Town-mouse?" she said.

"The chardonnay…I guess."

"Great. It's buttery. You'll love it. All the girls do."

The waitress bounced away and Teddy sighed. "Just look at this place. These little people living there little lives. They seem happy, but I don't get it."

"Get what? That teenager just out wine snobbed you."

"Yeah, but this is what these people consider fine dining."

"No, Teddy, it's not. This is what *I'll* pay for. You know how Degrasse is about *per diems*."

"Good times, good times." Teddy chuckled, "I'm glad there is no animosity between our publications. It's great to be working with you, Lucy."

"Well, we still haven't done any work, have we? You just keep telling me the monumental importance of the information you've got...up in your room."

"Well, I wouldn't call it *monumental.* But it's gonna shake up the race. So," Teddy asked gently, "what's the story with you and that Deke Kipling? You guys are pretty close if you're staying at his parent's house. I didn't think he covered much politics."

"That little bastard is full of sneaky surprises."

"Tell me about it. He was out all night with some harpy last night."

"Oh I know."

"Sounds like there is a little tension –"

"Teddy, what did I tell you in the car?"

"I know. I'm just saying that if you need a place to crash, you can stay in my room at the Sunflower."

"No I can't."

Through the front door came a local television news crew ahead of the Wallaces. Betty Sue was hometown causal in jeans, cowgirl boots and an untucked but crisp button down. She was moving through the room, stopping to talk to the diners. Casper came around the commotion and slid into the booth next to Lucy. "Lucy Burton of the *Daily Brute*? I'm Casper Wallace."

"Hi." Said Teddy.

"Listen, when we are done with the local press, would the *Brute* be interested in a national exclusive?"

"What about SLAMNEWS!"

"Teddy here –" said Casper.

"Theodore–" said Teddy

"Theodore says you two are working together on the campaign story."

"Well, we're pooling our resources." Said Lucy. "Sort of. Maybe."

"We're still working out what kind of marriage this will be." Said Teddy.

Lucy cringed and handed Casper her card.

"Great." He said, sliding out of the booth, "Oh Betty Sue."

She breezed through the restaurant with poise leaving a path of disrupted Sunday diners. "Hello Lucy Barton." Betty Sue said, "I'm all yours."

"Hello Mrs. Wallace." Said Teddy.

"Hello Teddy." She pointed to a table and sat down, motioning Lucy to join her.

Teddy ignored the snub and sat on the other side of the candidate as the waitress came by and set a beer in front of Lucy and a glass of wine in front of Teddy. "Aw Lawd," Betty Sue exclaimed, "You're drinking wine with catfish?" Before he could answer, she leaned towards Lucy and said, "It's a new day for the Mississippi politics. Gone is the two party lock on good ole boy politics."

"Ma'am, you're running as a Republican."

"This isn't your grandfather's Republican party, is it Lucy?"

"My grandfather was English."

WENDY X sat in the first tree line nestled against a Beretta 687 .12 gauge shotgun that was entirely too large for her. She'd watched Deke sitting on the porch with the Old Bear and Eunice's brother making plans for the patriarchy. It occurred to her that she might do the world a favor by getting rid of all three of them, but it also occurred that shooting a sitting senator would be the last favor she ever did womankind. Except, perhaps, as some gadfly in the women's prison system.

So she waited. As the heat pressed down and the insects swarmed and little pokey twigs and branched scratched, she decided to never give any more money to environmentalists again because, to put it bluntly, the environment sucked. Then she saw *him* moving off the back gallery and looking at his phone. She held her breath and took aim.

That Barrett .50 caliber machine gun that she'd bought in Tennessee was bigger, but most of its recoil had been absorbed by the Prius. She'd thought about using it for the job, but a) it was really heavy once you started lugging the thing around and b) there was a certain plausibly deniability with shooting someone with a shotgun during dove season. That raised the question: Why wasn't anyone else at said shoot? Then a squirrel jumped on her bottom. This thought, along with her the upper right side of her torso, were knocked violently out of focus when she pulled the trigger in surprise.

Deke was looking at his phone and wondered how, exactly, Lucy was going to react when she learned about his *Front Street* assignment when something stung his face and shoulder at the same time – hard. He stumbled into one of the long, empty tables as he heard one of the upstairs windows break.

He'd never even heard the report of the shotgun but within seconds, Beau and Laudermilk were out on the gallery. Beau was looking for the broken window. Aubrey called to Deke, "You all right?"

"Yeah, I think someone got excited and started a day early." He was pointing to the tree line. One hand went up to his cheek and felt a streak of blood. The smartphone was laying shattered and useless on the grass.

"Deke, your coat!" yelped Darla.

There were three small holes peppered in the upper arm, two blooming red around the edges. Then it really started to hurt. "Swell."

ELEVEN:
SKULLDUGGERY

Deke walked into the front door of his parent's house and was not greeted with the sympathy that a man who'd just been shot might expect from his mother. "Where have you been all afternoon?" she barked.

"Nice to see you too, Mom. Over at the O'Conners, I thought Lucy was coming over. Where is she?"

"Deke! What happened to your face?"

"I was sort of shot. Darla picked two bits of brass out of my arm. The phone is a goner, though."

"Your face! Do you need to go to the hospital?"

"Naw, it barely broke the skin. But this was my favorite sport coat."

She sniffed the air. "You're drunk."

"It was the haint punch. It retards the infection."

"It retards something, alright." said Booey. "Was it Eunice?"

"No. Well at least I don't think so. Some boob just got excited about dove season, I reckon. Mom, where *is* Lucy?"

"Army! Where did you take Lucy?"

"To the Sunflower Inn." Boomed the voice from the study, "Said she had a meeting."

"A meeting?" said Deke, "with who?"

"Whom." Said Booey

"How the hell would I know!" called Army. "I thought you two worked together!"

"Language! The boys."

"Yeah, the boys…" Deke muttered, "Hey Derrick, come here."

There was the sound of rushing feet. "Hey Uncle Suitcase, where have you been?"

"At. The. O'Conners." Deke said, glowering at the boy.

As his uncle spoke, something shortly forgotten began to float up in the back of Derrick's mind; unidentifiable as of yet, but there nonetheless. In his mind's eye, the leather cat suit snapped away revealing a host of otherwise normal adults all secretly going commando and having some great secret adult laugh about it at a bar or a boardroom or some other place adults gather to talk about underwear and/or money. He was in trouble, Derrick could sense it. The vibe from Uncle Suitcase had turned ugly. But why? He was wearing his…. "Underpants!" he yelled in a panic and took off through the kitchen and out the back door like a bottle rocket. There was another rush of feet and Peter now came tearing by screaming "Underpants!" and followed his twin brother out the back door.

Deke and his mother stared at each other for a long time. "What was that all about?"

"Eunice…" Booey growled and dropped her head in her hands.

The front door opened and in walked Lucy. "Hello all." she said quickly.

"Lucy, great news! – hey where'd you run off to?"

"I was working Deke." she snapped. "Why do you think I'm down here?"

"Whose car is that?" asked Deke eyeballing the rental Spark in the driveway.

"Don't worry about it. I've got to get my voice recorder, that's all and I'll be out of your hair." Lucy went upstairs without another word.

The vibe from Burton of the *Brute* had turned ugly, Deke thought. But why? He turned to Booey for help. "Deke, honey, don't be an idiot." she counseled gently.

"Do I talk to her?"

"It depends what you did."

"I don't know what I did."

"Then you need to find out."

"Do I go up and ask?"

"It depends what you did."

"..." Deke took the steps in a few strides and knocked on Lucy's door.

"Just a second." She opened the door and her face went tense. "Deke, what do you want? I've got to work on this story. You knew this is why I came down here. I was going to do the story and you were going to be on vacation. Remember?" Her eyes welled up.

"Lucy – look…"

"Deke, if I can't do this story from here I'll go to the Sunflower, okay? I'll get the expense out of Degrasse. She's not a monster."

"No… don't do that. Can I get you anything?"

"You can let me get my gear and go to work." She shut the door.

Along the stairs, a picture fell from its pin. "Not my fault." he called down.

"Yes it is!" came the answer.

Deke shook his head started down the steps, righted the picture – a perfectly normal graduation photo of Ashley graduating form a perfectly normal law school – and was suddenly jealous of both his brother and his nephew. It had never before occurred to him that screaming "underpants" and running out the door was a viable solution to life's more mysterious problems, but now he was beginning to see the genius behind it. For his part, Ash never actually seemed to have mysterious problems. When he turned on the landing he barked. "God's Holy Trousers! It's you!"

The pasty-faced cherub the world called Teddy Landry smiled smugly. "And it's you, Deke Kipling. Hope your vacation is going well. Lucy ran into to get her voice recorder, but she seems held up. I was wondering if everything was okay."

"It's fine." said Army, "She'll be down in a second."

Then Lucy came down the stairs and went immediately to the kitchen, "Thank you Mrs. Kipling, but I've got a story to file for tomorrow and I just can't stay for dinner." Then she circled around to the foyer.

"Hey Lucy, can I talk to you for a minute before you head out?"

"Maybe later Deke, my ride is here."

"With SLAMNEWS!?"

"You don't have to yell it."

"We're working together on a story." she said.

"Partners, really." Teddy clarified.

"Oh, shut up, Teddy." Lucy said as she barreled out of the house.

"We'll leave the light on for ya!" yelled Army and shut the door. "So… five for dinner then?"

"You'd better count me out." said Deke as he bounded upstairs to his room. He was pulling off his suit and looking at the wrecked shirt beneath.

There was a knock on his door and in came Army. "Well played, Son."

"This is why I don't cover politics, Pop. I'm more comfortable in some sadistic war zone where at least I know the rules."

"The rules depend on what game you're playing."

"Listen Dad, you've been married to Mom since, well, forever. You've got to know something about women…"

"You'd think." Army sat down on the edge of the bed. "I've been married to Booey for 45 some odd years – which isn't quite forever – and I still don't know what the hell she's talking about half the time."

"I'm glad your grandchildren are around to absorb that sage wisdom of yours. It'll help them through the hard times."

"Says the chronically unemployed bachelor who just had a marital spat with a gal he was never even dating. Deke, I say this as your father and I say it with love: If I knew how to outsmart a woman you wouldn't exist."

"Fair point." He dropped his face in his hands, "Jesus, Pop. What did *I* do?"

"Why don't you quit trying to figure out what you did and figure out what it is she thinks you've done. Or not done. Like, I don't know… accepting an assignment to cover the same story for a rival magazine and, apparently, not telling her."

"How do you know about that? Was it Ashley? That Judas. Dad, It's not the same story!"

"Alright then, why haven't you mentioned it to her?"

Deke thought about it. "Honestly I was hoping something terribly clever would come to me before the story ran."

"I see. You've really thought this one out, haven't you?"

"Lucy and SLAMNEWS!," huh? I wouldn't have guessed that."

"Apparently, that ginger gummy-bear has got some damning file on Kabler he's going to share with her."

"But haven't they been together all afternoon?"

"That's what I thought."

"Then why hasn't he shown it to her yet?"

"Deke, forget about that little rube, would ya? I may not know what your mother is talking about half the time, but the fact is that she's the most sensible woman I know. I think she's right on this one. You *are* an idiot." Army planted a paternal hand on his shoulder. "Don't worry about it, Son. You come by it honestly."

"That's strangely comforting. Thanks Pop. I gotta go."

DEKE AND FERG sat in the Land Cruiser behind of the Sunflower Inn. "Here, take another slug." Said Ferg.

"No. We've got to stop drinking that damn stuff." Deke took the jar and had a gulp.

"I'm sorry, Deke. I thought that you said you felt hung-over."

"Now I'm starting to feel drunk again."

"See, you're cured."

"Look, Ferg, you ready to do this?"

Ferg thought for a moment. "It seems kind of Watergate-ish. It might ruin my political career."

"You haven't got a political career." Deke handed the jar back, "Laudermilk is drunk."

"You don't think I can win?"

"Well, if we can find whatever dirt our boy Teddy has on your possible opponents, you just might."

"I want to run a clean campaign."

"No, you don't. Your only hope is that Kabler and Betty Sue eviscerate each other before they figure out you're running." Deke stopped and thought. "Actually, that's not a bad plan."

"Well, if that's the case, then why don't just we let them have at it. Why should I get involved in this political… skullduggery?"

"Because we've got to be – nice word choice – because I think Teddy is gonna to screw Lucy over."

"And you're the only one who gets to do that?"

"I haven't *done* anything. Besides, you owe me a favor."

"Why?"

"Because I stripped your glistening sister nekkid this afternoon."

"Oh, come off it. It wasn't anything you hadn't seen before."

"Everything was so much smaller before the hormones."

"Jesus, that's my sister. Well, I suppose that I do owe you one. That dehydration really took the air out of her sails. She's weighed herself like four times this afternoon. Over the moon, Eunice is...almost pleasant now."

"That's dear."

They both looked at the back of the hotel. "How do you know what room he's in?" asked Ferg.

"I called out here before I picked you up. The kid working the desk gave me the room number. He asked if I was a friend of Louis Guillory of all people."

"That can't be good."

"No, I can't see how. At any rate, the guy even offered to let me in the room – seems to hate Teddy with a pleasant sort of passion."

"Deke, how're we gonna do this?"

"Climb the balcony up to his window go in from there."

"How do you know the window is open?"

"I'm sure it's not, but I'm also pretty sure the lock is older than we are."

Ferg looked at the mason jar in his lap. "I'm not sure I'm in any state to scale a balcony."

"Nonsense. It's like flying, Ferg. The tricky part is getting back down."

The boys got out of the car and scaled the wrought iron lace to the second floor gallery and then the third.

There was a door into the room but Deke reckoned the window would be easier to pick. It was. Moments later he stepped through the window into Teddy's room. On the desk sat a laptop and an old nylon computer bag nearby on the floor. Deke inserted a flash drive and began to copy the files from the folders marked "Kabler/Corsair, Inc." while they were being written onto the flash drive. Deke searched through the computer bag until he found a stiff envelope from Casper Wallace. Under it was another, unmarked envelope. He peeked inside and was looming at the franchise agreement between Grande Terre and one Chad Wallace for Digger Stations 25 and 27. "Hello nurse."

Then Deke looked up and saw it. On the bed was an AR-15. "Jesus God! Ferg! This guy has an almost assault rifle!"

Ferg poked his head through the window. "For a dove shoot? He's not even invited! You think it's a political assassination?"

"How? Neither Kabler or Wallace have been elected yet."

"You think he's after the Old Bear?"

"Laudermilk?" said Deke, "No, implausible. Even his enemies like him. Maybe he wants to kill Eunice. They did have an encounter last night."

"Huh." Said Ferg. "Well we can't have that, can we?"

"Will you get back out on the gallery and look out for a small red Chevy Spark?"

Ferg stepped outside almost impressed that sister had finally driven a man to contemplate homicide, but not altogether surprised. Eunice had always had potential. Then he saw the small dirty Prius pull into the lot. Out stepped a vaguely familiar girl who was dressed like she just left a cocktail party through a thorn bush. She yanked the gun case out of the car and went inside.

What he missed while watching the Prius, was the aforementioned rental car pulling into corner space on the other side of the building.

Teddy put the car in park, and let a little *Quiet Thunder* roll. "Lucy, I'm so glad you decided to come up this evening."

"Let's watch our phrasing, shall we? I want to take a look at this smoking gun of yours."

"Yes." He said as they climbed out of the car. "A highly-placed source leaked the information to me. It's good to have people on the inside. You'll learn that soon enough."

Lucy stepped out of the car and looked around the seemingly deserted stretch of downtown. Teddy was telling some heroic tale from the night before while Lucy stepped to the intersection. *Dammit, Deke!* she thought as she caught sight of the back of his old Land Cruiser, *who is that bastard interviewing now?*

"Hey," She heard Teddy saying behind her, "I like a good time too, but it's time to get to work."

"Yeah, sure. I'd watch those Wallace's if I were you Teddy. They look set to drop you at the first whiff of national press."

"I doubt that. They seemed pleased enough that I brought you on." He opened the lobby door and grandly bowed for Lucy to pass. "We go a long way back. They are very grateful for my coverage."

"That's good to know."

Upstairs Ferg poked his head back into the room. "Hey Deke? What color car am I looking for?"

"Red. Did they just pull up?" Deke hopped over to eject the flash drive – the light was still blinking. "C'mon…." When he heard Teddy's voice in the hall and leapt across the room, snatching up the envelopes and slipping through the window as the door from the hall opened.

"Damn! I left the flash drive in there." Deke hissed.

"Tough titties!" Ferg said, snatched the envelopes and climbed over the balcony railing. Deke followed to the rail, "Ferg, get down to the truck, wait for me."

"Hell no! We've got to get out of here!"

Deke padded back around to where he could peak inside.

"Nice assault rifle!" Lucy was saying as she came into the room.

The little light on the flash drive was no longer blinking. "Well, it was here somewhere." said Teddy, scratching his head before resuming his search through the computer bag. "I swear."

Lucy looked around the mussed sheets and the underwear on the floor. "Hey, Teddy, when did you book this room?"

"Just the other day – actually it's a funny story–"

"Like within the two days?"

"Yeah, the lady said I was lucky, that there had been a last-minute cancellation."

"Really?" she said, but she was no longer listening. She was picturing the ghoulish smile of Mrs. Degrasse. "Something is not right." She muttered to herself.

"What's that?" Teddy was still rifling through his stuff.

"How are we coming on that smoking gun."

"It *was* here."

"You can't find it?" Lucy was rolling her eyes.

"It's here. I swear. It's not like I was trying to lure you up here." He laughed nervously.

"Teddy. This is just pathetic."

"I wasn't lying! This is the smoking gun!"

"Then can you just tell me what was in the envelope? Just the important points, so I know the nature of the issue. Maybe we can reverse engineer the evidence. Just the broad points."

Teddy stopped. He was looking through the computer bag. "Well I haven't actually read through it… entirely."

Deke heard his car start. Below Ferg was pulling away from the hotel. Inside, Lucy had had enough. She now hated all men. Her eyes dropped to the laptop and the flash drive poking from the side. As Teddy crammed his face back into the bag, she snatched the flash drive out of the computer and slid it in her pocket.

Then the rape whistle went off in her ear. "Sweet Jesus!"

Teddy was blowing the whistle and pointing through the window. "What are you doing here?" Teddy screamed through the window.

As soon as Lucy realized he hadn't blown the whistle at her, she turned to the window and said, "Yeah Deke, what *are* you doing here?"

"Well, if you must know…" he cleared his throat, "I'm waiting on Leo Kabler to get off the phone."

"What are you doing outside *my* window?" demanded Teddy.

"It's a wrap around balcony you half-wit!" said Deke, "I stepped outside to give the man some privacy!"

Deke had no way of knowing that Kabler was staying on a higher floor. Had Teddy given it a little thought, he'd have likely seen the flaw in Deke's story, but before those two points of fact had time to collide, Lucy's voice broke through the room. "I thought you said you weren't working on a story, Deke! I thought you said this was a vacation! Or was that the problem, I believed something that you said?"

Teddy blew the whistle again.

"What the hell man?" Deke plugged an ear, "Is that a rape whistle?"

"Why is my window open?"

"How should I know? It's your room!" Deke said as it occurred to him that the only way to get off the balcony without a room key was to climb through Teddy's window.

It is the very rare occasion when the call for police support goes out by a civilian and a constable is, in fact, within a short stone's throw. Which is exactly where Officer Crenshaw was, talking to André outside the Crossroads, when she heard the first blast of the rape whistle.

"Well give him some privacy somewhere else." Teddy was saying and blew the whistle a third time.

With all the nonchalance he could muster, Deke climbed over the back of the balcony and started the shimmy down the supports. He got to the sidewalk about the time the patrol car roared around the corner, "Stop right there." screamed Crenshaw. Deke stopped. "What are you doing?"

"Going for a stroll."

Teddy and Lucy stepped out onto the balcony and looked down into the street. "Officer," Teddy called, "that man was breaking into my room."

Crenshaw looked up and saw Teddy. "Oh, it's you. Have you got a room?"

"Yes, it's me and I'm pressing charges!"

"Officer," said Deke, "I stepped outside onto the balcony, I was interviewing Congressman Kabler who had to take a call. Then this clod starts blowing a rape whistle."

"He broke into my room." called Teddy.

"If I was in his room ask him what I took. You can search me." The khakis and white button down didn't leave much room for stash.

"What's your name?" she asked.

"Deke Kipling."

"Alright Mr. Kipling come with me." Deke got into the back of the patrol car.

Teddy smiled at Lucy, "Looks like your boyfriend is the jealous type."

"Teddy, why do you have a rape whistle?"

"Those D.C. streets are dangerous."

Lucy was contemplating calling the patrolman off Deke when Wendy X appeared in the door with a very pretty shotgun leveled at Teddy.

Down in the patrol car, the two sat in silence for a moment before Crenshaw pulled away from the Sunflower. "Can we go talk to the Congressman?" Deke said. It was a risky bluff but he figured Kabler's burning hatred for Teddy Landry and SLAMNEWS! would provide some covering fire.

"Where is your car, Mr. Kipling?" she asked.

"Oh...Ferg O'Conner has it."

"Ferg O'Conner? Beau's son? Did he drop you off?"

Deke thought for a moment. "No. He stole it."

"What? Ferg O'Conner *stole* your car?"

"Yup."

"Deke Kipling... Are you Booey Kipling's boy?"

"Yup. Are you taking me to the station? On what, empty handed robbery? Breaking into a hotel room I never set foot in? But I'll tell you what is a felony, grand theft auto. So yes. We need to get to the precinct as fast as possible to file charges."

"You're gonna file felony grand theft auto charges against Ferg O'Conner?"

"Right. And you are gonna arrest him. I'll call the mayor, he'll be so pleased. Hell, I think that I'll use him as my phone call. I think he's headed out to the O'Conners tomorrow anyway."

The patrol car was now rolling along the street at a thundering 15 miles an hour. No Crenshaw thought, The mayor will not be pleased. Nor, for that matter neither will the chief. And Crensha saw no good reason to risk a city wide hurrah for that fool caught out sleeping in the street last night.

"That Teddy fellow has an assault rifle in his room." Deke continued, "Now I'm all for the Second Amendment, you understand, but they aren't exactly designed to shoot birds. And there are some political heavy weights in town."

"You shittin' me?"

"Nope. But first we've got to charge Ferg O'Conner with grand theft auto."

"If you weren't in the room, how do you know about the assault rifle?"

"It was laying on the bed. I wasn't in the room, I was on the balcony giving the congressman some privacy for a phone call. Why do you think I was standing outside? Who keeps an AR-15 on their bed?"

"Who *is* that kid?"

"Well, I *thought* he was a reporter. Anyway, you might want to look into that tonight after we get to the station, book me for whatever it is you think I've done and I'll report Ferg's felony and y'all can send the squad out to the O'Conner's to get my stolen car back."

"Well, look, Mr. Kipling, we haven't filed any charges yet."

"Yeah, but when you do it'll be a mountain of paperwork. I hate that."

So did she, for that matter. "We haven't started any of it yet. Look, are you sure you wanna file charges against Ferg? Didn't you two grow up together?"

"Officer Crenshaw, that hardly excuses stealing my car."

"Why don't I just drop you off at your parents?"

"Why don't you take me out to the O'Conner's farm?"

"W-why do you wanna go out there?"

"To get my car back, Officer. I'd have thought that was obvious."

BACK AT THE SUNFLOWER, Lucy had turned to see Wendy X in the doorway leveling a shotgun at Teddy, who was holding himself perfectly still. "That's right, hold it right there!" snarled Wendy. But there was something wrong with what she was seeing. She cocked her head to the side for a long moment.

Then Lucy said, "Oh, I see. Love the spirit – whoever you are – but you've got it backward. He's the one who blew rape, not me. Easy mistake."

"Who'd rape *him?*"

"He thinks he got robbed."

"Jesus, he stole it!" Teddy squealed.

"Who stole what, Teddy?" asked Lucy.

"My smoking gun."

Wendy nodded to the AR-15 on the bed. "Your gun is right there."

"He's mashing up his metaphors." Lucy explained, "He's not a very good writer."

Teddy looked around the room in a panic. "Deke Kipling stole my smoking gun!"

Wendy's eyes went wide. "Deke Kipling was *here?*"

"Well," Teddy said proudly. "he's down at the police station now."

"Teddy, if you don't know what was in it, how do you know it was a smoking gun?"

"How much longer are you going to let him treat you like this, Lucy?" asked Teddy, "The lying, the duplicity." Then came the *Quiet Thunder.* "You need a real man."

"You do *not* need a man" said Wendy from the doorway. "Certainly, not that one."

"Him?" Lucy thumbed toward Teddy.

"Oh, well, probably not." she said, "I was talking about Deke Kipling. He's a bad guy, Lucy."

"I'm sorry, who are you again and can you please put the gun down?"

"Oh, sure." Said Wendy and leaned against the doorjamb with the barrel drooping to the floor. "Deke Kipling... he's a misogynist, Lucy. And most of them are. You know we have a past. We went skinny-dipping together and he never called me again."

"That's a larger club than I'd imagined." She thought for a moment, "Listen, Teddy, why don't you take me back to the Kipling's."

"W-why? I think you should stay here."

"Yeah, about that... " She thought for a second, "we've got to maintain cover."

"But he's already seen you up here. Trust me, your cover is blown. I know a thing or two about black ops."

"Racist." spat Wendy.

"You need to stay here." Teddy pressed.

"Are you keeping this woman here against her will!" screeched Wendy and raised the shotgun.

"What? No! I just thought..." Teddy stammered, "Hey put that down!"

"Whoa... Hey... I don't think that's necessary, really." Lucy interjected, "Listen Teddy, I've got a story to file."

"I AM WOMAN, HEAR ME ROAR!" yelled Wendy.

"You don't actually have to roar it." Said Lucy.

"You don't need him!" barked Wendy, "*I'll* take you to Deke Kipling's house."

"You know... sister... I'm just not... I'm just not sure about you." Said Lucy. "Thank you though." She and Wendy walked out into the hallway while Teddy locked the door behind him. "You do this often?"

"What's that?"

"First responder to distress calls."

"No. I'm really more of a social justice warrior."

"Wonderful. There is a lot of that around here. Are the benefits good?"

The three started down the stairs together until it got awkward. Wendy cleared her throat. "Well, this is my room, right below you. That's how I could hear the whistle so well."

"It was nice to meet you." Said Lucy, "Thanks for the covering fire."

"You want me to come with?"

"Oh, Teddy here is harmless."

Wendy went into her room, put the gun in its case and checked her phone. The blue dot was gone. "Damn." She said, "Now I've got to hack another phone."

When the red Spark got to the House of Kipling, Teddy stayed in the car as Lucy hopped out. He didn't linger while she went up the drive and knocked on the front door. Army answered. "Hello, Lucy. Are you with Deke? He said that he was going to find you. Had some big news."

"Deke's in jail."

"Again? What did he do?"

"I'm not sure, I just saw him getting hauled off in a police cruiser." She went upstairs and opened her laptop on the bed and inserted the flash drive. There was the folder *Leo Kabler Corruption* which had just been copied onto the drive. She scanned the older files; *Syria, Klansman AA, Hong Kong* and *Gypsies*. She clicked on the last and saw a draft of Deke's incredibly weird feature that ran in *Whiskey/Barrel* a few weeks before about some belly-dancing Roma who were robbing the tourists blind in New Orleans. "Deke Kipling you bastard." She said to herself softly, "You *were* stealing his files. You knew I was working with him and you were stealing his files."

Outside, she spotted Army grumbling to himself as his climbed into a battered jeep and pulled out of the driveway. Then everything went blurry for the tears.

OFFICER CRENSHAW pulled the patrol car up the O'Conner's long drive and stopped before the house. Deke reached for the interior door pull that police cruisers don't have. Crenshaw turned around, "Look, Deke. You still wanna file car theft charges against Ferg?"

"Well, not now. The car is right there."

"Cause there haddn't been any paperwork filed and well, if this a buncha nothin', I'd rather not start a shitstorm."

"Fair enough. Thanks for the ride. Can you let me out, please?"

"Tell Ms. Booey I said 'Hi.'"

"I will." Deke was barreling across the front yard and through the house. In the den, Eunice was laying on the couch watching a reality show about unemployable hipsters living in one big house designed to foster sexual intrigue. Deke walked through the kitchen, where he saw Teddy's mailer and the envelope on the center island and stomped into the mudroom. "Hey Deke," said Ferg without turning around, still making last minute adjustments to the punch to counter act the ferocious thirst of the angles. Deke gave him a fearsome wedgie.

"What is wrong with you?" said Ferg turning around to cover his flank.

"You left me at the Sunflower to get arrested!"

Ferg started readjusting his boxers as he held Deke at bay with a dripping serving spoon. "Deke, keep it down. Daddy and Uncle Aubrey are in the study with the Wallaces." He started to laugh. "You got arrested? By Juanita?"

"Well, no. She didn't book me when I threatened to file grand theft auto charges against you."

"You were gonna charge me with grand theft? That's cold Deke. That'd sunk my career right there."

"You don't have a career!"

"You just hide and watch. Uncle Aubrey and I have talked about it more this afternoon."

"Then why is he in a closed, door super-secret meeting with the Wallaces?"

"Well, it's like this…" Ferg stirred the haint punch with the spoon and dipped the sticky teacup back in. "… have I got this right?"

"I'm not drinking anymore of that devilment."

"You aren't drinking, you're tasting."

Deke tasted. "That *is* good. So why are you excluded from the super-secret meeting? Other than you're almost certainly drunk."

"Aubrey has got to hold his cards close to his chest."

"I'll say."

"You know, as a senator, I won't stand for anymore wedgies. That'll be a federal offense."

They walked out of the mudroom and settled into the kitchen. "I'm going home." said Deke.

"How's Lucy. Kinda cold of her to let the cops haul you off."

In the den, some feline sense pricked up in Eunice, who was no longer watching "Dylan – 25 – IT Activist" tell the camera that he might be in love with Katilee, but he was in lust with Gillian. As intriguing as it was, Eunice sensed a real-life drama. "You and Lucy on the outs?" called Eunice. "Again?"

Ferg ignored her "…And that was after you got shot and lost your phone."

"Yeah," Deke was saying. "…funny thing about that. Two days ago, Ash and I went out to one of Bayoil's natural gas platforms and some damn protester took a bunch of shots at us and drove away. I'm not talking about a shotgun either. I'd say this was a .50 caliber."

"Don't forget some hippie tried to poison you."Ferg pointed out.

"What?"

"Got Louis Guillory instead."

"Huh... You're right. This is all to be a little too... something. I mean, who'd want to kill me?"

"Lucy."

"Every self-respecting feminist in the country." Called Eunice from the couch. "Hashtag: *damndeke!*"

"Thanks Eunice."

"Love you!"

"Louis Guillory certainly had motive. You know you two never really got along that well." Ferg was warming to his theme.

Deke was reaching for the envelope. "I'm heading home to see what fresh hell awaits."

"Isn't the Ballyhoo gang pissed at you as well?"

"Ballyhoo. I'd forgotten about them." Deke started counting on his fingers, "That is a lot of people. You think that's why Teddy Landry has an AR-15 in his room?"

The doors to the study opened and Beau, Laudermilk and the Wallaces came out into the kitchen. Beau seemed excitable, "Yes yes" and the Wallaces more so. The Old Bear was like still water. When Casper saw the mailer he squinted, then his eyes went wide and Deke tucked the thing under his arm. "Well, I'm off."

"Wait now." Said Casper. "Deke Kipling is it? You're the press. How about an exclusive interview with the candidate?"

"Sorry, I'm off the clock, Mr. Wallace." Said Deke and walked quickly out to the truck with the envelope tucked snugly under his arm.

He got home and tried to sneak in the back door only to find his parents sitting in the kitchen with the remains of a bottle of wine. "Deke, Lucy said you were arrested? I went down to the station and they didn't have any record of it."

"I didn't get booked."

Booey started, "Deke honey, I tried calling you but I keep getting sent straight through to voicemail."

"Phone got shot with me. Phone's dead Ma. They got mah phone."

"What happened?"

"That Teddy Landry fella, the one Lucy's been mooning around with, told a cop I was breaking into his hotel room."

"Were you?" asked Booey.

"Not at the time."

"Lawd Deke!"

"I was trying to fix things with…" he pointed upstairs.

"Well settle down, son." Said Army. "This is hard on your mother. It wasn't a week ago we thought you'd been blown up in Kentucky."

"I'd forgotten about that, too." Deke shuffled off upstairs. In the hall, Lucy was looking at an old picture of the three Kipling kids: Ashely the eldest standing larger than the rest, then Deke holding a small shotgun with very much air young Derrick would possess a generation later, and Jane standing with her hands on her hips. "Hey Deke…" she said when he got to the top. "caught me on the way to the bathroom."

"Don't let me stop ya." He turned back to his room.

"We need to talk."

"No, we don't. Hope your story is shaping up. You'll get lots of face time tomorrow with the candidates."

"Listen, Deke…. Army said you weren't taken to the station."

"He's right. I wasn't booked, so no worries." He sighed, "Lucy, I'm beat. I'm going to bed and you've got work to do."

She smiled weakly, "You said you had some good news!"

"Who can remember anymore." Deke stepped into his room and closed the door. Then he made sure the widows were locked and pulled the curtains. He left one light on, hoping it wouldn't attract a roaming Eunice, and began to look through the mailer. He went immediately to a list of campaign contributions to Leo Kalber. One entry caught his eye: Corsair, Inc. The last page was a simple account statement for Digger Station #27, owned by one Chad Wallace of St. Andrews Grammar School.

"God's Holy Trousers! that is a smoking gun." He flipped through them again, "God's Holy Trousers, it's two of them." Deke sat back and tried to connect some dots in his head but nothing seemed to make any sense. Of course there was that other distraction to consider. "Who the hell keeps trying to kill me?"

DANNY SPEWE was wedged between the hefty thighs of two Rebel Yell old ladies in the back seat of a 2012 Subaru Outback. In the front, where two more old ladies and in the way back, Trevor was curled up in the fetal position on top of some supplies. The station wagon trailed a phalanx of motorcycles cutting through the humid night.

"Hey!" called the denim clad monument to hopeful sizing behind the steering wheel, "Did J.E.B. say you was on the TV this morning?"

"I was." Said Danny.

"Shoot. Whadda they pay?"

"It was a news show, I wasn't paid."

"Huh? I guess it was just for kicks, then?"

"It was work."

"You don't get paid for work?" asked the one beside him with a nose-ring.

"Well, no. Yes. I didn't get paid for my television appearance."

"What do you do?" asked nose-ring, "you know, for money. I don't get outta bed unless it's for kicks or cash."

"Hah!" laughed the driver, "You get kicks and money in bed."

The old ladies let forth a thundering laughter. When they stopped they were all looking at Danny.

"Karla, watch the road!"

Karla turned back around but eyeballed him in the rear-view mirror.

Danny cleared his throat. "Just to be clear. You ladies are giving me a ride to Clarksdale right? We aren't hostages, are we?"

"You don't need to be so hung up on labels." said Karla. The old ladies all laughed again. "Naw, Spewe, we're just fuckin' with ya. Pencil Dechamp asked J.E.B. to give you a ride after those wetbacks wrecked your van."

"Who?"

"You don't know Pencil? We figured you did. I guess you know his brother Claudel. He's all into politics these days, dresses like a fairy."

Danny knit his brow, "No, I don't know him either."

"Well, he knows you. And you owe him."

"Hey!" came Trevor's voice from the way back, "I just got some bars. Landry is reporting from Clarksdale!"

"Was he the orangutan?" asked nose-ring.

IN THE SUNFLOWER INN, Blanche and Summer were bunked in the last available room. Summer was sitting in a comfortable chair with her laptop reading SLAMNEWS! of all things. "Dispatch from Ground Zero" by Teddy Landry. Until the Senate race, the boy would never have even appeared on her radar. His reputation was less the stories he broke and more the stories he was going to break when the time was right. Which it rarely was. Tonight, evidently, he was close enough.

True to form the piece told of a cache of damning information that Teddy had diligently dug up on that radical liberal Leo Kabler and would release when the time was right. But first, informed readers, he was going to let Leo draw out just a little more rope with which Teddy could hog-tie the man before his hanging. Then he went on to mention the *Daily Brute*, his former employers, and the "flirtatious alliance' he was having with its political correspondent down in Clarksdale, Mississippi. And, informed reader, if you had never heard of a place like Clarksdale, Teddy was there to assure you that it was ground zero for one of the nation's most important races of this election cycle.

TWELVE:
FLIRTATIOUS ALLIANCES

"IT'S A ZOO down here, Mr. Macastle. I think you'll be pleased." Deke was standing in his parent's kitchen, wiping down the lens of his camera. "I'll be out of pocket today with the shoot. Someone shot my phone yesterday...shortly after the leather cat suit incident... *then* I was arrested... You know, lazy Sundays. Listen, on the off chance that I survive this hootinanny, I'll call in tomorrow. Have a good Labor Day." He hung up the phone. "That ought to keep him interested."

On a sheet of paper adhered to the refrigerator were all the Kipling's important numbers. "This place is like a time warp." He muttered while his finger ran down to Ashley's number and dialed his brother up. "Hey Ash, this is Deke, I got a question... yeah I know it's early, this is important... Oh you heard about that, huh? Good news travels fast... No, it wasn't hard at all really, after a good tug she just sort of plopped right out of it... It was, it was *very* unappealing. I know, poor thing, Mom just wants to go to her grave without any more Eunice stories... Listen, I've got a question..."

"Deke, it's Labor Day." Said Ash.

"There is a company called Corsair – what kind of business do they do with Bayoil?"

"Officially... it's an off-shore catering company. In reality it's a floating bar. They run a boat out to the rig with music and drinks and hot wings. It gets the workers off the rigs for a few hours. They come back and the boat moves on to another rig."

"A floating bar, huh? Nothing else?"

"That's all we contract them to do. Whatever goes on, if anything does, it isn't on a Bayoil property or lease, so we can't say."

"So it's a floating brothel."

"I don't know anything about that, Deke." And then less convincingly, "What I can say is that we are doing business with a licensed contractor for catering. I'm the one who checked it out."

"Actually, that clears up quite a bit."

"Are you trying to ruin my career?"

"No! You're my brother, and I'd have to find a new place to live."

"Can I go back to sleep now?"

Deke hung up, stuck his camera in the back of his cartridge bag and poured a cup of coffee to go. Them he heard his parents stirring. He scribbled a note and walked out the back door.

Upstairs, Lucy's phone went off with a lovely little ringtone called "By the Seaside." She didn't know why, but the music just made her happy in a goofy, lighthearted way. Had she given the matter some thought she would have reckoned that it had to do with the fact that she'd become a political journalist because it sounded like fun when the modern reality of Washington and Hollywood and Silicon Valley meant dealing with sanctimonious, constipated monks who were either telling everyone around them why *they* were sinners, or begging forgiveness for something before some mob of self-righteous bigoteers whipped up in a social media rage. Which, on balance, wasn't very lighthearted at all.

At eight am on Labor Day, even that silly ringtone wasn't helping. It was Anna Degrasse, and that was even less helpful. "Hello." She muttered.

"Late night?"

"Not particularly."

"Where are you?"

"In bed."

"With whom?"

"No one, thank you."

"Lucy, I told you to keep an eye on Deke, not that buffoon Teddy Landry!"

"What are you talking about? Deke is down the hall in his room. And that's as close as I'm getting with his parents downstairs."

"Then why is Teddy Landry somewhere in the Land o' Cotton writing about a...what was it? *a flirtatious alliance* with my political correspondent?"

"WHAT!" now Lucy was sitting up feeling around the side table for her glasses. "Mrs. Degrasse, I have NO idea what you're talking about!"

"I take it you haven't read SLAMNEWS! this morning."

"I never read SLAMNEWS! ...and why do you?"

"Because he's going on about pooling resources with the *Brute* and some damn bombshell you two are digging up that is going to bury Leo Kabler."

"Mrs. Degrasse, we only met for lunch..." she thought about the expense report "...and dinner."

"You two are practically dating!"

"It was to compare notes! It was totally professional."

"Well.... I've heard *that* before."

"WHEN?"

"It's what you and Deke say about each other."

"Hey now!" Since she'd come to work for the *Brute*, Lucy had heard the odd remark that there was some friends with benefits package worked out between she and Deke. She dismissed it, but the misconception never really bothered her. But to be suspected of being squished into a romance with Teddy was not at all the sort of thing that popped into your head while playing "By The Seaside."

Degrasse cleared her throat. "The one I want you comparing notes with is Deke. If you pool resources it's going to be with *Front Street*, not some hysterical right-wing blog going on about bugaloos or juggalows or, wait, they can't say that? Can they? Either way, I don't want Deke to scoop us on this Aubrey Laudermilk story."

"I thought *I* was following the Wallace/Kabler race."

"It's all the same thing! Do you think anyone really cares about Mississippi? They want crooked politicos, puppet masters and a senate seat hanging in the balance. If you have to deep fry in some cornbread to make it work then do it!"

"Mrs. Degrasse?"

"Yes?"

"You're the reason I got into journalism."

"I'm certainly the reason you're still in a job! Snark if you want to but someone has to pay the bills."

"I thought that was Smut Butter."

"Young lady, I sent you down there to stay on Deke Kipling – "

"Yeah, about that –"

"I will overnight you a case of Smut Butter if I it will get the job done, but I want you ON HIM! And another thing, no more long, lingering dinners with Teddy!"

"Ehww." Mostly awake and fully horrified, Lucy got out of bed and dressed for the shoot in a pair of jeans and one of those quick dry safari shirts she'd bought when she thought she was being sent to Africa to chase down the Secretary of State. In the end, she didn't go.

The *Daily Brute* instead relied on "citizen reporters" to supply the Gordian knot of sputtering indignation young Francis Degrasse referred to "Cloud Journalism."

Downstairs, the twins were eating their eggs and bacon like a pair of ravenous wolf cubs. Booey was sitting between them. "Lucy, the is coffee on." Lucy poured a cup and was having trouble looking at her hostess in the eye after getting her son arrested.

"Boys!" Booey snapped, "Peter, don't clean your fork with your tongue."

"I thought I was helping!"

"Go talk to Granddaddy about gun safety."

This left them alone.

"Listen, Mrs. Kipling," Lucy cleared her throat, "I am sorry about − ehmm − last night."

"What's that dear? Missing dinner or sending my son to jail?"

"Yes, well, about that…in my defense I was being held at gunpoint."

"By that clod with whom you've been galavanting around town?"

"Oh, Teddy, no. I'm not sure who it was holding the gun, but she's staying in room 14 at the Sunflower. She seemed to know Deke."

"Where does he find them?" Booey asked without ever breaking eye contact.

"Well I don't… Oh… Oh no, Mrs. Kipling, I've never pulled a shotgun on anyone… I mean, I promise you that I'm not… *we* aren't a Eunice situation. I honestly don't know how she manages."

"And just what do you think the situation is?" Booey said with that iron maiden stare that Lucy decided she absolutely needed to learn one day.

Army came in, grabbed a beat-up canvas hat off a peg. "We're off headin' over to the O'Conners. Lucy, make that coffee to go if you want to ride with us. You want Booey's old .20 gauge?"

"I'd better not. Mrs. Kipling might want to shoot me with it later."

Booey sipped her *café au lait* and denied nothing.

BEAU O'CONNER was in rare form, a once a year form to be exact. For as long as anyone could remember he'd always gotten like this the morning before the noon start of the dove season. Also for as long as anyone could remember, everyone who could avoid the man on Labor Day morning, did. Hank couldn't.

"I told you to watch the smoke!" Beau roared from the porch. "The missus will have my hide!"

"No, I won't." Said Darla a little defensively, "You fire up a smoker you're gonna have smoke!"

Beau's laugh was filled with a big can of manufactured *bon homme*. "I'll hold you to that, Darla." Darla had been thrown out of her kitchen by the caterers and now her fiefdom was overrun with great bowls of coleslaw and egg salad and bourbon baked beans each only slightly less tremendous than that old whiskey barrel in which Ferg and Deke were mixing up that wicked haint punch. And what the kind of name was that for something you served respectable guests anyway? "What's the status of the kitchen?" Beau asked roundly.

"Fulla caterers."

"Well, we want everything to be perfect, so crack that whip. Hank! Where'd the smoke go!"

Darla retreated back in to the kitchen and further still into the mud room where the boys were seated around the whiskey barrel. "No," Deke was saying, "I'm not drinking anymore of that stuff."

"Well, that's a lie." Ferg pointed out reasonably.

"I'm not drinking it *now*."

"It's good for a hangover."

"I'll say."

Ferg was stirring the punch. "Hey Deke, will you hand me the long spoon? It's on the hook behind you. I want to really swirl it around, you know, to kick up the splinters. That's how we marry the flavors." The long wooden spoon was right by the hook holding Eunice's hosed out cat suit. "Why'd you have to hang it next to *that* thing."

"Ahh shut up you lace doily," said Deke, "the whiskey retards infection." He turned around to reach for the spoon and saw Darla. "Oh hey Mrs. O'Conner."

"Are you two drinking already? Aren't you boys about to go out and play with guns?"

"Not if I can't find my gun." said Ferg. "It's the Beretta. I thought I left it in here."

"It's a good thing God likes drunks and little children, 'cause y'all are both."

"How'd you lose the Beretta?" asked Deke. "Did you leave it Jackson?"

"You know I'm way too materialistic to forget that gun."

Laudermilk stuck his head into the room. "It the bar is open already? I just need a touch, just an eye opener. This too is off the record, Deke."

"Sure thing." Deke went in the kitchen as the baby monitor crackled. A trucker with the handle "Trapdoor" said that he couldn't stop until he hit Biloxi, and there he was gonna get him a card game and a pretty girl down at that number #27. Deke looked at the thing for a long time until one of the caterers moved around him quickly and in a huff.

Deke crossed over into the dining room where a shoot breakfast was laid, surrounded by guests milling around the spread. Leo Kabler chatting with his aide Kelly Makin and pretending not watch Betty Sue Wallace. Kelly leaned in, "Deke Kipling" he whispered.

"Leo." Deke said, "Good to see you. Did you recover from Saturday night?"

"Well, now, I had nothing to recover from."

"I wasn't talking about booze, Leo, I meant Eunice."

"Oh yes. So you're a friend of the O'Conners? Because I was led to believe the hunt was always press free."

"Me? I'm off the clock. I do have a question though: Do you know anything about an outfit called Corsair?"

"This doesn't sound off the clock, Deke."

"It's not a political question, Leo. Actually, it's about illegal casinos."

"It's *Congressman Kabler.*" corrected Kelly.

"Why would I know anything about that?" Leo said after a moment.

"Well, they are well connected in your neck of the woods."

Leo turned to Kelly, "And I can't have him throw out?"

"Honestly, I don't see how."

"Snuggy here is right. This isn't your district Congressman." said Deke. "Not your party either."

"Not yet." sniffed Kelly.

Outside, Blanche and Summer had pulled up and parked in the grass in front of the house. "I feel like one of those objectifying Ralph Lauren ads exploded on me." Blanche whined.

"You look great, and with your face it really is the only way you won't be caught out."

"What's wrong with my face?"

"Too angry."

"If you aren't angry, you aren't paying attention."

"Dr. Barker, these people are definitely paying attention. They're just trained from birth to hide it well. Try this…" Summer smiled. She really was annoyingly beautiful.

"So what's security like?"

"Security? Just try to look like you belong and walk on in. And smile! We're about to get back on track."

Walking casually, the pair found themselves inside with no harassment save Darla pressing iced tea into their hands. Blanche scanned the room to find Leo talking to a fellow in old khaki pants and a patched tattersall shirt who looked like an unretouched photo on one of Deke Kipling's book jackets.

"C'mon Leo, you gotta give me something." Deke was saying, "Aren't you gonna pass...something... stamping out corruption?" Leo whispered something to Kelly and Deke threw a free press bomb. "This is for *Front Street*. They published Hemingway back in the day."

"Sorry if I'm not impressed, but *that day* saw Jim Crow and no social welfare. Those weren't good days."

"As you say. But without the benefit of time travel, we can't publish the story back then, so you're off the hook! We both know you want to be quoted..."

"Deke, I am talking to ya! I've told you that I'm creating new jobs for Mississippi, within an environmentally responsible energy sector."

"Geez, Kabler, gimme something you didn't slap on a billboard."

Blanche breezed up. "Good Morning gentlemen!" She had remembered to smile but it was ghoulish. "Congressman Kabler How are you? And what strange company you keep. Deke Kipling! Are you surprised to see me on *your* turf after that hack job you wrote?"

"Nothing surprises me anymore Dr. Barker. It's the drinking."

"And you two are in the middle of an interview...? Careful Congressman, Deke Kipling is quite a fiction writer."

"Swell. Hey Dr. Barker, is the OLA trying to kill me?"

"Well I'm sure I wouldn't know anything about that."

Kelly leaned in "Dr. Barker, Leo wants you to know—"

"Dammit Kelly!" Leo barked, "I can speak for myself!"

"Hell's Bells," said Deke and slinked off.

Blanche kept smiling ghoulishly at Leo.

"Blanche," he said after a deep breath, "I didn't expect to see you here."

"Just a friendly little shooting party. What's the problem? I'm not the one joining the war on women with that misogynist Deke Kipling. Who knows where this will take us?"

Leo wasn't listening, but whispered something to Kelly, who darted off. "I'm sorry what where you saying?" He pushed his glasses up the bridge of his pug nose.

Kelly moved through the crowd scanning for that country-come-to-town hostess to tell her they had some party crashers, but was caught out by the face of Summer Greene. "Summer!" he said, non-threateningly.

"Yes?"

"Kelly Makin, Leo Kabler's aide. We owe each other a lunch!"

"Oh, of course. How did you recognize me? We've only talked over the phone."

The truth was in his off hours, Kelly was a bit stalkerish and if there was a photo of Summer Greene online that he hadn't seen, it was not for a lack of trying. *It was okay*, Kelly told himself, *I'm an ally*. What he told Summer was: "You came in with Dr. Barker."

"Well, it is nice to finally met you." Said Summer. Then she looked over his head, "My God, is that Congressman Elk Penis?"

"I just want to say how proud... proud and inspired... I am by the work you do." He looked deeply into her eyes with a gaze he privately called *Piercing Soul*.

On balance Summer found the exercise unsettling. "Well," she said, pointing to Leo and Blanche, "I guess they finally got their meeting."

Undeterred, Kelly maintained *Piercing Soul* with Summer's ear.

On the far side of the room Betty Sue Wallace was thanking Darla for another 'light' bloody mary and asked, "Now just how do you know Dr. Blanche Barker?"

"Who's that?" Darla asked.

She was the one trying to keep her voice level as she said to Leo, "I'm not threatening anyone, Congressman! All I'm saying is that if you think that you are going to sit this round out and play footsie with that sexist coon-ass Ronny Basco, well, you are mistaken. My Goddess! Is that Congressman Elk Penis!"

"Blanche, don't make a scene!" begged Leo.

"Look you, you're going to make a stand with us before the election or we are going to have a scene no one will ever forget."

"Dr. Barker, obviously when we passed the Kare for Kids act in...Oh hello Mrs. O'Conner..."

"Hi Leo!" Came Darla's twang as she appeared in their midst along a big man in khaki. "Is this lady bothering you?"

"Well..." Leo stuttered. It looked like Darla was about to fix his problem, but would it? Later, Leo would never be exactly sure what he'd replied to Darla, but to Blanche sounded like "jolly schmuel."

"I'm sorry, Ma'am." Darla smiled graciously at Blanche, "This is a private party."

"Leo Kabler," the congressman said, extending his hand out to the big guy, "you are the chief of police, right? I'd love to talk to you later about various crime reduction initiatives I'm hopeful for. When we passed the Crime is Bad bill in '12, we were only getting started."

Summer was watching Deke because she couldn't bear anymore compassionately creepy eye contact with Kelly. Sensing a stare boring into the side of his face, Deke looked her way. "Oh look, here comes that misogynist brute." said Kelly. "Aren't you glad you go for a more sensitive man, Summer?"

"What?" Did he just tell me what type of guy to like? She turned to find herself eye to eye with *Piercing Soul*. It gave her a small start.

"Summer Greene is it?" said Deke, closing the gap between them. "Deke Kipling, how are you? What brings you to Clarksdale?"

"The hunt." She said innocently enough.

"Well Hastag: *Damndeke*, I hope you're talking about the dove."

"Mr. Kipling, you joke, but 75% of the violent language on social media is from men directed at women."

"And I don't doubt it. Little boys are awful in their own way. But I'm not 75% of men. I'm just one. It's a vulgar world. We got rid of manners and now we can't figure out why so many people act like savages."

"Manners hide a lot of..." Summer looked over at Blanche, now approaching with what appeared to be an out of uniform police officer.

"We need to go." Blanche said ordered, then to Deke, "This isn't over."

"I'm sorry, I've got to run." said Summer, "Well, *Vodka, Bears and Furry Hats* was a good book. I hate everything you stand for, it was nice to meet you, though."

"Nice of you to say...sort of."

"And you didn't think I have manners." Summer was off.

Deke and Kelly looked at each other. "So, whaddya shoot?"

"Don't even." said Kelly. "She'll never love a man like you."

"Love? I think she's trying to kill me."

Darla walked up. "She was pretty. Looks familiar."

"Oh, a delight. Her mother was an actress, did a movie called *Clam Whiskers* in the 90's. It was terrible."

"Is she a 'friend'." Air quotes.

"Sworn enemy!" corrected Kelly before he scampered away.

"He's right as it turns out." Said Deke, "Isn't that a hell of a thing?"

In the front of the house Summer and Blanche made their way to the car under the watchful eye of the chief of police. "Great plan, Summer. We flew all this way for nothing. You said 'smile and act normal.'"

"Dr. Barker, you glommed onto Kabler like a guided missile. How is that normal behavior? You had to know that the hostess would be making sure Leo was having a good time – the man's is running for senate. You're like talking to my mother."

"I think Leo sent that prissy aide of his to tell Mrs. O'Conner. It's humiliating us being thrown out like that."

"Us? You're the one who got thrown out. I'm just babysitting."

"You watch it."

As the mid-sized rental car carrying Blanche and Summer pulled away from the house, it was passed on the road by Army's old jeep, which roared up the drive onto the lawn. "Say, Miss Lucy!" asked Peter from the backseat, "what are you going to shoot?"

"Sweetheart, I'm just here to chat. I don't have a gun."

Army cut the engine. "That ought to put Deke at ease."

"Very funny."

Young Derrick said nothing. He'd not been his usual zippy self this morning. He was, in fact, somewhat quiet and sheepish. It was a something he'd overheard Grandaddy say to Booey about Deke, Lucy and a 'marital spat.' Granddaddy had said it like a joke, but Derrick felt weirdly guilty somehow. About what, though, he couldn't say.

"Take your guns around the house, boys. And leave them in the case until I get there." They leapt out of the Jeep.

"Thanks for the ride, Mr. Kipling." Lucy wrestled with the ancient seatbelt.

Army looked at the wheel for a long time before turning to Lucy, "You two nimrods were really cooking up a scheme until it blew up in your faces, weren't you?"

"Yes sir. Yes, we were."

"Well, now, Lucy, I *know* where Deke gets it. And it's not his mother, either. The one I'd like to meet is *your* momma. You know, just to see how you got yours."

"Yes, well… sometimes mother can't leave well enough alone."

"At least you come by it honestly."

They climbed out of the Jeep and started towards the house. Burton of the *Brute* cleared her throat, "So… Mr. Kipling… where would an unarmed girl find your son. I called him earlier but his phone seems to be off."

"It was shot yesterday." Army looked at his watch, "Season doesn't start until noon so he's probably in the house. After that he'll be in the field. Look for a spot in the sky where the birds fall two at a time. That kid is the best shot I've ever seen."

"Now where'd he learn that, Mr. Kipling?"

"I thought it was from me, but that can't be right. One day, about 20 years ago, he commandeered my old double barrel after I bought a new .12 gauge pump and has never upgraded since. If I shot like that neither would I."

They stepped into the foyer of the house and Beau bellowed "Well if it isn't Lucy Burton, the gal who finally settled Deke Kipling!"

"Leave that poor girl alone until she's had some iced tea!" came a sympathetic twang from further in the depths of the house. "Or would you like a cocktail?"

The damage, however, was done. Hearing the name, somehow, from the back gallery Betty Sue Wallace suddenly appeared before them looking like a woman determined to make the steamier parts of the old British Empire a little steamier. "Burton of the *Brute*." She said. "I so enjoyed our conversation yesterday. I'd love to talk just us gals, without that fool Teddy Landry around. I mean, he's nice enough, but why send a man to do a woman's job. Am I right?" She took Lucy by the arm and led her away.

Beau harrumphed.

"Mrs. Wallace, I'd love to talk…"

"Then let's talk."

The candidate had a point.

As the two walked off together, Casper Wallace watched them go. Then he scanned the room for Leo Kabler who had attached himself to the mayor. He stepped out to the back gallery and looked out over the impressive spread. Beyond it the lawn turned to field. In truth, he wanted to just go shoot something, then he saw Deke Kipling talking to Burt Carlson.

"Deke, Deke Kipling?"

"Yes. Casper Wallace right?"

"Yes, can I have a word?"

"Deke here is on vacation, Wallace." Burt slapped Deke on the shoulder.

"It won't take a second."

"You *are* on the clock." growled Carlson

"Oh shut up!"

"I'm gonna…" Carlson marched off in the direction of the Old Bear.

Casper cleared his throat. "Is he always like that?"

"Carlson? Couldn't say. Barely know the man. You wanted to talk?"

"Yeah. Maybe you'd be interested in a profile of the candidate. After the hunt, of course. I understand that you're working for *Front Street*."

"Good news travels fast. Look, I'm not doing profiles, you see. I'm a little more interested in what's happening behind the curtain, as it were. The rest of it is just theater."

"How do you mean?"

"Okay. Have you ever heard of the Dechamp Brothers?"

"Who?" said Casper, "No, I can't say that I have."

"They run Digger Stations 25 & 27."

"We've got a 150 truck stops. I can't know everyone."

"No, I don't suppose you can. Don't know anything about them, then?"

"Nope."

"So you'll be shocked to learn that they pay your son Chad over \$150,000 a quarter. I think it's great that the boys has got himself a job, but that is a hell of a lot of milk money, don't you think?"

THE SUNFLOWER'S pleasant little bell tinkled when Blanche swung open the door in a fury. "*It's nice to meet you!* My Goddess Summer, why didn't get him to sign your copy of his book. Or your tits while you're at it?"

After two years it all just sort of crashed over Summer like waves of briny water. What did catch her attention, as Blanche stomped past the front desk, was a mousy little figure sipping coffee and looking strangely out of place in her preppy clothes. Summer charged into the dining room toward the woman. "What are *you* doing here?"

Wendy nodded silently to the corner where Louis Guillory sat reading the newspaper and largely ignoring his breakfast. Wendy popped a grape from the plate of fruit on the table. Summer lowered her voice, "Who's he?" Wendy nodded and pushed out the other chair.

Summer sat. Meanwhile, halfway to the second floor, Blanche realized that no one was listening to her tirade against the patriarchy and backtracked her way to the dining room in a huff. "May I join you ladies?"

Across the room, by the window, Guillory peaked over his newspaper, looked the trio over, and quietly returned behind the page.

"Look." Wendy was saying in a hushed tone. "I know that Kentucky ended... badly."

"Wendy, you killed someone." hissed Summer.

"Ladies, let's not get hung up on details." Wendy said. "The plan was simple. The OLA knows it needs ISOP for above ground support –"

"We aren't just *support*–" Blanche hissed. "We are the movement!"

Wendy smiled sweetly and hissed, "...while *we* fight the battle. Certainly since Dr. Barker's interview for the 'Hell's Belles' piece..."

"'Now just hold on!"

"We needed to stop *his* momentum." Wendy pressed on, "But we already had the campaign to do it."

"Can I get you ladies more coffee?" The boom of Mrs. Wilson's voice shocked the trio, now hunched low over the table to hear each other whispering.

"No thank you," said Summer, "we're about to head upstairs."

"Okay. Holler if you need anything."

"What were you going to do?" Blanche whispered as the others leaned in low again.

"The toilet bombs. We were going to wreck his career and let him know it was the OLA by blowing up the toilets *everywhere* he went. Just imagine leaving a trail of them. Who'd ever grant him an interview then? No one! I mean, toilets are expensive to replace. Right? Anyway, after that troglodyte at the distillery oppressed my personal space all oppressively... that ought to be the next campaign... the stress being around men cause. We should ship them to Bulgaria... these micro aggressions must stop!"

"Wendy, focus." said Summer.

"Okay, so I got spooked in Kentucky and left the bomb in the warehouse. What's the difference? There's your symbol of the patriarchy. Big barrels of rape juice."

"Yes...good," said Blanche. "I like it."

"No, Dr. Barker," Summer pleaded, "you *don't* like it!"

"And after that security guard got blown up I figured, what the hell? We've already knocked off one fella, why don't I just kill Deke Kipling while we're on a roll."

"No... Wendy... bad. Why some writer?" Summer rubbed her eyes and dropped her voice again. "This is the stupidest thing I've ever heard."

"Is it?"

"Yes!"

"But is it?"

"Saying is slowly doesn't change what you've done. A man is dead and now you're on the run from the law."

"I'm not on the run. I'm on a mission. I'm underground."

"You haven't been to work in a week."

"Now look…wait… how do you know that?" asked Wendy, but Summer said nothing. "It was Eunice wasn't it. When we were at Berkley, well, you know we used to be—"

"Yeah, we know."

Teddy lumbered into the dining room like a big, sleepy orangutan. He scanned the room, spotted Wendy but wasn't about to go over there. She was sitting with Blanche Barker and some vision he didn't recognize. The ISOP was in a huddle with a woman who'd held him at gunpoint. Was she part of the Ovarian Liberation Army? Was it true? The ISOP and the OLA are in cahoots! It pained him to admit that Deke Kipling was write about something but… the wheel turned over in his head as he dug into his pocket for his phone. This picture would be so SLAM!

Then he heard Wendy yelp "Hashtag: *notyourpenis!*" and hurl a banana at him. She missed, but that was little consolation. He beat a retreat upstairs. Guillory peered around the paper again and quickly ducked back.

"Was that gimp from SLAMNEWS!" Blanche asked.

"I guess." said Wendy.

"I wouldn't worry about him." Summer said, "That blog is comic relief. Try not to kill him too, Wendy."

Wendy thought for a second. "Well, I'm not sure he's who *you* think he is, Sis. I thought he was raping Burton of the *Brute* yesterday afternoon and went to his room and he had an assault rifle."

"He was assaulting Lucy Burton!" yelped Summer.

"No, I just thought he was. Turned out it was chubby who'd blown the rape whistle."

"Who'd rape *him*?" asked Blanche.

"I know, right! I went to the room when I heard the whistle and he had an assault rifle on the bed."

Summer pinched her brow, "Are you sure it wasn't a meatball hoagie?"

"I know an AR-15 when I see one."

"How?"

"Never mind. Look, I had a thought. Is it possible that this ridiculous blog is a cover for something darker? I mean, who takes an assault rifle to a bird shoot?" Wendy leaned in close, "So the question remains, just who is Teddy Landry planning to kill?"

Upstairs, Teddy was stepping into his insulated camouflage coveralls and starting doubt that his kit was going to keep him cool. It was like wearing a comforter. He started to zip himself up and looked down at the sales tag: *BLLTPRF*. It was also worth noting, Teddy thought, it didn't *feel* bulletproof. The words of the sales guy rang in his head: "Hey man, Kevlar is just fibers too. These are just fluffier. Think of it like Kevlar down."

Yet, he did have to admit that he felt like thicker than a June bug in August.

Teddy had long railed against government snooping in the digital pages of SLAMNEWS! until the leftists started complaining about it. It all made him a little nervous, searching on the Sunflower's Wi-Fi for how to operate an AR-15. He sat on the bed, feeding rounds in to the magazine just like the website told him too. He slipped the rifle into the case and had just finished zipping it when there was a knock on the door. He didn't move. There was a scratching at the lock and the door was opened by the man from downstairs with the bandaged hand.

"Teddy Landry is it?"

"Who the hell are you?"

"I'm Davison diddles. Well, that's not what my mother named me, but you get the picture. I'm the one who leaked you the Davison sex tape."

"Oh." Said Teddy.

"All kitted out are we?"

"Yeah. How'd you open the door?"

"Just wanted to see if you'd looked over that information I slipped into your bag yesterday while you were out."

"Does that lock even work?"

"Why don't you get that envelope out of your bag, Teddy, and tell me what you've got on Leo Kabler?"

Teddy crossed over to the bed, knowing the bag was empty but he looked anyway. "My room was broken into last night. Someone stole everything in my bag."

The angry throb on the side of Guillory's hand began to make itself known. "Teddy?"

"Yes?"

"Now who would do a thing like that?"

"Deke Kipling."

Teddy felt the padded collar go tight around his neck and he was being pushed back into the room. The door slammed shut but there was too much face in his field of vision to see. Guillory's forearm pressed hard into Teddy's throat. "Dammit! I did not drive all the way up here to give that ass the lead of the year! That story is going to blow somethin' up and if it comes from Kipling, they are gonna come after me." Guillory's eyes went tight. "And I will fucking kill you first!" He let the boy loose, opened the door and disappeared with a slam. Perhaps it was the coffee or the fear, but he felt the warm trickle down his leg. Bulletproof or not, that the lining was absorbent.

One floor up Summer was in the room phoning a contact to tell them where a certain congressman from Nebraska was hiding. Blanche said she was going down for more coffee. She stopped on her way to the lobby and stopped to knock on a closed door.

Wendy swung the door open. "Dr. Barker?"

"Listen, Wendy, it was nice to finally meet you this morning. I realize that we don't know who Teddy going to assassinate, but if you did happen to kill Deke Kipling, that'd be great. Just super."

THIRTEEN:
IDIOTS AFIELD

EUNICE STOOD before the mirror in her room in the House of O'Conner and assessed herself. She was wearing what she'd dubbed her Dove Hunt Protest outfit. Which was thankfully more breathable that the Ovary Squeeze Protest outfit she'd worn yesterday. It consisted of a grey leotard and leggings with a cape designed by a protest collective in Knoxville to look, when she spread her arms, like the wings of a dove – all poetic and theatrical. On her desk was the latest of three placards she's made: *I'm Protesting Blood Sports and Land Raping*. On the third try she thought she'd really gotten the lettering particularly well-spaced. Most Americans, complacent as they were, didn't know it, but that was the tricky part.

Wee Mavis was playing with some plastic measuring cups in the middle of Eunice's bed. "I'm gonna raise you right, Mavis." she said. "Or Molly… Your big sis Eunice is going to see to that. I may only come out once a year but…" the flaw in her plan to rear Mavis with the correct sexual ownership started to make itself clear. "well, it's not *quantity* of time but *quality*." Mavis dribbled and snatched at her wings.

Downstairs, Wendy came around the house in a suit of brand new olive clothing she'd bought yesterday. She set Ferg's Beretta shotgun case back in the mudroom where she'd found it and moved confidently into the house, up the stairs and knocked on Eunice's door. "Hey there, Girlfriend!"

"Oh, Wendy!" Eunice said without enthusiasm. "You're still here. I thought you were heading back to Knoxville."

"You're wearing the protest suit I made you!" Wendy closed the door behind her. "Does it work?"

"Yeah. But the wings make it a little tight in the chest."

"I'm sure I measured you correctly."

"Well, you were thorough. I thought you were going to milk me." Eunice scrunched around in the leotard, "Are you staying?"

"Would I leave my best girlfriend to protest these land-rapers alone?"

"Oh, sweetie," Eunice said, "I know you came a long way, but this is my time to be with family."

"Aren't I like family?

"Not really."

"Remember Berkley? Witchcraft? We were close then?"

Eunice laughed. "Not like family."

"Closer...?"

"You always gotta bring that up, doncha, Wendy?"

"But wasn't it fun?"

"Yeah...I guess...the jello shots helped."

Wendy pursed her lips and propped her hands on her hips Wonder Woman style, "This is about Deke Kipling isn't it?"

"What? No, of course not."

"He's all you've talked since that Hell's Belles article came out."

"Is it?"

Unseen by the two was Teddy's rental car rolling almost to a stop in front of the house. Still at a creep, he decided that parking out front of the O'Conner's and walking through the front door was a low percentage thing to do. He needed to proceed with caution, and walking right up to what appeared to be a well-armed cocktail party lacked stealth. Finding a service road, he crept down about half a mile before locking up the car and making his way through the field with the AR-15 slung over his shoulder. It was hot. By the time Teddy had made it to the perimeter of what looked like the O'Conner's lawn, he was sweating like a pig. With mounting desperation he found some shade and began to study the party through the zoom of his camera. People stood around drinking bottled water on a clearing on the far side of the house where SUV's sat parked with their gates open, gun cases leaning this way and that. He looked at his watch, its face was fogged with the humid heat. It was 11: 30. People were moving towards their guns. Teddy snapped a few shots. "This is the belly of the beast." He muttered to himself and crept out of the cover of the sunflowers.

From her vantage spot on the second floor, Eunice watched the carrot top of Teddy watch the party. Then she saw it. "Hey Wendy, come here and look at this." She squished up next to Eunice. "The window isn't that small. Look, do you know that goofy right-wing blogger? Has he got an assault rifle?"

"It's an AR-15. I saw it in his hotel room."

"You were in his room? Why?"

"Eunice, I don't have to hang around you *all* the time, do I?"

"Well, you hadn't been to work in a week."

"Jealous?"

"More like overwhelmed – those hashtag: *layoff!* Flyers didn't print themselves." Eunice looked hard at Teddy, standing unseen at the edge of the soybeans.

"Maybe I've misjudged the little dweeb. Di'ju think he's an *agent provocateur?*"

"Maybe. Is that what you want?" teased Wendy.

"He is! He's a damn revolutionary! Leo Kabler said he wasn't even coming to the hunt so who is he after? Uncle Aubrey – Land-rapey true, but likable. Hey Wendy, why is your arm holding my ass?"

"Where else would I put it? Small window."

"I guess so. Di'ju think he's gonna shoot that Wallace crack-pot! Perhaps. Perhaps. Is Teddy a double agent? A deep-cover revolutionary? But what is he wearing? He looks like he a fuzzy tree. Why is his hair so shiny now?"

Wendy's heart jumped, "Ewe – I didn't think that you went in for the underground stuff!"

Mavis cooed and threw one of Eunice's bras to the floor. "Hold on now," Eunice said aloud to herself, "If I have any hope of saving wee Mavis here from Darla and Daddy's obvious sexual repression then I've got to come back here. To this house."

"Yes, we do."

"...and fomenting a peacetime political assassination during Daddy's big hunt might not get me invited back." She cut a look to Wendy, "It'll certainly get *you* crossed off the list. I've got to look at the big picture...family."

"Eunice, you hate your family."

"I know I do." She sighed heavily. "Daddy, the things I do for you and yours, you misogynistic, patriarchy bastard, you." She was halfway down the hall when she turned around and came back to find Wendy standing forlorn and alone. "Well, Wendy, are you gonna help me protest these one percenty shitheads or not?"

"I thought you'd never ask! What'll I wear, do you have another protest suit?"

"Not one that doesn't need a good hosing out." Little Mavis was looking over the edge of the bed reaching for

Eunice's 'Saturday night' bra on the floor. It was shiny. "You'd better grab the kid."

DOWNSTAIRS, FERG came into the mudroom very annoyed by Ferg standards. "Look," he said to the caterer. "Don't mess my baby up." He said, waving to the half barrel of haint punch. "At about-"

"At about three" The caterer cut him off, "...we'll take the punch to the gallery and drop a few of those massive ice blocks in it. Cool it off but don't water it down too much."

"Exactly. I hate to think I'm becoming my father, it's just..." suddenly the cloud lifted, as the Ferg saw his beloved Berretta case in the corner of the mudroom. "How long has that been there?"

"Hadn't noticed it."

Ferg unzipped the case to look at the prodigal shotgun, "Hey! Why's it all smudgy?"

The caterer shrugged and said, "Punch out at three, right?"

From the soybeans, Teddy watched as Ferg came out onto the gallery grinning from ear to ear and wiping his gun down. The other hunters were gathering up their guns. Teddy noticed that their guns looked different from his AR-15, for one thing, his looked way more bad-ass. This gave him confidence. Whatever strange musketry they were armed with, hunters started to move out into the field. On balance Teddy thought it would be wiser to drift out into the field and just return after the shooting was over just like part of the crowd. Then he saw an unarmed Betty Sue Wallace on the back gallery holding Lucy Burton by the arm and waving grandly with what looked like a bloody mary.

"Wow, these are good." Said Betty Sue taking another loud slurp. "Not too spicy, just enough heat."

"Yes." Said Lucy, "C'mon, give me something? What would you say to critics who might point out that your only leadership experience was the Ladies Guild at a Methodist Church in Jackson?"

"What's wrong with a Methodist Church in Jackson? I mean, I'd steer clear of the Catholics, am I right?" She got serious. "I'd say there are a lot of ways to make cornbread, but you just know that the way your momma made it was *just* right."

"Okay, how would you address the charge that your momma's cornbread recipe is not a legitimate qualification for US Senate."

"You mix the right ingredients, in the right way, and add a little heat. Wham-o, you've got cornbread. You know the 'lamestream media' calls me ultra conservative, but I'm just a Jeffersonian liberal at heart. Jefferson, most of our founding fathers, knew how to make cornbread."

"I think a lot of them had slaves for that, actually."

Betty Sue made no immediate comment but the look on her face, Lucy thought, was something akin to wistful.

She tried another tack: "So what made you want to join the senate race, Mrs. Wallace?"

"Wow!" Betty Sue said looking at the dregs in her glass. "That went down fast." She took a bite out of the pickled okra she'd been using to stir the thing. "Let's go to the bar, girlfriend."

"Should you have another if you're going to go play with guns?" By this point most of the hunters were out in the field.

"Let the boys play and come back sweaty." She smiled at the bartender, "Two bloody marys please." She turned to Lucy, "Oh, get into politics? Well to serve the public. Address the pressing issues of the day."

"Alright, immigration reform is on the top of the list for Mississippi voters, so Mrs. Wallace, what's your 'secret recipe'?"

The recipe that Lucy found herself jotting down was Betty Sue's grandmother's recipe for deviled eggs which, she had to admit, sounded scrumptious.

FROM HIS HIDDEN spot in the soybeans, Teddy continued to watch the hunters move off the gallery to move out to the fields. He'd seen Deke head out earlier with a spastic dog and a gun that looked like what he was something which folks went at each other with during the Civil War. On the gallery, Leo was in jeans and a new, olive green shirt with big orange patches. He had a gun, but he also looked confused, chatting nervously with Kelly, dressed in loafers and a short blue blazer.

"Where do I go?" Leo asked Kelly.

"I don't know."

"You were supposed to find out."

"Well Sir, I had to be a little discreet. I mean, did you really want to show up with a $2,200 shotgun and not know what the protocol is? We've got to make it look like this thing is old hat for you."

"I don't see why, down on the coast I just need to go fishin' from time to time."

"We're casting a wider net, sir."

"Okay, dammit. What'd you find out? Where do I go?"

"I don't know."

"Certainly were discreet. Useless, but discreet. Where'd you get the gun?"

"I borrowed it."

"Really? It looks brand new. Who'd you borrow it from?"

Kelly cleared his throat. "Claude Dechamp." He said into his cup.

"Ah sweet Jesus. We don't need to go to *that* well too many times. I swear to God if you got me a gun that's been used in a hit, I'm gonna use it on you!"

"Let's hope it doesn't come to that." Kelly looked at the shotgun, "It looks a little fancy for grease work don't you think?"

"Greasework?"

"Anyway, Congressman, I *borrowed* it. It wasn't a gift, and it wasn't purchased. I may be useless, thank you, but I am discreet."

"Go find our hostess, Darla the Texan. Ask her, surely she can't be *too* political."

From inside the house, Darla's eyes moistened. She was chatting pleasantly with Booey Kipling and the mayor's wife, but she wasn't listening. She was looking, transfixed, at the beauty and grace and power that was Betty Sue Wallace. Little Darlene, daughter of Mavis and Tom Tick, from Gun Barrel City, Texas, was hosting the future senator who would shake up the old boy's game in politics and restore the country's greatness. After the Chief got through draining the swamp, it'd be Betty Sue who's sit in the Oval Office. And she was in Darla O'Conner's, *nee* Darlene Tick's, back gallery talking to that cute little gal who'd she thought was Deke's girlfriend but had apparently thrown him over for the hard-hitting investigative reporter, Theodore Landry. While she felt bad for Deke, the boy had seemed to land on his feet with the girl whose momma had been in *Clam Whiskers*. And where had she run off to?

"Well, Ms. Wallace," Lucy was saying on the other side of the window, "thanks for the face time and the recipes. I know you want to get out to the field. And there is Leo looking a little lost…"

"Why do you want to talk to Leo?"

"He's the other candidate." She redialed the last number called on her phone and, again, it went straight to Deke's voicemail.

Betty flinched and peered over Lucy's head, a fairly easy maneuver, and gave Leo the stink eye. "Why don't you come out to the field with me? We'll talk about guns."

From the other side of the gallery, Leo grabbed Kelly's arm and pointed to Betty Sue and Lucy. "Those two idiots seem to know where they're going!"

"Yeah but Betty Sue is a country girl."

"You fellows look a little lost." said Burt Carlson. Leo smiled sheepishly. Burt lowered his voice, "All this shouldn't be a qualification, but it is. Same in Nebraska. Sure as shit in Mississippi." He slapped Leo's arm, "Even for a Democrat. C'mon, I'll get you to the right place. Might want to leave college boy on the porch." He turned to the aide, "Don't look glum, you'll have the ladies to yourself."

The two congressman marched off into the field. "That's a hell of a gun you got. I *know* you didn't buy it for this shoot."

"Borrowed it from a friend."

"Friends are nice, aren't they? Said Carlson, "Especially after the week I've had. That *Brute* interview gave me all kind of hell."

"I don't know," said Leo, "I thought you did alright, considering. I thought the bull cock walking stick was a fair diversion."

"I didn't like it. That was Laudermilk's idea." Carlson thumbed back to the house. "You know O'Conner actually has one. He thinks he's doing me a favor by hauling it out. I just need it to go away. If you win the election stick close to your senior senator, that man is a genius... but he does keep his cards close to his chest."

"Let him haul the walking stick out." said Leo, "That'll water it down. Your real problem is the hashtag: *notyourpenis* crew. What did Laudermilk say about that?"

"His genius has its perimeters. Hey, listen, you know more about these feminists than I do. How do I get them off my back? Or at least distract them?"

Leo laughed, "Do nothing. But do it deliberately." "

"Huh?"

"Do them a political favor. Tell 'em you're ignoring the Nebraska bombing by calling it vandalism. Quietly so it makes it hard to them to use your name if you think it's gonna get you in trouble back home."

"Back home they want blood."

"Doing nothing doesn't leave much of a paper trail."

"Huh," Carlson had always seen himself as a doer, not a thinker, but he was warming to the oily strategist beside him. "No. I don't suppose it does."

"Listen, Carlson, you think you're gonna bag your limit today?"

"I always do down here."

"Then don't. You don't want to be too masculine. Not with the Hell's Belles at your throat."

"Huh," muttered Carlson yet again. Then he stopped. "You need something for the bag?"

"I've never shot one of these in my life." Leo said.

Carlson smiled, "Then why don't we split the difference?"

LOUIS GUILLORY pulled the BMW in line with the cars in front of the O'Conner's house. The exercise was more painful than he'd imagined it would be. While in college, he'd joined Ferg for a couple of these Labor Day shoots – two exactly. He'd graduated from W&L with the world at his feet: joined up with a boutique securities firm and made a suspicious amount of money as their young buck. Then he got busted and sent to a white-collar prison that was doubling as a leper colony in Louisiana, which killed his spot in the right firm and parties like this seemed beyond his grasp. Now he was a social connection for an ambitious gangster and posing as a political fixer. On balance, the private games seemed the more civilized profession.

He got out of the car and walked toward the single figure sitting on the front porch with his head in his hands. Guillory looked at his watch then heard shots fired from the fields beyond. "You're missing the shoot." Casper looked up and the surprise of recognition hit them both. "I see you got your invite. Don't waste the opportunity. Is Mrs. Wallace out back hob-nobbing?"

"Hey, Louis." Casper said, "What brings you up to Clarksdale?"

"Went to W&L with Ferg. I love the opening day shoot."

"Huh? So you know Deke Kipling? The writer?"

Guillory gripped his bandaged left hand and the pain shot up his arm. "Yeah..."

"Listen, Louis. You need to do me a favor... this is bad..."

Which was about the time the Rebel Yell motorcycle club arrived. He looked up and said to his mopey client, "I can't see how *that's* not going to muddy the water."

DEKE STOOD OVER his camp stool in his usual spot, scanning the sky, the old double barrel propped upward on his knee. Between his feet, a gallon jug of water, frozen solid this morning now melting in the heat. Maxine sat twitching in the shadow of the stool. A trio of dove flew overhead. Deke and fired. The bird spun and dropped as Deke pivoted and fired again, dropping another. Maxine darted from under the stool after the quarry.

Deke opened the breach and reloaded. That's when he noticed Teddy on the ground face down with his hands covering his head. "Hey Teddy, what's up?"

Teddy looked up. "Oh, hey. You surprised me."

"Nice AR."

"Nice musket." Teddy said.

Deke closed the barrel and put the shotgun over his shoulder. "You know you can't shoot birds with that thing, right."

"The second amendment says –"

"It's not a question of the second amendment, Teddy. You'll never hit them, not with an assault rifle. You need a shotgun."

"A what?"

"A musket, Teddy." Deke tapped his shotgun.

Out in the stalks Maxine followed the line with her nose straight until she came upon the bird. She took it up and pivoted on her haunches. The degree to which she pivoted was a mystery even to her. So was the minor adjustment afterward. She darted forward.

"So," Deke was asking. "Did Lucy invite you? You know there is a strict guests of guests may not bring guests policy to this shindig."

"Well, we *are* collaborating." Teddy said as he struggled to his feet and dusted himself off. He felt woozy.

"Good exposure for SLAMNEWS!" All caps. "You know, to pair with a real news site."

"Hey, slamnews has a global reach."

"So do viral cat videos."

"When I created s l a m n e w s ..." a keen observer would notice that not only did Teddy not say it in all caps, he said it in a smaller font. So great was his desire to get people to stop yelling it at him that he'd taken to never uttering the name of his own website in anything over a whisper. "I wanted to create a site that was honest and unafraid. And I don't have to break into other journalist's hotel rooms to steal their research."

Even Deke had to admit (at least to himself) Teddy kind of had him there. "Listen, I was interviewing Leo

Kabler until you blew rape. But tell me this, who are you planning to kill out here, Kabler or Betty Sue?"

"What do you mean?"

"You don't know what the smoking gun in your bag was, do you?"

"Of course, I do."

"Where'd you get that video of Davison screwing that gaming lobbyist?"

"That was investigative journalism. I went after the story and got it."

"Who sent it to you?"

Across the field, unseen under the sunflowers, Maxine cocked her head to the side. Over the years hunting, she had learned a clever trick. According to Army, it was about the damnedest thing he'd ever seen a dog do, and begged Deke to show him how he'd trained her up. After about half a season, Deke confessed that he had no idea, as near as he could tell Maxine had simply taught herself. It involved not mouthing the bird around the torso, but around the head and neck. That enabled her to carry two birds at once with the bulk of either torso bobbing on either side of her mouth like saddlebags. Clever dog, that one.

Deke watched her come out of the soybeans with two birds held softly from the same mouth and not one but two smoking barrels went off in his head at once. "Oh Maxine, you're a genius!" Deke cooed as she came up. Deke gave her a treat and topped up the little steel water dish from the jug. He kissed the dog on the head and scratched her behind the ear.

"I see you are a dog person. How is she a genius? All she did was go fetch."

"Teddy, there's no call to insult my dog. I didn't say she's a genius of *your* caliber. That was some King-Hell research you did on Davison affair. And who says you aren't the story?" Deke fired into the air twice – it seemed to unhinge Teddy, who swung the AR-15 off his shoulder. Deke didn't want him that unhinged. Maxine stared up in the sky and bounced around. Deke gave her another treat.

Teddy fiddled with the rifle, "Well, it is a good story, I'll admit. Brave young journalist goes after the establishment, forms an alliance with the same publication that dared spurn his vision and a romance blooms."

"Romance?"

"Well, I tell you, it started as work. Like you guys I guess. But who can tell how these things happen, Deke. Who can tell?" He mopped his head again. "Don't be jealous, man. You seem to like them a bit crazier – that girl you came in to the bar with was bat-shit."

"Eunice... She's just misunderstood. I think she really liked you."

"She assaulted me! With an orange!"

"She doesn't do that to just anyone, you know. I thought you two really hit it off. I could feel something. Alright, she's a little causey, but aren't you? That's passion, my friend."

"Huh." In his darker moments, when the *Quiet Thunder* went quiet, Teddy had to admit that he was not, in fact, an ace with the ladies. It was possible that his unerring nose for news did not extend to the murky arena of love. Have I misread the whole Eunice thing? Thought he, Imagine what a girl like that must me like when the lights go out. But what about Lucy? So pretty, so level headed. Hell, she's practically doing my job for me. She was the sort of girl you brought home to mom. At least Deke Kipling had thought so. Honorable. She was off talking to Betty Sue Wallace right now.... Teddy's thought process jammed as Deke fired into the air again, twice.

"So where is your Woodward, Bernstein?" Deke asked.

"Huh?"

"Where is Lucy?"

"Oh, she went off with Betty Sue Wallace into the field." He mopped his face again, and thumbed over his shoulder.

"You better watch it, she might scoop you."

From over the soybeans a shot rang out and then so did Betty Sue's voice. "Good shootin', Sister."

Huh, Teddy's mind continued to spin forward, maybe this private interview with Betty Sue isn't a good thing... that bitch has been trying to drop me since she won the primary, fobbing me off on her husband like that. And now a loop is being formed without me. Is Lucy Burton using me to get to Betty Sue Wallace...? Perhaps it was the perfuse sweating but the situation suddenly became clear. But Eunice....

"Did Lucy scoop *you?*" Teddy asked mopping his head with his padded sleeve.

"Naw, I'm on vacation."

"I thought you were interviewing Kabler?"

Damn. Evasive maneuvers. "Teddy, aren't you hot?"

"Yeah." He looked at the partially melted ice water between Deke's feet. "I sure could use a drink of water."

"I'll bet." Deke scanned the sky, "Teddy, why the hell are you wearing those coveralls?"

"They're bullet proof."

"This is a dove shoot, not the *Hunger Games*, you twit. Take that damn thing off before pass out. I've already played that game this weekend."

"I can't."

"Why?"

"Water... please."

Deke put his shotgun down, picked up the water jug and took a long, cool pull. "Teddy, why can't you take that thing off?"

"Just one sip…"

"Teddy?"

"I'm not wearing any pants under this thing." Deke burst out laughing. "Shut up! It's hot, dammit! How do you people wear these things?"

"We don't until it gets cold. And they aren't bullet proof either, Spanky."

"That bastard." Teddy growled and Deke handed over the water jug. While Teddy started soul-kissing the plastic bung, Deke took up the AR-15 and fired two three-shot blasts in the air. Teddy jumped. "What was that for? I thought you said you couldn't hit a bird with that thing?"

"You can't." Deke wiped down the rifle with a kerchief and handed it back. Teddy sat staring at the weapon and not wanting to let go of the jug. "Teddy that was obscene." Deke said snatched back the jug and wiped the lip off.

"Sorry." Picking up the assault rifle with his sweaty hands. "So, what were you shooting at?"

"Teddy, I want you to listen to me. That was an AR-15, the preferred gun of really theatrical psychos. Now everyone in this field – save the two candidates, apparently – knows it has a distinct sound from a shotgun, which all the sane people are using today. Do you understand?

"Yeah, thanks for the ballistics lesson."

"I don't think that you do. Out in that field, there is one sitting senator, two sitting congressmen and another unlikely but possibly future senator, as well as an equally unlikely but rumored presidential candidate. The local mayor, the chief of police and two sitting Judges."

"So?"

"And you are holding the assault rifle that was just fired."

"You fired it."

"No. You're holding it," Deke smiled "and you're all smudgey." He picked up his double barrel, scanned the sky and took another bird. Maxine who was about to explode with all the pointless gunfire took off like a rocket. "Now Teddy, I'd run if I were you."

Teddy slung the weapon over his shoulder and started a fast trot down the field. About the time Maxine came back, Deke looked over and saw Teddy bent double and heaving about five hundred feet way. He trotted a few more paces and fell down.

"Aw hell!" said Deke. He took the water jug and walked over to the mumbling Teddy. "I'll get somebody. Why doesn't anyone dress for the weather anymore?" He patted his pocket for his phone. "Swell." Then Deke looked toward the house and there, standing on the overhang above the back gallery, Eunice stood with her arms spread like the wings of a dove. Held aloft was a sign that read:

I'm Protesting BloodSports
and Land R a p i n g

Unlike Sunday's protest, she wasn't alone. Beside her, suited up in a bed sheet with eyes cut out like a ghost, another held sign that read:

H e l l s B e l l es say
N o t y o ur penis

"That's nice." Eventually, Deke strode up to the house and called up to the protesting dove, "Hey Eunice,

I see you brought a date this year. Listen, we've got a man down out in the field."

"Deke, good to see you. Back from killing God's defenseless creatures for sport?"

"For dinner, actually. I didn't think you believed in God."

"We are all Mother Earth's children."

"Eunice what's the difference? There is a man passed out in the field about to get heat stroke. Go grab your…" He looked bewildered at Wendy. "….ghost… get the ATV and bring him back to the house, please."

"Why don't you get him?"

"Think of it as karma. I got you out of that ridiculous get-up yesterday and you lost seven pounds. Now you have to pay it forward and get him out of his bad choice."

"Yesterday up in my room was hot…"

"It was heat stroke Eunice! That's not the same thing."

"I'm protesting your penis!" howled the ghost.

Deke and scanned the women on the gallery looking at him. "Oh, hi Mom." Deke had never actually witnessed his mother polish off an entire gin and soda until that moment. "She was passed out…" *remember your phrasing…* "heat exhaustion…"

"Who is it?" Eunice called from the overhang.

"It's that clod Teddy Landry. You pelted him with the orange Saturday night."

"Redemption!" she fairly screamed.

"Retardation…"

Eunice dropped the sign with gusto and scrambled across the overhang to an open second story window with the ghost following.

Far afield, young Derrick shaded his eyes against the sun. He'd been watching Ms. Eunice on the overhang in her body suit and assumed she had gone commando again. But he wasn't so sure about the ghost until he saw her having trouble climbing back through the window. She whipped off the sheet, revealing buff colored undies and nothing else. "Hey Granddaddy, that ghost has gone halvsies."

Army, whose attention had been skyward, looked down at his grandson. "What are you talkin' about, boy?"

"The nekkid ghost."

Army looked at the child with a vague concern he hadn't felt for a generation. "Derrick, have you ever rebuilt a duck blind?"

Unseen from young Derrick's vantage, Eunice appeared out of the mudroom, still dressed like a dove with the mousy girl now wrapped in a bed sheet like a Winged Victoria both heading toward the ATV.

FOURTEEN:
WHISKEY SPLINTERS

Casper Wallace had retreated from the front porch to the relative safety of the foyer as the Rebel Yell motorcycle club roared into the front lawn followed by a Subaru Outback. "Well," said Karla, "here we are."

"Take another cut of this!" said nose-ring as she put the bottle of Tequila up to Danny Spewe's mouth.

"Ohhh…"

"Hey gimme some!" called Trevor from the back.

"Alright!" said nose-ring, "Hey Spewe, your boy here is about out-pace you?"

"Now stop it." Karla chided, "We're here so get these little fellas outta my car before they blow chunks!"

The old ladies expelled the Ballyhoo from the car as the motorcycles roared around. The sudden standing up caused Danny's head to swim and he fell against Guillory's BMW and vomited all over the windshield.

"Well, you're here." roared J.E.B. as he dismounted the motorcycle.

"Where is here?" asked Danny.

"Hell if I know. I got a call from that fella who works for Pencil Dechamp. Said Pencil wanted us to bring you two twinks up to this address in Clarksdale and I done it."

Danny's head swam, "Again, who is Pencil Dechamp? Why am I here? Is this a kidnapping!"

"Not really."

"How is it not kidnapping!"

"Well I don't see it that way. Listen fella, are you alright? There is supposed to be some big political to-do going on. I thought you'd know why you were here."

"Hey J.E.B.," said nose-ring who was sharing a bottle with Trevor, "can I keep him?"

DEKE HAD JUST started back afield when the french doors connecting the living room the back gallery flew with great ceremony and the caterers brought out a sloshing half whiskey barrel of haint punch with a two ice cubes the size of car batteries in it. There was a polite round of applause from the women who'd forgone the actually shooting. They were also, in general, smart enough not to the drink the stuff.

With the shotgun over his shoulder, Deke stomped back to the gallery where he plunged a water glass into the blood orange and yellow concoction. "Deke!" screamed Booey politely.

"Yes, Mother?"

"Deke you can't... Oh what's the difference?.... the cocktail napkins are on the sideboard."

"Thank you. Where are my manners?" He started back into the field. "Maxine! Heel!" About eight ounces into the sixteen he'd commandeered, Deke started to think he should have added ice, or at least chosen a smaller glass. Lucy emerged from the soybeans. "Burton of the *Brute*, where'd you come from?"

"Betty Sue Wallace. That gal couldn't hit the ground if she shot her foot."

"From where I was I thought she did okay."

"That was me! Gimme that punch! I had to go fetch 'em too."

"Didn't you get my message yesterday? Derrick was supposed to tell you to meet me at the O'Conners after church. You never showed. I serve Laudermilk up like a pudding and you run off with Teddy for? That reminds me, I may have killed your boy. I sent Eunice to rescue him." Deke wiped the sweat from his face, "I guess I have time to break back into his room and try to get—"

"Break back into his room? I knew that's what you were up doing. Deke Kipling you knew this was my story —"

"I was copying the files for you!"

"You're such a liar! Why would you swipe some files for *my* story?"

"Because you're pissed at me! Why else would I do it?"

"I'm pissed because you're chasing the same story for *Front Street!*"

Deke wiped his face and took another slug of the warming punch, "I haven't written it yet. And I really feel like hell about it. Who told you?"

"Who do you think, Mrs. DeGrasse."

"The one who canceled your room at the Sunflower so you could spy on me?"

"It was my story first, Deke!"

"I know, Lucy. It's *Front* Street, that not an excuse, just an explanation. Look I've got some info for you, not a disk, it's a hard copy. It's on my desk at home. Lemme get you the paper work before you spring anything on Betty Sue."

"It wouldn't do me any good," grumbled Lucy, "Every time I try to take her to the mat and she gave me another recipe. The last one was a tomato pie"

"I love tomato pie. So where'd you learn to shoot like that?" Deke took the glass back and took another slug.

"I'm from South Carolina, you knew that." She dug a mound in the soil with her foot. "Listen, Deke. You don't have to go back to the Sunflower. I've got your flash drive."

Deke laughed. "You're a shady bag of tricks. Listen, I hate to ask but you couldn't broad stroke it for me could you? It's not for *Front Street*, I promise. There is something strange going on here. Now I've got to go find Laudermilk."

"Why?"

He handed the glass back. "We've got two smoking guns, I need to find the target. C'mon Lucy, just the broad strokes."

"Will you tell your mother I'm no Eunice?"

"What the hell, Lucy?"

The arrangement regarding who claims what spot at a dove shoot is not arbitrary, at least not in Mississippi. Age gets you the sweet spot more than station in life. So Deke knew exactly which shady little spot near the small pond where Laudermilk would be stationed with his jug of water, some beef jerky and a thermos of "coffee" that smelled suspiciously like haint punch. "Hey Deke, mah boy." The Old Bear looked at his watch. "Don't tell me you've hit your limit already."

"No, Mr. Aubrey. We've got to talk."

"Let's talk over supper."

Shotguns cracked off in the distance. "Mr. Aubrey, we've got to talk."

"Well, keep your voice down boy, I hadn't hit my limit yet." Laudermilk stood and fired, "Pullin' to the right."

Deke turned and fired. Maxine darted out into the field, happy all over. "How many more you need, senator?"

"Hell, boy, the Navy didn't teach *me* to shoot like that."

"We gotta talk."

"Okay, Deke, you win." Laudermilk looked Deke over. It wasn't a mean look, just hard and intense. "Alright, whadda we gotta talk about?"

"You say you don't care if Leo wins, right?"

"I care about the will of the Republic."

"No, that's not it."

"Actually, young man, that is *exactly* it!"

"You hadn't let me finish… You're the one who called Kenneth Macastle at *Front Street*, aren't you?"

Laudermilk smiled, "You're welcome, mah boy. I didn't know you were gonna bring Ms. Burton along. Heh heh. Army says you got yourself a little girl problem."

"I'll say. Most of them are trying to kill me."

"That is unfortunate. Better kiss and make up."

"Why'd you set up the *Front Street* assignment?"

"Thought you could use the work."

"That's not it."

Laudermilk laughed, "That's not it *exactly*."

"Why, then?"

Laudermilk's hard look went away with a long pull on the water-jug. He smiled devilishly. "You tell me."

"This isn't a game."

"No, it most certainly is not. It's a test. I want to see if you passed."

"Okay, you insane old man…" Deke took a pull from his glass. "You weren't – God's Holy Trousers this stuff is harsh when it heats up!"

"You were saying?" Laudermilk's hands were neatly folded on his belly.

"I was saying that you weren't doing me a favor, I'm doing you one. You called Macastle and wafted that rumor of a presidential bid under his nose so he'd give me the assignment without raising red flags. But you aren't going to run – so why the splashy profile on a man who *not* running for president?"

"Granted, that lacks zip."

"What about the only honest politician in America?"

Laudermilk laughed, "Nope, that can't be it. I haven't exactly been up front, have I?"

"No, you wanted me digging around on the senate race. You wanted to see what I came up with."

"Not entirely."

"Not entirely." Deke repeated to himself. "Okay – this would be easier if you'd throw me a bone. No... you didn't want me to just dig around. You already knew the rumors about Leo Kabler's bribes to ensure Corsair's gaming licenses stayed current without much fuss. Now Bayoil is more or less clean, but the Dechamps aren't. They're using Corsair to launder the money from the illegal casinos and whores and out of the Digger Stations. The Digger Stations that paid the Wallace's nine year old son half a million dollars last year for what I assume is corporate cover."

Laudermilk smiled again. "Interesting. How'd you suss it out?"

"Well I'm a little embarrassed to say but it was Maxine. You know that trick she does with two birds hanging out of either side of her mouth? That's when it hit me, both candidates are the target.

"Yeah, that's a clever pup. But Macastle ain't gonna take your dog as a confidential source. Can you back it up, verify any of this?"

"Yes. That's it. You told me that you didn't care which candidate won, but I wasn't asking the right question. It isn't that you don't care who wins at all. It's that you want both candidates to lose!"

"Interesting theory, Deke."

"You wanted me to dig up information that would set off a chain reaction that would blow up the Wallaces *and* Kabler because they are both owned by the Dechamps."

The Old Bear laughed, "That's a lot of influence for a pair of Dixie mafia goons, dontcha think, Deke? Now, all I did was suggest an editor hire you for a job, mah boy. Remember that."

Deke was wiping the sweat from his face again. He hadn't smoked in years, but now he suddenly wanted one. "But someone *has* to win. For this to work, you'd needed to find an independent candidate to pick up the pieces. But why? Why do you care about a couple of crooked politicos in a house full of them?"

"Because it's Mississippi and it's my home and I reckon I got tired of it being run into the ground by grasping crooks. It's my country too. The parties carry one like they're polar opposites. Shit. They're just throwing slogans to hide the fact that each is trying to steal the other's votes, skimming off the same damn purse — not to make this Republic could be, or maybe even what it once was. Nobody wants to govern, they just want to squeeze the hell out of the concession." The Old Bear squinted into the sun. "...And do I need another reason?"

The sun stared down at the two mercilessly. "No." Deke thought for a moment. "I don't reckon you do."

"You did good, mah boy."

"I don't know about that. I'm in a little bit of a mess with *Front Street*."

"Not again."

"Alright, fair enough. I was trying to wrangle a staff job out of this."

"Why? You think corporations are any different from politics? Advertisers, voters, and customers: they are all the same thing. They'd have your nuts in a sling because the money is good. The Macastles, the Barkers, the Kablers and the Wallaces — they've been bought and paid for and they hate anyone who isn't, and that includes you. Hashtag: *damndeke!*"

"Still, it was the chance of a lifetime."

Laudermilk laughed, "The article or Miss Burton?"

"You sound like my mother."

"Me? Naw, I ain't that smart. The way I see it, is that y'all are the only two journos down here at the implosion of a senate race that has inexplicably caught the national eye. You might try workin' together. I mean, if the national press is running scared of the sort of people who spend their life on their phones screaming in single sentences, and you two have *the story*, well don't you have the leverage? I could be wrong, Carlson tried to explain it to me but the whole thing just sounded like a big pecker joke." In the distance they heard a several sirens. "Now I have a question for you. You got two smokin' guns – as you say – and two targets. It might be worth askin' who pulled the trigger."

LIKE A GREAT MANY of his confederates on the Hill, Leo Kabler was fairly used to passing laws that required other people to do all the heavy lifting. His chosen profession never required him to be a personally brave man. And the sight of Louis Guillory beside him gave him a start. "Guillory, what are doing here?"

"Old friend of the O'Conner's. Went to school with Ferg. Just thought that I'd come up and check on my investment."

"I don't know where Kelly got this shotgun. He told me it was his uncle's."

Guillory smiled, "No he didn't. That boy isn't related to anyone who owns a gun like that. Don't worry Leo, no one's asking for it back. Listen, have you seen Deke Kipling?"

Leo had not. But what he did see was Eunice returning with the nearly unconscious Teddy strapped like a deer to the front of the ATV. Wendy X was riding snugly behind Eunice, her ghost outfit cum toga flapping wildly behind them. Red flags went up. Eunice hopped off the ATV and commanded Hank and a bartender to take Teddy up to her room, where it would be quiet and cool. That surprised him, Eunice may have been fit for a straight-jacket, but she was the sort of crazy that tended to side with Kabler's progressive people. Landry was the other kind of crazy. Not the endearing sort.

From the memory of the weapon under Wendy's flapping toga, Guillory drew a line from there to the .50 caliber machine gun in her car. "Maybe we ought to go skinny-dipping to cool him off." He heard her say as she leapt from the ATV. Then, as if the clouds opened, he could see Wendy perfectly on Esplanade Street holding that damn martini. Over the commotion he could barely hear the motorcycles out front.

Leo saw the assault rifle strapped to the back of the ATV. "What's that?" Leo asked, but Guillory was gone.

"Oh, that's a semi-automatic rifle, Congressman." Booey said calmly. "I don't think the boy is much of an outdoors type."

"If you'll pardon me ma'am." Leo went inside. The first call he made was to the Clarksdale police department, reporting his own foiled assassination attempt. The second was to his campaign manager, reporting a windfall of electoral gold. "That buffoon Teddy Landry just tried to assassinate me."

"Really?" said the manager, "are you alright?"

"He didn't get a shot in. He passed out, of heat stroke I think."

"Then how do you know he was shooting at you? Aren't you at that damn hunt? Isn't everyone armed?"

"With an assault rifle?" Leo was excited. "I mean, Jesus, what else could it be?"

"I see what you mean." Said the manager. "So how do you know that he was there to kill *you*?"

"Teddy Landry has been out to get me since the campaign started. You know that!"

"Do I?"

Leo took a big slug of punch and felt better. "He's in bed with Betty Sue and Laudermilk's GOP."

"Everyone is in bed with someone, Leo."

"This implicates the Wallaces."

"If true, yes. Have the police been called?"

"They are on their way."

"Good boy." Said the voice on the other end of the line. "Now we can make it true."

As the crowd watched Hank and the bartender hoist Teddy's limp body inside, as Eunice followed. Wendy stood looking at the AR-15. "Hmmm." She picked it up, and walked around the house as if it were the most normal thing in the world.

Casper was still squatting in the foyer watching the Rebel Yell make camp in the front yard. So lost was he in his thoughts that Casper leapt clean seven inches off the ground when Guillory told him to move. "Dadburn it! Don't sneak up on me like that! Did you talk to that Kipling fella? He'll ruin us both."

"Nope. Only you." Guillory opened the door.

"Hey Guillory! Where are you going?" Casper demanded. Across the lawn, J.E.B. looked up at the name.

"I left a file in the office."

"In New Orleans?"

J.E.B. called out, "Hey Mr. Guillory, what's Pencil want us to do with these sweetmaries?"

"Ballyhoo!" Danny managed to retch.

Guillory smiled. "Pencil say you can keep him. They'll pay you when you get back in town." The old ladies cheered and force fed Danny more tequila. "Just pop in to the office this week for the expenses."

It wasn't until he'd slid into the driver's seat that he was aware of both the sight and smell of the vomit slowly heating on his windshield. He pulled out to the highway and was turning left when he heard the sirens. He turned the other way.

OFFICER CRENSHAW wasn't happy. If what she thought had happened had, in fact happened, it was going to be a blemish on an otherwise fair to middling record. So it was almost with a sense of relief that in answering a report on a possible political assassination, she found a small army of Rebel Yell motorcycle clubbers. That was bound to muddy the waters.

J.E.B. turned to Karla and called. "Cops are here, Karla, guess you can't keep the little dweebs."

Wendy slipped unnoticed to her car.

MEANWHILE, UPSTAIRS, Hank and the bartender dropped Teddy on the Eunice's bed before being shooed off. Alone, Eunice looked at the helpless figure on the bed and unzipped his jumpsuit. Underneath, his tee shirt and briefs were soaked through. She pulled off the boots and rolled him out of the damp coveralls and underthings and gave him some water. Somewhere she remembered that fruit juice was good for dehydration and she spied the jar of punch on her dresser. She was pretty sure than stuff had fruit in it.

Teddy's vision was still ebbing back and forth in blurry globs of light. He felt sick to his stomach and dizzy at the same time. He concentrated on a focal point on the ceiling fan as it whirled away. "I know something about you." Eunice said gently, sticking her blurred face in front of his. "You were going to shake things up out there, weren't you?"

The strange figure above him looked down, a hazy, bright light behind her golden hair. Does she have wings? Is she really an angel? Am I dying? Focus on the light. Is the angel speaking to me? What is she saying? Is this the end? So many things I have to get off my chest to make amends at this, my final accounting. Okay, Okay, I was fired from the *Brute*, and not even for professional reasons. I kicked in the candy machine when it stole my dollar. There was the Tut's delivery guy…well, screw him on second thought. He called me a blogger.

Then there was a sweet sensation pouring into his mouth, followed by a warm bloom. Teddy lapped at it and Eunice whispered into his ear. "You can tell me." she whispered sweetly, "Who were you gonna shoot?"

The angel above was pouring the warm sweetness into his soul as she spoke in tongues. Well if this is death, soon I'll understand her. I really am sorry I've been pretending to be a journalist when I've more or less on the payroll of some ridiculous fraternity. But haven't I been punished enough? I believed in the Wallace's and they dropped me for that Lucy girl. Is that irony or poetic justice? Anyway, I have to get away from the Wallaces, they are bad people.

"Who?" Eunice whispered in his ear.

"Betty Sue…that bitch." he mumbled.

She hugged him close to her bosom.

"Eunice!" came the voice from the hall. It was Darla.

"Can't you see I'm taking care of this man?"

"By giving him that awful hoochie punch?"

"Ferg said it was non-alcoholic."

Darla burst out laughing. "When did he tell you that? Your brother is pulling your leg. Here's one of those sports drinks. Now put that boy down. He's got a himself a boner."

FIFTEEN:
THE SECRET CORNBREAD RECIPE

The Rebel Yell rode off in a fury as Deke slipped quietly to his truck parked by the side of the house. And there he stumbled upon Wendy's spare nudity entirely by accident. "Whoa! Sorry about that." He looked the other way and opened the back of the truck.

"Back off!" she barked, "It's Still. Not. Okay!"

"What's not okay? Public nudity?" said Deke, cramming his head into the truck bay like it was a bucket of sand. "You know, they've got some bathrooms inside with doors...locks even." Maxine was not entirely sure what to make of the situation.

"This is my body. It doesn't matter where I am or what I'm wearing. This is Still. Not. Okay!"

"Why are you naked in the O'Conners front yard? You're about thirty feet from the highway! The police are here, and not to mention that there must be 200 people back in the house!"

Wendy X stood her ground. "Still. Not. Okay!" What looked like a blouse was in her hand and some shorts in the front seat.

He straitened up and looked at her. "No, Miss, it's not okay! What about *my* rights? You just ruined nudity for me!" Then something struck him, he looked back at the underfed, naked woman. "Wait a minute, don't I know you?"

"Stop objectifying me!" Wendy shrieked, shimmied into her blouse as she opened the back of the Prius and reached under the sustainably sourced Peruvian blanket when she stepped on something pointy. "Goddamn nature!" She slammed the back gate shut and trying to hop into her shorts. "Still. Not. Okay!" she hissed again and jumped into the driver's seat. The car pulled away as fast as Priui are typically able.

Upstairs, Eunice was in a state of controlled euphoria: Ever since she was a little girl, she'd dreamt about that special day when she would barricade herself in a heroic stand against the onslaught of the Fascist Police State. No silly princess gowns for her − despite Daddy's attempt to fill her closet full of them. No No. Why wait for some dumb man to rescue her from the tower when it was more fun to just burn the whole damn thing down? Of course, as she grew older, her childhood fantasies became more realistic and she knew that Daddy probably wouldn't be there but merely watching, mortified and stunned, on cable news. And now, as she heard the wail of the sirens chiming in her soul like the bells of the angels in which she didn't believe, she knew that her special day was here. What's more, she would share it with − or at least inflict it upon − her father personally.

She looked out the window in the hall as the first of three patrol cars roared into the front yard followed by the news truck bouncing into the drive. She snuck back into her room and barricaded the bedroom door with her desk.. "I'm sooooo happy!" she clapped her hands.

Outside, Deke walked around the police interviewing the two wildly drunk Ballyhoo boys who'd been left on the O'Conner's front lawn. "Oh hey Danny Spewe, what brings you here?"

"Goddammm Deke Kipling! We're not wankers!"

"Settle down!" barked Crenshaw.

Deke sighed and went back into the house trying to rub the image of Wendy in-the-all-together out of his eyes. He found Lucy. "You need to talk to Ferg about the senate race."

Before she could react, Leo grabbed her arm, "Alright Burton of the *Brute*, this is the political story of year, the decade! Teddy Landry just tried to assassinate me."

"Teddy? He did not!"

"He did! He's got an assault rifle!"

Lucy rolled her eyes, "Oh he doesn't even know how to load it! I don't think." Now the police were fanning throughout the house. "Leo, did you call the law on that poor idiot?"

"Ahh good, the TV news is here. Sorry Burton, print is dead." Leo moved away like a leaping gnome.

"Don't I know it." She grabbed her camera and found young Derrick on the gallery standing next to Booey, who siting on the porch swing, tickling Maxine behind ear. At the sight of Lucy, the boy muttered "underpants" sheepishly.

As Lucy approached and bent down to his level, Derrick wanted to bolt again, but couldn't. Miss Lucy was very pretty, you see. "Sweetheart," she was saying, "I don't know what that means, but I need your help. I need *you* to be my cameraman. Can you do that for me?"

"Yes ma'am."

In the mudroom, Deke took the plastic cup of punch from Ferg. "Alright, I think it's time you take charge of the situation."

"What is the situation?" he asked.

"Hell if I know! Just take charge!"

"How?" He reached for the cup.

Deke held it at arms length. "No more for you! Just act like your father and take charge! He was faking it too!"

They walked into the living room where, unfortunately, Beau was also acting like himself. "Ferg! Dammit! Go talk some sense into your sister! She's barricaded herself into her room with the assassin!"

"Ferg!" Deke said, "This is two... two Eunices you owe me for. Now take charge!"

Ferg and Beau stepped outside at the same time like two horses facing the same finish line. Beau looked at his son and snorted, "Let me handle this."

A tremendous cloud of delicious smoke wafted past the two O' Conners. "Gee Dad, you are never gonna get that smoke out of the living room drapes." Ferg noted with concern.

"Careful boy!" Beau bellowed as a furious eye fell on Hank, who was trying to guess what the Wilson's would do when they found out he'd sold the offending AR-15 for a political assassination. Hank began to casually slink away, thinking that Bora Bora might be a fine change of pace from Clarksdale. "Hank, get back here!" Beau screamed and strode off in pursuit.

Ferg faced the television cameras, brushed his hair out of his face and cleared his throat. "I know we've had a lively time today, but let's let the police do their jobs. They've got their work cut out for them today! We've got plenty of good food and punch. We've had a little spook here today, but there is no reason to be scared or panic until we know *what actually happened*. It might not be as dramatic as it looks."

Upstairs, Deke passed the phalanx of police standing outside Eunice's closed door. "Excuse me fellas." He opened the window at the back of the house and stepped out onto the gallery overhang, slid over and knocked on her bedroom window.

A small nose and half an eye poked from between the curtains. "Deke!" a voice squealed. "I knew you'd come back. But it's too late."

"Open the damn window, Eunice!" She threw the latch and Deke climbed in and looked at Teddy, lumpy and naked under a sheet. "Is he okay?"

"I think he'll pull through. He's a fallen soldier for the cause."

"I don't know that he is."

"There is more to him that you think." Teddy let out a little gas in confirmation. "Deke, I'm glad you're here."

"That makes one of us."

"We've had a lot of history, but, eventually we all have to grow up."

The police were banging on the door outside. "Miss O'Conner, you need to open this door!"

"It's Ms!"

"Hey fellas," said Deke, "Why don't you give us a second?"

"Open the door!" came the voice.

Eunice continued, "See, Teddy here, he's given himself to the cause. Think about it, he left a great job at one of America's top newspapers...sites...whatever you call the *Daily Brute-*"

"I don't think that you call it the top anything, Eunice."

"Left his job as one of America's top political reporters"

"Do you know what that word 'top' means?"

"Shut it! He went undercover, Deke. Undercover to expose a crooked GOP senator and set the Wallaces up for a downfall."

"Well, about that – "

Eunice was rolling, "He told me that was the plan all along."

Teddy mumbled something.

"What was that?"

"Oh," said Eunice with a wave of the hand, "We were talking about the moon landing hoax when you came in."

"Well, he fooled me. You know the police are gonna haul both of you off."

Eunice put her hand on his cheek. "You'll grow up one day, Deke, if you'll just let the world change you instead of writing those silly books."

There was a pounding at the door. "Miss O'Conner, please open the door. Has Mr. Landry got you in there against your will?"

"YOU'LL NEVER TAKE US ALIVE!" Eunice shrieked.

"Now Eunice, don't do that." Said Deke. "I think they're serious."

From the other side of the door came the Midwestern shriek of Darla going full Darlene Tick to tell the police not to kick in her freshly painted doors.

Deke moved the desk and opened the door. "They're all yours."

The police poured into the room with enthusiasm and Deke was sure he heard Crenshaw telling Eunice not to bite. Deke took the stairs three at a time, hit the landing and scrambled towards the back gallery where his nephew watched the almost operatic figure of Betty Sue Wallace in her polo boots, khaki twills and safari shirt gently clingy with sweat. Young Derrick was still holding Lucy's camera because he was afeared of dropping the ball again after yesterday's fiasco that seemed to have put Uncle and – potentially – Aunty Suitcase on the outs. Betty Sue was still jabbering about some secret cornbread recipe to Lucy when word that the police had taken Eunice and Teddy cracked through the walkie talkies and the guests exploded with wild chatter.

Ferg jumped inside quickly and returned with his now gleaming Beretta. He fired into the air and the crowd went silent. Ferg cleared his throat. "Everyone stay put. The police need to do their job and they may need our help later so stay put, please. Again, there is food and punch. And let's let our brave men and women in blue do their jobs. The best thing we can do right now is sit back and have another plate of ribs!"

Lucy said to Betty Sue, "I gottta go!" And crossed over to where Ferg was standing with the shotgun over his shoulder. "Ferg!" she said, "I didn't think you had it in you."

"I think it's the haint punch."

"It's working. We need to talk."

Young Derrick failed to follow Lucy, or even realize that she'd left. He'd discovered he could use the camera's zoom to settle the nagging issue of this magnificent woman's underwear policy. Last night, he'd mentioned his thoughts on the matter to his brother who stated flatly that it was against the law for adults *not* to wear underwear. Young Peter maintained that it was written in the Napoleonic Code. In point of fact, he had lectured, the emperor himself had invented boxer shorts and wrote a law about it himself. Still, Derrick wondered. This was Mississippi – which wasn't Napoleonic at all – and now Derrick knew the strange and titillating truth about Miss Eunice's obvious lack of lumps. He zoomed in closer and... bra strap! *Well that's that.* thought Derrick. Still, it was an intriguing heft of flesh being harnessed in there. *How close does this thing go?*

Somewhere out of the boy's keenly focused field of vision, Leo Kabler trying to wrest control of the situation from Ferg. "Oh, we know what happened, Citizens! This is a threat to our democracy."

"Now Leo, you just hush up!" drawled Betty Sue, standing with her fists on her hips, which had become something of her trademark: a sort of a matronly, *standing athwart the corruption of Washington* pose. "That poor boy didn't try to shoot you! He's touched."

"You can say that again."

"Get over yourself, Leo, quit talking down to me from your pedestal."

"You two have been bankrolling that kid for months, now he's tried to assassinate me!"

"We didn't bankroll anyone and he didn't take a shot at you!"

"Betty Sue, was this part of the Wallace campaign strategy all along! Wipe out the people's choice?"

"Oh, so now *I've* tried to knock you off!" She turned to the guests, "Well, that ain't the most, y'all. How about it people? Y'all think I tried to have Leo here killed?"

"Lot's of good barbecue." Ferg said. "I think the candidates need to take it inside."

"Cut out the cornball routine." barked Leo, "I happen to know that you got your grandmother's secret recipe cornbread recipe from the Junior League cook book."

Booey, still on the porch swing tickling Maxine, looked up quite alarmed. Darla choked on her first glass of haint punch. The mayor's wife gasped. The second wife of Mary Katherine Shanks' first husband guffawed. Mrs. Laudermilk, who'd thought she'd seen it all, hiccuped faintly. Betty Sue Wallace's shoulders went back, lifting her ample bosom into an aggressive attitude; her eyes widened, then went tight; a curling snarl replaced the enthusiastic smile. Sensing he had the advantage, Leo stepped down from the gallery. He sensed wrong. It was one thing to falsely accuse a Southern lady of political assassination, murder, mud raking or bank embezzlement, but to impugn the authenticity of her grandmother's recipes was not something a creature like Betty Sue Wallace could abide.

"You dirty little shylock!" she hissed and unplanted her hips.

"What did you say?" said Leo, "Just so we're clear-"

Betty Sue Wallace came around with a right hook that was no less surprising or effective for its apparently girliness. This was a punch throw by a cheerleader, but an angry one who had spent her life burning off excess calories, not avoiding them. Combined with the forward thrust of Congressman Kabler the hit created a force that knocked the man, despite his low center of gravity, backward off the step and flat on his back as his skull bounced of a paver stone.

"Oh shit!" Casper Wallace said for the second time in his life.

On the other side of the open french doors, Eunice came down the staircase in handcuffs escorted by Officer Crenshaw. "I'm a hostage of the state!" screamed Eunice.

Ferg looked at Lucy, "Oh yeah, I'm running as an independent for Senate. The Old Bear is endorsing me."

Now Lucy's eyes went wide. "Ferg, does anyone know this!"

"Well, Deke, Uncle Aubrey... hadn't told Dad yet..."

"Derrick Kipling!" Lucy shouted, "Bring that camera over here, I thought you were behind me!"

"I think we're almost out of time, Miss Lucy." The boy said, scrambling to her side.

"How? Didn't you stop the camera?"

"You didn't tell me how!"

"Swell, we'll do it quickly. Derrick, stand on this chair." He hopped up and aimed the camera as Lucy cleared her throat, "So just to confirm, Ferguson O'Conner has just announced that he is running for Senate for the state of Mississippi as an independent candidate."

"Right-o. Just look at the choices." said Ferg, with his shotgun over his shoulder like some friendly country squire. "What option do I have? What option does Mississippi have?"

The crowd began to murmur. Deke was moving down the hall and snatched Ferg's shotgun. He moved towards the front of the house, loading it as he went. About the same time Beau was coming through leading Hank in a headlock. "Mr. O'Conner, I'm sorry" Hank was gasping. On the front porch, two reporters and camera crews stormed into the foyer. Alone in the yard, Deke took aim. The first shot crippled the satellite antenna on top of the van, the second took it clean off. "Lucy Burton, the things I do for you."

The shots went unnoticed as Beau was bellowing on the back gallery, "You there, Officers! Unhand my little princess."

"Can it Daddy!" Eunice was screaming, "I'm willing to pay the price for the cause." She tried to bite Crenshaw again.

"Now look Eunice, you bite me again and I'm taking you downtown!"

"You'll do no such thing!" ordered Beau. Eunice tried to kick the Crenshaw in the crotch.

"Allllrrright!" she said and dragged Eunice screaming through the house towards the patrol cars in the front yard. "Oh hey Deke!" she called as they came through the yard. "Sorry about the other day."

"No blood. No foul!" Deke hoped he looked like he was gazing out at the late afternoon sun as opposed the antenna-less news van.

"Sorry I didn't get chance to visit with your mother," Crenshaw was saying as he guided the theatrically struggling Eunice to the patrol car. "Just crazy about Ms. Booey."

"Deke!" Eunice screamed offering her two cents, "It's a police state."

"Officer, you're gonna watch those legs, she's a stocky little thing."

Having just shot up a small fortune in satellite equipment, Deke retreated inside as Crenshaw locked Eunice in the back of the patrol car. Alone at last, Eunice smiled and melted back into the vinyl seat. "Wow. This will really get Daddy's goat."

Congressman Burt Carlson sat alone at a table at the edge of the clearing, eating some ribs and drinking a beer. The let out a deep sigh and he watched the chaos with a gathering sense of peace and tranquility. He watched Beau thundering to all from the gallery like a Roman senator, "Officers! I believe this young man has something to tell you." Hank was still in a headlock.

"Well, let him go!" someone yelled. A rib bone flew through the air, missing the pair by a few inches. Beau released the kid.

"Hey look," said Hank, taking off his Wilson Hardware cap and scratching his hair. "Uh. I don't think that Teddy fella meant to hurt anyone. I sorta told him that it was a good idea to shoot dove with an AR-15."

"C'mon, Hank. No one is *that* stupid." The chief of police said.

"Well, he might be." opined Casper generously.

"Why would you do something like that, Hank?" said Crenshaw

"Well, Officer, have you ever met that fella? Look what he was wearing." said Hank, "He came in asking if we took Federal greenbacks and wonderin' if we slept on straw down here. So I sold him that discontinued insulated coverall and told him it was bulletproof. He was scared the other hunters would shoot him."

"Well, that does explain it." said Crenshaw. "Anything else, Hank?"

"Charged extra for the bulletproofing."

"Good Lawd!" screamed Beau. "Hank, I've misjudged you. I am sorry."

The guy from the TV news came out in front of the camera man and yelled at Beau, "Hey, O'Conner, one of your guests just shot the satellite off our van! How are we supposed to broadcast?"

Beau took the camera, handed it to Hank, and proceeded lead the reporter off his property in a headlock. Carlson smiled: He'd bagged his limit, and about half of Leo's and was pretty sure the world had forgotten about his elk penis.

"Ferg," Crenshaw was saying, "we've got the boy handcuffed to Eunice's bed."

"Again?" came a voice.

"That'll do!" she called. "We've got an ambulance coming though. He's in lousy shape." Then she looked at the unconscious Congressman Kabler. "Maybe they have room for two."

The chaos was starting to sort itself out in Lucy 's head. She looked at young Derrick, still standing on the chair. "So you never turned the camera off?"

"I'm sorry Miss Lucy, but that woman with the bosoms knocked that little fella clean out. I forgot!"

IN FERG'S old room, Lucy was uploading the footage that young Derrick had shot to her laptop. It wasn't a perfect: some of the early shots of Betty Sue looked like a Jane Russell screen test, but the mini-Deke had gotten every frame of the knock out along with sound. "Wow," she said, "did Betty Sue call Kabler a shylock on camera?"

"He's not Jewish." said Deke, coming in with Ferg's shotgun. "But... she still said it. You need get that footage up fast. I shot the satellite off the local news van, that'll give you some time."

Lucy tossed Deke his flash drive from the Sunflower. "Looking for this? Deke, I want you to be honest, did you break into Teddy's room to do me a favor?"

He laughed, "Yes! You don't know what you're like when you're pissed. Are you still working with Teddy?"

"I'm going to thump you." She put her nose up to the screen. "Leo Kabler has taken some pretty damning gifts from outfit called Corsair – an off-shore gaming company. That' pretty garden-variety corruption and might not be the end of the world, but Corsair is owned by the Deschamp Brothers – "

"That's bad for Leo, but that's just half the haul. It's not just gaming, but money laundering for Corsair's more unlicensed operations." Deke added. "The high rent ghost casinos and the low-end brothels which operate mainly out of two Digger Stations owned –"

"By Chad Wallace of St. Andrew's Elementary."

"Right. What do you need me for?'

"Petty thievery and opening jars. Was there proof in the bag? Because I don't think that Teddy knew what he had."

"I don't think he did either. What I can't figure out is how Teddy got the information in the first place."

"Maybe he got it from two different sources. The Casper's hired a political consultant out of New Orleans, a guy named Guillory."

Deke looked up, "Louis Guillory?"

"Yeah, you know him?"

"Went to college together. That would explain the dirt on Kabler. But why would he want to sink the Wallace's? They're the ones who hired him."

Lucy had a more pressing question:"So how are we going to do this? What about *Front Street?*"

"Print is slow. I'll figure something out. Listen, Lucy, I really do feel rotten about that."

Then Ferg appeared in the doorway. "Ferg, I always knew you had it in you! Great speech, brother."

"Well, I've talked to Missy."

"Who?"

"His wife." Said Deke. "Lucy, keep up!"

Lucy still had her face buried in the computer screen, "I forgot that you were married. You don't seem like the sort."

"Honestly, I'm not very good at it."

"What'd she have to say about the senate race?" Asked Deke.

"Hates the idea. Says I don't have a chance. Hey Lucy, that's off the record."

"Don't have a chance!" barked Deke, "This is America my friend – the republic was founded on giving blockheads like you a chance. Hell, JFK took us to war against Cuba and *lost* – and he's got a cult following. So does Reagan and he napped through cabinet meetings! Ferg, listen to me! You are just as qualified as the next guy to go to Washington and screw everything up eight ways from Sunday! Just look at the Kabler/Wallace fight. Wait till Missy sees that!"

"Gee thanks, Deke. You've always been there for me. So Burton of the *Brute*, what's next?"

"Listen," Lucy said, "Ferg, you're a nice guy. And I really do agree with Deke that you are just as big a clod as everyone else on the Hill, but I can't really be on your side."

"Is it Eunice?"

"No! It's journalistic integrity."

"Have you turned on the news lately?"

"I know, I'm old fashioned. I just can't be gunning for you. I only *report* the news."

"That makes me blue."

"Teddy Landry became a crusader, and look what happened to him."

"Yes. That *was* unfortunate. I think that Eunice is in love with him now. Sorry Deke."

"One survives, one must."

Lucy's phone rang. She put it on speaker. "Lucy Burton."

"WHAT IS THIS?" squawked the voice over the phone. Ferg, who'd had neither opportunity nor reason to build up immunity to the banshee-like squall of Anna Degrasse, couldn't tell whether she was furious or pleased.

"What does it look like?"

"It *looks* like G-rated MILF porn directed by an eleven-year old. Then it takes a turn into what seems to be Betty Sue Wallace calling Leo Kabler a shylock, whereupon he insults her grandmother's cornbread recipe and she knocks him out."

"You've got the broad points, Ms. Degrasse."

"Who else has this footage?"

"No one. But the ambulance just took the congressman and Teddy off to the hospital. We won't be able to keep the media at bay for long. Edit quick. I've sent you 500 words. Stand by for more."

"And you did this without that sleazy travel writer Deke stealing your story?"

"Mrs. Degrasse..."

"Never again! I am never hiring that aborted love child of Hemingway and Shecky Green-"

"HEY NOW!" called Deke.

"Lucy! Have you got me on speaker phone?"

"We're kind of celebrating."

"Kind of celebrating? I've got a news site to run. Lucy, send me the follow-up, ASAP." She hung up.

"You two work for her?" Ferg asked.

"*I* do." said Lucy. "Fancy-free over there has to write a story for *Front Street*."

"Okay." Deke got off the bed and shooed Lucy out of the chair.

"The old cow *pays* me sometime, I'll grant her that. But lately she'd been too busy signing my death warrant." He plopped into the chair and stopped.

"...and you think that Guillory boy sent Teddy the Kabler info?" asked Lucy

"Louis Guillory?" asked Ferg.

Deke turned from the screen, "I got the impression Louis worked for the Deschamp brothers."

"I got that impression too." Said Ferg. "I swear I saw him today."

Deke scratched his head. "The information on Kabler leads back to the Deschamps."

"So would the information on the Wallaces." Said Lucy.

"Ha! That bastard." Deke laughed, "It *was* Guillory! He didn't want to sink either candidate, he wanted to sink the Dechamp Brothers!"

"But why sabotage his own employer?" Lucy asked.

"And live out the dream of killing your boss?" said Deke.

"Well," said Lucy looking at her phone, "I see your point."

CLAUDE DECHAMP was sitting behind his desk in the out of the way office park in Biloxi. The nondescript glass door read, in Helvetica, **Corsair Corp.** He was watching the video footage originally posted on the *Daily Brute* but now making its viral way across the cyber-sphere to every news site in the known universe, save SLAMNEWS! which had mysteriously gone inactive that morning.

Pencil came into the room wearing the baggy jeans and long sleeve tee shirt with skull & crossbones on it that he lived in when his brothers wasn't nagging him into a black suit. "Well, Brother, been watching the news lately?"

"Yes." Claude said curtly.

"That's some influence you bought us. I tell you whut." Pencil eased into the chair on the other side of the desk and put his boots up.

"Feet."

"The way I figure, Bro, this really throws things up in the air. On the one hand, you got one candidate in our pocket, Betty Sue Wallace throwin' a punch at the other'n. Also paid for, you tell me… hedging our bets. That would normally be enough to knock punchy outta the race. I reckon one of them *had* to loose. Except that punchy was a woman, and she knocked out that Leo Kabler clean out. I mean, a fella might survive getting' whupped by a woman in Vermont or New Hampshire. But not in Mississippi."

"Thank you for your astute political analysis, Pencil."

"I won't lie to you…"

"Please try."

"I'm kinda turned on by that bass-ass Southern Belle bit."

"Well, Pencil, go downstairs and get a girl. I've got to track down Guillory, he's gone AWOL."

"Where the hell is he?"

"I don't know, I haven't heard from him since you penciled his hand, you ape!"

"Ah, c'mon! I didn't mean nuthin' by it. Why's he so sensitive all the sudden?"

"I'm sure he'll be pleased you didn't mean it personally. But we've got an issue with the candidates and he's our political fixer, so he needs to get his ass over here."

Pencil thought about this. "Hell, the way I figure, they're both unelectable."

"I'll call CNN and tell them you think so. They can't both lose!"

Pencil shoved his phone in Claude's face. "Wanna bet?" On the mobile version of the *Daily Brute* was Lucy's latest dispatch: Ferguson O'Conner Announces Bid For Mississippi Senate; Laudermilk Endorses Independent Candidate.

"Ye Gads!" belched Claude, "Who in the hell is Ferguson O'Conner?"

"No clue, other than The Rumble in the Delta, happened at his house... or his father's."

Claude sunk in his chair. "Shit, now we gotta figure out what kinda girl *he* likes. I wonder if Guillory knows him?"

Pencil's phone began to vibrate. With a put-upon grunt, he dug the thing out of his pants and took a look at the caller ID for a moment before putting the phone to his ear. "Hey J.E.B. you comin' down to the 27 for a game and a screw?" He laughed and then Claude watched the humor drain from his brother's face. "Who the fuck is Danny Spewe?...Okay, here's a better one – who told you to take this kid to Clarksdale and why do you think I'm gonna pay you ten large to do it?... Well fuck you... You and what army?!?"

The phone went quiet and Claude asked, "Who was that, Pencil?"

He thought for a moment. "We...ahh...we may have a problem with the Rebel Yell boys."

BEAU O'CONNER strode back and forth in the Clarksdale jail while the mayor and the chief of police talked in a hushed huddle. Crenshaw came up to the huddle and Beau eyed the trio suspiciously. "Lord, Eunice," he muttered to himself, "You've out done yourself." His ears pricked up. This time he turned and continued his paces, but closer to the trio.

"What can't you find, gentlemen?"

"This is a police matter, Beau." said the mayor.

"But you're the mayor."

"That's true."

"So it's not *strictly* a police matter, but a city matter."

"Perhaps…"

"So what can't you find? Since you were so good to raid my house, perhaps I can help."

The chief sighed. "Beau, we can't the find the AR."

"Your team raided my house on the tip from that buffoon Leo Kabler, wrecked my shoot and arrested my daughter for conspiracy to assassinate a Congressman and … there is no gun. Correct?"

"Now, there *is* a gun. Hank admitted to selling it to him."

"We know that Wilson that sold him a gun. Just not that he had one at the farm. All my sweet princess did was –"

"Who?" the chief asked.

"Eunice…"

"Oh, right."

"All Eunice did was care for some damn fool who got overheated."

"She barricaded herself in her room and refused to come out." The chief pointed out.

"Ohhh, pooh! She did that once a month in grade school. I understand it got worse at boarding school. The calls I used to get…"

"She bit me." said Crenshaw.

"Well you went barreling into her room trying to jostle the frightened thing."

"Would we call that frightened?"

"Quiet you!" Said the chief, "That'll be all." He and the mayor huddled again.

"Well?" Beau tapped his genuine bull penis walking stick on the ground. He thought it intimidated people.

"So…" said the chief. "When is Eunice leaving town?"

"Ferg is gonna fly her to Memphis tomorrow."

"For sure?"

Beau sighed, "It can't be soon enough."

"We'll release her right now, Mr. O'Conner."

AT THE SUNFLOWER INN, Summer Greene was scrolling through the feed on her phone. "Oh, this isn't good at all."

"Dear Goddess!," came Blanche, "if I hear any more bad news, I'm literally going to die."

"I'll miss you. It looks like Hashtag: *hellsbelles* is the top trending story write now."

"What do they think we did now?"

"Nothing."

"Great."

"Not great. That's the problem. It's not about us. It's about Betty Sue Wallace. Now *she's* the fiery Southern belle. At least you're off the hook, Dr. Barker."

"Yes…I suppose. Still…"

They stared at each other for a long time.

"Well, if she's gonna win…" said one.

"It's always nice to have people on the Hill." agreed the other.

"You know, we need the grant money…"

Summer bit her lip and sighed. "The FBI will almost certainly find out who blew up the rickhouse."

"Which we had nothing to do with."

"I know. But still. Maybe it'll be a boom to mom's career, my kid sister being a terrorist and all. Well, Dr. Barker, let's get this done."

The two climbed the stairs and knocked on the door marked 31. On the other side, sat Betty Sue who had wanted to eat downstairs. Casper had insisted that after her performance, she needed to steer clear of anyplace where the press might find them, and there were a lot of them downstairs. They had Mrs. Wilson bring up some sandwiches, drew the shades and bolted the door, switched on the news and watched the computer.

When the knocking started, the Wallaces looked at the door then each other: Casper still in sweat stained field clothes, Betty Sue in yoga pants and a tee shirt with hair still unmoved by the day's events. Twice in Casper's marriage to Betty Sue he'd seen her actually look sheepish. Once when she's gone out with the girls and wrecked the brand new sports car he'd bought to celebrate his 100th Digger station. This was the other time. "Should we answer it?" Betty Sue whispered.

"We should not." Casper whispered back.

"Mr. and Mrs. Wallace, my name is Dr. Blanche Barker." came the voice.

"The candidate is very tired," said Casper, "she's not granting interviews right now."

"Oh I'm not a reporter, thank Goddess."

"What?"

"I'm not a reporter, thank *goodness*. But there are an army of them downstairs, in from Memphis and Jackson. No, I run a women's rights organization with chapters throughout the country. After today, you're a great −" Blanche choked back a bit of vomit on the words, "a role model for young women."

Casper cracked the door, leaving the chain on. The older one, Dr. Barker he assumed, looked sour and angry despite her ghastly smile. The one behind her looked less so. Casper opened the door. "Well, come in." Casper shut the door quickly behind them.

"Excuse me, I look a fright." Said Betty Sue at the first sight of Summer. She gave her husband a sneer and rolled away from her club sandwich to pad off to the bathroom.

"The candidate has quite a punch." Blanche said.

"Yeah," Casper said, "May have knocked herself clean out of the race."

"Casper, it's not that bad. At least I won!" said Betty Sue.

"She may have a point, Mr. Wallace." Blanche said. "That little man came down the steps shouting awful things and she walloped him... *yesallwomen*, *metoo*, *timesup*, hear me roar, all that good stuff." Summer handed Casper her smart phone. The hashtag: *hellsbelles* was blowing up social media."

"I don't like that talk of hell," said Casper, "Look, I'm trying to get hashtag: *steelmagnolia* started."

"And how's that working?"

"It's thing in Jackson. It's been liked, like 86 times."

"*Hellsbelles* is at quarter million and counting."

"And that's the female vote," said Summer, "You can hardly expect the Southern gents of Mississippi to ignore the Southern belle thing." From the bathroom, Betty Sue was starting to like what she heard. Casper sat still at the desk, looking at the computer screen crackling with the now viral footage that always started with his wife's admirable breasts. The hashtag: *votefortits* was blowing up too, but with an entirely different demographic.

"Where'd you say you're from again?" asked Casper.

"I work for a women's right organization in Virginia."

"So these aren't Mississippi voters?"

"Shut up Casper." Said Betty Sue, "We're a quarter million strong and growing. We're national now!"

SIXTEEN:
A JOB CALLED AMERICA

BEHIND THE HOUSE of O'Conner, Hank was stacking the rental chairs and taking his sweet time about it too. He didn't really want to hear about his little bait and switch from Mr. Wilson, and how it violated the sacred trust stitched into his hat. His cell phone had not rung, though, and that was a good thing. So was the fact that, unknown to Hank, that Mr. Wilson was at that exact moment across town counting receipts, himself unaware of the drama that had unfolded in his sleepy dale. His wife was too plowed under with reporters from Memphis and Jackson to get word down the street. "We'll I'll be a monkey's uncle." Mr. Wilson said to himself. Hank just moved one of those discontinued coveralls for double the price at the opening of dove season *and* an AR-15 ...that boy needs a raise. "...or some store credit." He muttered to no one.

Back in front of the house, Beau and Eunice came through the door. "Darla!" Beau called. "You, Ferg and... Molly..."

"Mavis!" Darla called from the kitchen, "The baby's name is Mavis!"

"...yes...well whoever you are, I've sprung Eunice from jail."

"Where is she?" asked Darla, coming out of the kitchen with Mavis on her hip.

Beau turned around twice. "Eunice? Princess? Well, I suppose she's gone upstairs to change out of that ridiculous get-up."

Darla went upstairs to put Mavis in her crib and passed Deke headed to the ground floor in a couple of leaps. In the den Aubrey, Army and Lucy were talking and Beau was staring out the french doors looking glum. "I've sent a short story to *Front Street*." said Deke, "They've already posted your video on their site Burton of the *Brute*."

"I guess we *can* work together." said Lucy.

"Degrasse will be horrified."

Army cleared his throat, "Well, Booey's gone back to the house with the boys. Will you two be home for dinner? Or are you meeting Teddy at the hospital, Miss Burton?"

"Hah, very funny, Mr. Kipling."

Laudermilk cleared his throat, "Listen, you two need to get out of here, that TV news crew is gonna fix that truck and they'll be back. And take Ferg with you, the boy has had enough coverage for the day. Carlson tells me the Sunflower is swamped. That poor idiot is trapped in his room."

"I'll tell Booey that Ferg is coming for supper." said Army.

"Hey Ferg!" Deke called upstairs, "The Old Bear is ordering you into hiding."

"All right, I'm changing now." He called.

"Quiet, y'all will wake the baby!" twanged Darla.

Outside they heard Ferg's Porsche start and move off rapidly down the driveway. "I guess she isn't changing." Beau sighed, hanging his head low.

Ferg came down the stairs looking strangely fresh in an olive poplin suit and a rep tie. "You know we're just going over to Mom and Dad's?" said Deke.

"I'm running for senate now. This is how we dress."

"Sweet Jesus." Observed Lucy.

"Son…" opined Laudermilk.

Ferg clomped off to the mudroom and loudly rooted around in one of the closets. From upstairs, there came a baby's cry followed by a frustrated Darla wailing, "Whoever is trashing around down there, you woke the baby!"

"Sorry, Darla." called Ferg.

"Its Darlene!" Mrs. O' Conner screamed back. She was on a Betty Sue Wallace high.

Ferg came back with a plaid thermos. "We'd better get out of here. Geez… that Mavis can really wail."

"Son, your sister stole your car again." Beau muttered.

"Ferg, can you make the bottle for the baby?" came the voice from above.

"I gotta find a job, Darlene."

"Now? It's about damn time, but it's Labor Day! What job?"

"…a job called America!"

"Dammit, Ferguson Beaumont O'Conner, you put that bottle on right this instant!"

Had Lucy, Ferg, Deke or Maxine heard that last order from upstairs they might have felt bad for leaving Darla/Darlene in the lurch with Molly/Mavis. As it was, they fled ahead of the wailing child and piled into the Land Cruiser.

A few hundred feet away, nearly at the intersection of a farm service road, sat Wendy X in her car contemplating a cigarette. This business with Eunice and Deke had gone far enough. This business with Deke and Dr. Barker, Deke and the ISOP, Deke and the OLA – it had all had gone far enough. At the center of all of it, oppressing everything in a big micro-aggressive ball of goo, was Deke Kipling. Granted, he may not have actually *done* anything, but he was at ground zero of a problem so deep, destructive and systemic that Wendy – still on the lam – had been forced to retrieve her revolutionary black beret from the glove compartment.

At a distance, she saw the headlights go on, and was vaguely aware that Deke wasn't alone in the car. Wendy looked at Teddy Landry's AR-15 in the passenger seat and murmured, "Collateral damage." It was just part of war and, she was starting to realize, you couldn't have revolution without war.

In the backseat of the Land Cruiser, Ferg sipped on the thermos. "You know I'm glad you two made up."

"That'll do." Said Deke, "You know senators aren't supposed to drink like that."

"Like how?"

"Like constantly."

"I'm not sure you're right about that."

"Between Eunice and that other girl…" Lucy started, "I didn't get her name."

"What other girl?"

"Oh you know her, Deke." said Lucy, "Some old flame of yours. By the way, is there anyone in the Delta you haven't been skinny-dipping with?"

"What are you talking about?"

"Some little mousy girl at the Sunflower told me that y'all used to go skinny-dipping."

In the rear view mirror, Deke could see lights of a small car approaching fast. There had been that weird hippie chick that bought me a martini, she said something about skinny-dipping. Where was that? The ghost casino on Esplanade… He could see her, barely, and popping down the steps past the Prius with Knox county plates. The Prius with Knox County plates… did I see it before, on the way out to the Bayoil field station? It had been at Bardstown… surely not… the skinny gal in the toga he'd accidentally oppressed by trying to avoid her nudity, she drove a… "Prius with Knox County plates."

"Pardon?"

"She's not an old conquest, Lucy."

"Who is she then? And why were you skinny-dipping with her? Do you *not* own a pair of swim trunks?"

"I think she's been trying to kill me all week."

"Who? Wendy?" said Ferg, "You aren't her sort, I'm afraid. She had a flame for ole Eunice in college. Sis went through a Wiccan phase. We try not to talk about it. Wendy followed her from Berkley to Knoxville of all places. Frankly I'm glad she left town. I mean, she's harmless enough, but it's like having Eunice in stereo."

Deke's eyes flitted from the deserted road to the lights in the rearview mirror. "She's coming along side us."

The Prius pulled into the oncoming aside the Land Cruiser. A spray of bullets came spitting out the passenger window. Deke slammed on the breaks as the Prius swerved ahead and came to a hard stop, blocking the narrow two-lane highway. Wendy X came out of the car in a black turtleneck, beret and assault rifle to fire another burst. Deke hit the gas and swerved as the bullets glanced off the hood and cracked the windshield. "Don't go towards her!" shrieked Lucy.

"She's not aiming!"

"People get lucky!"

A headlight exploded as the truck hooked around the Prius, careened off the highway, over a dry drainage ditch and plowed into the soybeans.

"Daddy is not going to be pleased about this." said Ferg.

"Ferg! Where is the next service road?"

"Keep going Mannix, you'll hit it!"

"What was that?" screamed Lucy, "what have you gotten me into! Dammit Deke! You could swim in your boxers if you had too!"

"Gotten *you* into? The political story of a lifetime. *I've* been doing your research-"

"You've been doing your own research, boy-o!"

"Maybe you'd have a firmer grasp on the situation if you hadn't been playing kissy-face with that demonic love child of the Wallaces."

Ferg cleared his throat. "Now Deke, to be fair, y'all were on break when that happened."

"Shut up, Ferg!" They shouted as the truck crashed through the soybeans.

"And what do you do on a first date that makes these women want to kill you? And me?!? I swear Deke Kipling if I die because you can't make a day-after-sex-at-the-lake call I'm gonna haunt... haunt... hell there is nothing to haunt! You don't love anything but your career!"

"You're haunting that pretty good right now!"

"Deke, you really need to get this thing out of the beans." Ferg explained. "With soybean futures being what they are now."

"You know Lucy, I'm not the one making *flirtatious alliances* to get a story. Hold on!" The truck bounced out of the field and onto the service road. The Prius was coming at them in a rolling cloud of dust.

"Where you trying to lose her?" asked Lucy.

"You wanna drive?"

"I'm telling you right now, Deke Kipling, I didn't play kissy face with anyone. And I certainly didn't get nekkid to go swimming with half the state of Mississippi."

"I never - she got that story from Eunice!"

Ferg cleared his throat, "Now quit fussing, you two are startling Maxine here. That's all in the past. Darla told me that Teddy really fell for Eunice. They have a Florence Nightingale thing going or some such nonsense."

"Good for them." Spat Lucy and turned back to Ferg "Wait – Teddy fell for *Eunice?* What has that silo got that I haven't got?"

"Hey, that's my sister."

Deke cleared his throat. "Given your curiously long on-ramp to romance, Lucy, I think what she's got is accessibility."

"Curiously Long? Jesus, can't a girl be particular?" she barked, "And don't you get all high and mighty! If Eunice is tending Teddy, who are you gonna go out and poon-hound with?"

"She forced me!"

"She carried you out the window, I suppose?"

"Lord woman, you sound like my mother."

"Your mother is a delight!"

"Yeah but I don't want to –"

Then the back window exploded.

Maxine dove into the foot well. "Can you two kiss and make up?" called Ferg. "That one just about parted my hair."

"Hey Ferg," said Deke, "do you mind shootin' that gal?"

"I'd rather not. Mind driving faster?"

"I've been putting off a tune up, this is as good as it gets."

From what he could see with one headlight, the road ahead seemed straight. Deke set the cruise control. "Alright, Lucy. I've got this thing on cruise control-"

"I really don't like where your head is at right now."

"You're gonna sit on the console and take the wheel while I drop the seat back."

"Deke…"

"Because you're up here and you're wee and the country squire in the back is drunk again. So is Maxine apparently."

Lucy scooted onto the console and took the wheel. Deke dropped the seat back and slid back out of the driver's seat as another burst was fired. Pings and twangs sounded off the roof. Lucy plopped down into the driver's seat, pulled the release as Deke shoved it forward and seat back sprang back up. "Ferg, get up front, I need some room to operate back here." Ferg climbed into the passenger seat as Lucy hunkered down and disengaged the cruise control.

"Now why don't you two work together more often?" Ferg asked, straightening his suit jacket.

"Because Uncle Suitcase back there likes it when people shoot at him. Makes him feel important!"

"Lucy, that is simply not true." Deke was pulling his side-by-side out of the worn case and rummaging through his ammo box.

"Deke," said Ferg, "how hard is it to load that thing?"

"I'm looking for buckshot. Ah, here we go!" He loaded the barrels as another burst rang out.

"He's got a death wish." Lucy swerved the car wildly. "I ran a word search, Ferg, do you have any idea how many times the boy uses the word 'cordite' in his work?"

"That is a great smell." Ferg mused.

"Will you two shut up!" Deke was climbing into the way back.

"It's true."

"Embrace it, Lucy." Ferg advised. "The boy can only be himself."

"Okay Miss White Kidd Gloves, I suppose you like politics because it's so much more civilized?"

The front windshield exploded. "Sweet Jesus!"

Ferg started to knock the ruined glass out of the frame so Lucy could see. "Lucy, are you hurt?"

"Soup!"

"What?"

"The wind! It's like hot soup in my eyes!" She blinked hard against the humid Delta air now basting her eyeballs. "Soouup!"

"Oh, what are you complaining about, now?" called Deke, "You're from Charleston!"

"Where we have coastal breezes and windshields! Will you stop that car already!"

Deke aimed and fired as the car hit a dip in the road. The Prius's front windshield exploded.

"Brother, she's still coming!"

"Ferg, I can see that."

Lucy flipped the sunglasses down off the top of her head down to save her eyeballs. With one headlight and no street lamps, the world went really, really dark. "Oh dear."

"Lucy are you sure that's wise?"

"Ferg, you wanna drive?"

"Lucy, keep it straight." Deke called.

"You too!"

Another burst of wild fire and a .223 slug hit the interior of the truck.

"Deke…."

He braced his foot against the back of the seat. "Brake!"

Lucy stomped as she and Ferg lurched forward. Deke pushed back against the seat and fired a .12 gauge buck shot into the engine block of the oncoming Prius. The hood flew up over a spray of oil and steam.

"Go!" Deke screamed.

Lucy went.

As the Land Cruiser began to put space between it and Wendy , Deke laughed and climbing over into the back seat. "Lucy Burton of the *Brute*! Spectacular driving! Can't say it enough. Well, Ferg at least your first political assassination attempt was more dramatic than Kabler's."

"Now she was after Ferg, huh? I'll tell ya, the whole thing had a sort of 'hashtag: *damndeke* vibe to me."

"Lucy, you think everything has a 'Damn Deke' vibe. Besides, he'll get more mileage out of it than I will. Look Ferg, call the police, ask for Officer Crenshaw and tell her we – you – just immobilized the Kentucky Bourbon Bomber." Ferg dialed his phone. "Lucy, how can you see with those sunglasses on?"

"I can't."

"Well slow down for God's sake, she's not coming after us anymore."

Maxine climbed out of the floorboard and into Deke's lap. She licked his sweat-streaked face and he tickled her behind the ear. "Did you see me save the day with my epic bad-assery? Didja girl? Didja?"

"Have some punch." Ferg offered. "Quickly."

NO, I DO NOT have a ride, and I don't live here so I can't really call anyone." Teddy was telling the formidable ER nurse. "But I feel fine. The doctor said I was fine."

"Not that fine or we wouldn't have carted you in from that ambulance moaning like a haint." The nurse looked at Teddy from behind the tall counter of the nurses station. He was still in his paper gown. "Still, insurance says you can't be released without a ride. That's policy. Say, weren't you brought in from the O'Conner place? Well, all sorts a people were out there today for the to-do. You must know *somebody*. Call one of them."

Teddy cleared his throat and wished for his vaporizer. "Well, I wasn't exactly invited."

"Riiighhht. Say, you didn't really take a shot at that congressman – the little fella – did ya?"

"I'm a journalist!"

"What? No writer ever freaked out and went Old West on somebody?"

"Then no."

"So you're a journalist, huh? You know a fella named Deke Kipling? Local boy. I love his folks. He wrote a book about Ukraine – had a funny name –"

"I don't remember." He lied.

"*Vodka, Bears and Furry Hats.* Yeah that's it. Anyway, there is a chapter in there about a TV weatherman from a local station went off and joined up with the bad guys and started shootin' people left and right."

"Fascinating."

"Well, I guess that's not you because the police said you could go when the doc thought you were ready."

"I'm *am* ready. I feel fine and the doctor said I was fine."

"You aren't *that* ready," she noted, "you haven't got a ride."

The nurse saw her first, standing in the wide glass ER doors as they gently whooshed open. She stood behind the patient, in a grey leotard and what looked like wings when she raised her arms up toward him. On seeing this, the nurse reached down and gently pulled the pre-filled syringe of thorazine they used when the full moon and the meth heads combined to make the admission area of the little hospital a little too vivid.

"I'll carry him home." Eunice said, "I'll take his pasty white behind home."

Realizing that his gown was open in the back, Teddy turned to Eunice. While no firm believer in the metaphysical, to him she looked like a vision, a dream.

"You two know each other?" said the nurse, still fingering the syringe.

"I think so." Said Teddy slowly.

The nurse looked down and saw a light go off for room 207. She handed the paperwork to her desk partner and said. "I gotta go talk to the congressman."

Outside room 207, Kelly sat in snit. "The congressman needs me."

"You're still here? Look, the Congressman needs quiet. Family only. Doctor's orders." Inside, Leo was tired and groggy. "Nurse, where's my phone?" he asked.

"No, Sir. You've had a concussion."

"What?.... How?"

"Well, to judge from the shiner and the knot on the back of your head, someone popped you in the eye socket and you fell back and knocked your head on a brick."

"My phone…"

"Doc says you don't need to messing with the blue light on your phone right now. Just be quiet. The fracas is over, you aren't missin' anything."

BURT CARLSON sat in his room, looking at the hysterical tornado on his smartphone. *#notyourpenis* had been largely replaced by *#hellsbelles* and *#votefortits*. Then his aide Tim called. "Congressman, I just heard that the FBI think that they have located the Kentucky Bourbon bomber."

"Good for them."

"In Clarksdale. They haven't released a name but she appears to work for a foundation called the Institute for Sexual Ownership and Parity, but claims to be a soldier for the Ovarian Liberation Army. That's not pubic information."

"…"

"Sir," Tim slowed down, "that means the crew that blew up the men's room at the Nebraska Union are now considered terrorists."

"..."

"It means, Congressman, the feminists have victimized *you*. Or at least you can claim it. That's the QED."

Carlson was exhausted but the wheels eventually caught. "This I can work with! They found her in Clarksdale, eh? After the boxing match between Betty Sue and Leo, nobody is gonna be talking about walking sticks anymore!"

"Is that what they were talking about, sir?"

"Shut up. Good work, Tim. Listen, the lobby is full of press and I've got to get down there." Carlson shot up and instinctively looked in the mirror: He was dusty and sweat stained. He needed to change – then no – he looked *manly*.

Screw Leo, he thought, *that spaz of a she-man. Didn't even bag his limit*. Carlson strode down the stairs like the point guard he once was to link his tormentors with domestic terrorism before half a news outlets in America. He stepped into the lobby of the Sunflower only to see the last stragglers of a press stampede away from the hotel. "Wait." He screamed, "Kentucky Bomber!" as he ran outside to see a small army of journalists clamoring out of the Crossroads Blues club as well and all of them diving into their cars and peeling away in a fury. "Wait! I'm a congressman!"

"ARE WE OUT or range of that mad woman?" heaved Lucy.

"Yes. I hope."

"Then you drive." Lucy stopped the truck and got out into the swirling cloud of dust that overtook them.

Deke got out of the back and swapped places, but he didn't start the car.

"Deke. Go. If she starts moving-"

"That car is toast."

"You didn't shoot her legs."

"We've got to wait for the police." said Deke.

"Just because *you* like being shot at doesn't mean that I do?"

"Lucy," Ferg interjected, "You know how I like to agree with you, and your boy Deke here *is* a spastic blockhead-"

"That's not helpful."

"But at the moment – shut up – *at the moment*" Ferg explained, "He's right. I dropped a pin from my phone for Officer Crenshaw."

They could hear the sirens in the distance. "Lucy, you've got your story," said Deke, "Now let me get mine." He reloaded his shotgun and crammed his camera into the cartridge bag. The sirens sang in the distance. "Ferg, your gun is in the truck. For God's sake shoot a warning over head first if she shows up." He started walking back to the Prius. "Ferg, what did you say that gal's name was?"

"Wendy…Wendy Greene. You know her mother was an actress… remember *Clam Whiskers?*"

Deke kept walking as one patrol car roared past and came to a halt in a cloud of dust as Crenshaw leapt out. "Deke you need to stay back. Let us handle this!"

"We found that AR 15 y'all were looking for."

"You mean she's armed!"

"Yeah, did Ferg not make that clear?"

"Jesus Ferg!" Crenshaw barked into the speaker on her epaulette, "Keep your distance. Suspect is armed with an assault rifle. Who is she?"

"Eunice's college roommate, Wendy… Greene, I think it was. "

"We've got her." came the voice from the patrol car about 500 feet ahead.

"I've got a visual." Crenshaw jumped into the patrol car and didn't notice Deke had climbed, mostly at any rate, into the passenger seat. "Deke, you can't be here."

"Yet here I am."

She roared ahead and slammed on the breaks behind the other patrol car, sending Deke into the floorboard.

"Ow."

Crenshaw got out the bullhorn. "Miss…"

"Greene, Wendy Greene." Deke rolled out of the floorboard and onto the ground as he took the camera from his cartridge bag.

"Miss Greene! Listen, to me." Crenshaw was saying. "You need to stop this and give yourself up."

"Don't call me by my father's land-rapey name! Call me Wendy X!"

"I don't think she's got much ammo." said Deke from behind the car door.

"How much does she need?"

"Stay back!" Wendy screamed and fired a burst of shots over their heads.

"What is it that you want? Maybe we can work something out. Just calm down."

"End the patriarchy!"

"OK. Could you cut that down into manageable chunks? Something a little less abstract, Ms.… Wendy?"

"You'll never take me alive!" she screeched and shot a short burst into the air until the gun dry fired. "Oh…"

The officers rushed in as she threw the weapon to the ground and darted off into the soybeans.

Back at the Land Cruiser, Ferg cocked his ear. "Hear that? She's out of ammo. Your little Dekey Bear is safe… or already dead. Either way, that's settled." He started towards the patrol cars.

Lucy followed. "You know, I don't understand that boy."

"I know you don't, Love. That's because you play chess with your emotions." Ferg handed over the thermos, "He's just playing checkers. Really vigorous checkers, granted."

"He's gonna get himself killed."

"Maybe."

"And you don't care?"

"Sure, I do. I'll miss him. Love the man like a brother."

"You don't carry on like that baffoon."

"I'm married."

"I thought you said you weren't very good at it."

"Oh, I'm not. Still, Deke just needs something to live for. You know the right gal would calm him right down."

Ahead of them, Deke was standing with Crenshaw filming two officers trying to wedge Wendy into the back of a patrol car. "You're oppressing me!" she screamed.

An irate voice answered. "I'm about to oppress your head wide open." The door shut.

Deke switched off video and started snapping pictures. Lucy cleared her throat, "Hey Deke, I think that we're expected at your parents."

"You're hungry?"

Ferg blew his nose. "You aren't?"

BLANCHE CAME BACK to her room to find Summer frantically packing their clothes. "What's going on here?"

"They just arrested Wendy, and someone has already fingered her for Kentucky, Dr. Barker. When they start looking for hard proof, they'll find it."

"A causality for feminism." growled Blanche.

"Did you tell my sister to kill Deke Kipling?"

"Not expressly."

"I've got to call Mom and tell her she's got a new cause."

Blanche prided herself for never making a move without weighting the implications. Summer's phone pinged with yet another alert. Blanche cleared her throat. "Should we alert Betty Sue Wallace? She might be very grateful."

"Oh, screw that sweet tea swilling banshee." said Summer, "I'm heading back to Memphis. The car leaves in five."

"Well when we get back to Virginia-"

"Oh no! I'm not going back to Virginia. When we get to Memphis, I'm flying home."

"To LA?"

"Life is simpler out there – it's just narcissism and Scientology. At least I know the rules."

SEVENTEEN:
OBITUARY COCKTAIL

LUCY STOOD looking at Deke who was looking at himself in the three-way mirror. "I don't need another sport coat." He grumbled and looked sourly out the window in the men's shop in the French Quarter, full of people not currently being fitting for sports jackets.

"Sure you do. Radical feminists tried to kill you in the other one. Put holes right in it." Said Lucy.

"Right, I'll patch it up, wash out the blood. You know seersucker is machine washable if you don't care how you look."

"Put the olive one back on." She ordered.

"I wanna go eat."

"I'm with you, I can still feel that last drink, what'd you call it?"

"An obituary cocktail.   Derrick told me that the pirate Jean Lafitte invented them, but that sounds like drunken history to me. Anyway, it's become one of those symbols of... being the same sleazy pirate colony Bienville founded 300 years ago... this city."

"Oh, quit bragging, Charleston is a sleazy pirate colony founded in 1670."

Deke pulled on the other sport coat. "Good for you, Blackbeard will be so proud. Yet here you are, in a foreign city getting me to buy you dinner."

"New Orleans isn't a foreign... well not completely. But Ferg wouldn't fly me to Memphis to make my flight."

"I like this one that's pretending to be tweed." Deke said into the mirror. "Now quit whining about that, he flew us down here. Ferg's not an airline, you know. My car got shot up by the idiot brigade and we had to get the boys back here for school. Besides, you could have driven up to Memphis with Eunice. She offered. She even rented a car."

"I'll take my chances with the pirates." She looked him over, "Yes, that's the one. Good fit. Besides I've knocked out a hell of a story. Degrasse is so happy she's paying for the flight transfer." She looked around for the salesman who'd gone off to get the tailor, "On Tuesday, Smut Butter clicks went up by 700%, and then another 200% again today. She's is so happy I'm almost not mortified that that stuff is attached to my byline."

"You're still mortified."

"I know. You can't just let me have a moment, can you? Thanks for putting me up while I'm here. Or I guess I should thank Peggy and Ash."

"Lucy, there was plenty of room in the carriage house."

"We must set a wholesome example for your niece and nephews. They are at an impressionable age."

"The boy is setting me up with absinthe martinis."

"Comfortable guest room, though."

The tailor approached and started pulling at the sleeves. Lucy wandered off to a television in the corner. On screen was a shot of Ferg O'Conner and under his face: Senate Candidate, MS (I). "Could you turn that up, please?" she asked the lady at the counter.

"Well," Ferg was saying to the camera, "I'm personally appalled by the domestic terrorism of the Ovarian Liberation Army... although they get points for a clever name. Still, I support the right of groups to their legitimate forms of protest. Violence, however, isn't legitimate."

"Mr. O'Conner, would you say that the toilet bombing is a legitimate form of protest?"

"No, not really. Blowing up a fella's morning newsroom is a little off-sides."

"The Institute of Sexual Ownership and Parity has announced that Dr. Blanche Barker is stepping down as director and appointing Eunice O'Conner as Interim Director. Isn't Ms. O'Conner your sister?"

"And how."

"Do you have any reaction to her appointment?"

"Should I?"

This flummoxed the reporters until one of them braved a loud, *"Yes."*

"Alright. Clearly Dr. Barker got messed up with domestic terrorism and took the ISOP to a gruesome place." He smiled broadly, "I'm sure Sis'll do a great job. But that's her story to tell, not mine."

"But wasn't Wendy Greene your sister's...Ms. O'Conner's assistant."

"Well, not anymore – she's in jail. Look, trusty staff is hard to find. As for last week, I have it on good authority that Ms. O'Conner did NOT authorize the time off for a killing spree. Excuse me, an *alleged* killing spree. We must let the justice system take its course."

"Weren't you in the car she shot up?"

"Right-o. Next Question?"

"Do you have any comment about the *Front Street* story breaking that both your opponents, Ms. Wallace and Congressman Kabler were both taking kickbacks from the criminal Dechamp Brothers."

Ferg smiled, "I haven't read it yet. Sounds riveting, though."

Deke walked up to the counter. Lucy laughed, "Ferg says he hadn't read the article yet."

"Probably hadn't."

"You practically dictated the thing in the plane. He's the one that gave you the word *Rabelaisian* to describe Betty Sue's wardrobe... or was it her bust line?

"I don't know where he gets it... wasn't much of a student. Did they ask him what was in the article or if he'd read it?

"Sweet Jesus! Ferg O'Conner just might win this thing."

Deke rapped his knuckle on the walnut countertop. "You know he'll make good copy. Now I'm hungry. Can we go?"

They walked out into the late afternoon. "Let's go this way. I know a good place."

"You aren't going to make me drink anymore pirate cocktails are you?"

"You know Burton of the *Brute*, Ferg may have been right. I guess working together didn't turn out so bad."

"We almost got killed!"

"I said *turn out*. The actual process of working with you was fearsome. Let's never do that again."

BEHIND THE nondescript door in a wall in another part of the Quarter Madame Lemuex was looking out the window to the shabby courtyard. They weren't in what Guillory called the 'Mojo Room' but a back room that looked less *Li Grande Zombie and more* Office Depot. Phone lines and cables snaked across the floor and several flat screen computer screens sat on standard issue desks. "So, what are we gonna do without the Dechamps?"

"Keep the money." said Guillory. The black-eye was gone, but the hand still tapped up.

"That private game was a good feeder."

"I organized it, I think we can keep one going."

Lemuex reached for a plastic magic eight ball she kept on her desk as a private joke to herself. "Magic eight ball says those two coon-ass goons are gonna come at you pretty hard."

"I gave Basco the sex-video they were going to blackmail him with."

She laughed, "You took the video."

Guillory put his finger to his lips. "Basco's pissed, he's taking it personally. He thinks he owes me."

"He's no criminal, Louis! Dangerous game you're playin'"

"Bayoil has its own army. They do business in with dictators, Lemuex. If they want the Dechamps gone they'll go. Those brothers haven't got any cover anymore. Don't have any revenue either." Guillory scratched his head. "Listen, we do need to keep Basco thinking he's the master of the universe in all this. Have you or that eight ball got enough sway with *le gods* to keep Basco winning this season?"

"I might. You gotta keep him away from football, no one has that much magic."

Guillory laughed, "Yeah, magic." He got up to leave, "You keep the faith."

"SO, WHAT are you cooking up next to prove to Degrasse that the *Daily Brute* can't function without Lucy Burton?" Deke asked as they crossed the intersection into a beautifully dilapidated building.

"I'm not sure I should tell you." The stucco was in need of a coat of paint but the tiles were freshly mopped and gleaming in the light of the wide, tall windows. They moved to a table in the back of the narrow space and almost instantly a waitress appeared and asked for a drink order. "What does your twelve year old nephew recommend?"

"Sazarac. He's a big fan of the concept. At least I hope it's the concept."

"Wine is a little more my speed, today."

"White?" Deke ordered a bottle of white Boudreaux. "You really aren't going to tell me what you are up to next are you?"

"I'm afraid you'll call *Front Street*."

"Fair point."

"Actually, Degrasse called me today, she wants me to drive up to Jackson for a post-knock out interview of Betty Sue while I'm down here, and use your brother's house as the New Orleans desk."

"That sneaky bitch. Well, tell me before you post it. I want to buy stock in Smut Butter... for a numbered account in the Cayman's, off course. You don't want a thing like that in your permanent portfolio."

"You know that Degrasse wants you back from the clutches of Kenneth Macastle. Maybe enough for a staff job."

"Maybe not." Said Deke. "*Front Street* wants a series, and Laudermilk wants me in D.C to talk about some work over fried chicken. God only knows what that means."

"It means you'll be knocking on my door, begging for a couch. Is the Old Bear is actually going to run for president?"

"No. He wants to retire before too long."

"So what's the angle?"

"Laudermilk just wanted to muck out the stalls."

"The last honest politician?"

"I wouldn't go that far. Fairly heroic though."

The waitress came with a bottle of wine and poured out two crisp glasses. In the heat the outside of the glasses clouded instantly. Lucy toasted, "To one hell of a week!"

"Ta." Deke took a sip.

"You know I almost miss the haint punch."

"There is always next year. You know, Lucy, that perv Carlson seems to have made out okay. Now *he's a victim* of feminism."

She laughed. Deke thought that it was adorably vicious. "Oh, I haven't forgotten."

"It was the smurf comment, wasn't it? That really got under your skin." Over the sound system came the opening riff of Muddy Waters' *Boom Boom*. "I love this song."

On the other side of the window, a well-dressed Louis Guillory was walking along the sidewalk and stopped dead in his tracks when he saw the pair on the other side of the glass. Before either could take note of the halt, he was moving again and his bandaged hand came out of his pocket.

"Actually it wasn't that." said Lucy, "Well not entirely. It was that man hasn't had to consider the repercussions of his actions in a long time."

"You're gonna let it lie for a few weeks, let him forget about it until we're up against the election and really nail him to the floor, aren't you?" Deke said as he looked up and saw Guillory coming through the door.

Lucy tipped her glass. "That's about the thick of it, yeah."

"Shady bag of tricks, aren't you?... Hey, this is a friend of mine."

Guillory never stopped for an introduction but drew his right arm back as he moved forward, landing a flying fist square on the bridge of Deke's nose. His vision went black and stars exploded behind his eyes. He heard Lucy saying "Sweet Jesus!" the way she always did. Muddy Waters was still playing as the room warped and ebbed back into focus but not really for the blue and green blobs still dancing before his eyes. He watched Guillory walk back outside and turn down the street.

"Deke! Are you all right? Who was that?"

"Don't worry about it. I'm pretty sure I deserved that one."

A' boom boom boom boom.

THE END

ACKNOWLEDGEMENTS:

I actually had recently returned from Kharkov, Ukraine – about 18 miles from the Russian border – when it was suggested for some reason that I write 'the quintessential Southern novel.' With my keen and penetrating eye, I seem to have missed the mark entirely.

Still, to give credit where credit is due: My younger brother Bernie actually did go to Bora Bora on his honeymoon because it was the furthest he could get from Memphis without coming back. Joe Long, telling a harrowing tale from his childhood in Uniontown, Alabama, introduced me to the 'fistbath' and I've never really stopped laughing about it. My older brother Larry was indispensable with some of the more technical details getting this novel wrapped up. Tim Ferris, whom I've never met, coined the term 'bigoteer' and that's worth noting. I'd list all the activist organizations and social media accounts that provided such fodder for the fictional events in this story, but the ensuing lawsuits sound tedious.

Mostly I'm grateful to my wife, Maggie, for a great many things without which this book wouldn't have happened. Certainly, too many to list here and, Gentle Reader, they aren't any of your business.

About the Author

Richard Murff has covered humanitarian issues across Latin America, Iraq, Ukraine, Libya and Clarksdale, MS, to name a few places. Murff spent his early career in advertising and marketing for a handful of global corporations. His less impressive jobs included writing sermons for a preacher who is very likely certifiably insane. After several years in the financial sector specializing in capital markets for government debt and collateralized securities, the economy blew-up.

He has ghostwritten memoirs, business books and regional histories. His work has appeared in *The Bitter Southerner*, *Delta Magazine*, *The American Spectator*, *Sail*, *The Daily News*, and others.

His books include *Pothole of the Gods*, *Yellowcake*, *One Last Hour* and *Memphians*.

The Mint Julep cookie was created in his honor.